The Profit Doctrine

T0150472

The Profit Doctrine

Economists of the Neoliberal Era

Robert Chernomas
and
Ian Hudson

PlutoPress
www.plutobooks.com

First published 2017 by Pluto Press
345 Archway Road, London N6 5AA

www.plutobooks.com

British Library Cataloguing in Publication Data
A catalogue record for this book is available from the British Library

ISBN   978 0 7453 3586 5   Hardback
ISBN   978 0 7453 3585 8   Paperback
ISBN   978 1 7837 1993 8   PDF eBook
ISBN   978 1 7837 1995 2   Kindle eBook
ISBN   978 1 7837 1994 5   EPUB eBook

This book is printed on paper suitable for recycling and made from fully managed
and sustained forest sources. Logging, pulping and manufacturing processes are
expected to conform to the environmental standards of the country of origin.

Typeset by Stanford DTP Services, Northampton, England

Simultaneously printed in the United Kingdom and United States of America

To Anwar Shaikh and the late David M. Gordon for cultivating
my appreciation for theory in historical context.
RC

To Lisa Johnston. For everything.
IH

Contents

List of Boxes, Figures and Tables

Boxes

Figures

Tables

List of Abbreviations

AEH—Adaptive Expectations Hypothesis
ACA—Affordable Care Act
ACC—American Chemistry Council
ALEC—American Legislative Exchange Program
AEA—American Economics Association
AER—American Economic Review
AEI—American Enterprise Institute
CED—Committee for Economic Development
CFMA—Commodities Futures Modernization Act
CFTC—Commodities Futures Trading Commission
CPSC—Consumer Products Safety Commission
CR— Consumer Report
CCC—Copenhagen Consensus Center
DFA—Dimensional Fund Advisors
EMH—Efficient Market Hypothesis
EPA—Environmental Protection Agency
Fannie Mae—Federal National Mortgage Association (FNMA)
Freddie Mac—Federal Home Loan Mortgage Corporation
   (FHLMC)
the Fed—The Federal Reserve
FTC—Federal Trade Commission
FDA—Food and Drug Administration
GPS—Global Positioning System
GLBA—Gramm-Leach-Bilely Act
IMF—International Monetary Fund
LTC—long-term capital management
MRI—magnetic resonance imaging
NAIRU—non accelerating inflation rate of unemployment
NEC—National Economic Council
NTP—National Toxicology Program
NFA—New Financial Architecture
OSHA—Occupational Safety and Health Administration

OECD—Organization of Economic Cooperation and Development
PPM—part per million
REH—Rational Expectations Hypothesis
RBC—Real Business Cycle
S&L—Savings and Loan
SEC—Security and Exchange Commission
TSCA—Toxic Substances Control Act
WEF—World Economic Forum
WHO—World Health Organization

Acknowledgements

Like a racing motor car, the Chernomas–Hudson writing combination relies on a crack crew who ably toil away behind the scenes while the authors hog what limelight there is from academic publishing. Fortunately, the good people at Pluto Press have provided sterling service helping get this manuscript from the conceptual stage to an actual book. David Shulman has been involved in this project from day one and has been encouraging, patient, and insightful in guiding it through the entire production process. Robert Webb did a first-rate job of putting the finishing touches to the book. Our copy-editor Jeanne Brady ran a very careful eye over the book, catching many a potentially embarrassing typo. Our thanks to three referees who saw enough worthwhile in our draft to ensure we didn't make any wrong turns while advising us how to get the most out of our project.

We would like to acknowledge the generous funding assistance of the Global Political Economics Research Fund, which we used to hire Eduardo Regier as a Research Assistant. His careful literature reviews were an important source of information for us.

Finally, we also have the good fortune to belong to one of the very small number of economics departments in North America that contain a cadre of heterodox economists. We have had so many collaborations and conversations in so many places with Fletcher Baragar, Irwin Lipnowski, John Loxley, Ardeshir Seperhi and John Serieux that we often don't know where their ideas begin and ours ends. Their collegiality and friendship has been an important source of strength, protection and inspiration especially over the last few years when confronted by an environment hostile to our identity as economists. Because of the University of Manitoba Faculty Association – our union, our colleagues in the Faculty of Arts and the Canadian Association of University of Teachers, we all continue to enjoy academic freedom as part of a department of economics.

1
Prophets and Profits

As an economist, I often find myself defending "bad guys"—companies outsourcing American jobs, gas stations gouging consumers with high prices, Wal-Mart undercutting small retailers with low prices, Mexican immigrants sneaking into our country, the Chinese fixing their exchange rate, American companies opening sweat shops abroad, foreign companies dumping cheap goods onto our markets, and pharmaceutical companies profiting off other people's sickness and misfortune. Sometimes I feel like a defense attorney for economic criminals.

Unlike real defense attorneys, however, I get clients that are mostly innocent. The study of economics provides a cogent defense for these alleged evil doers.

Greg Mankiw (2006)

Despite the enormity of recent events, the principles of economics are largely unchanged. Students still need to learn about the gains from trade, supply and demand, the efficiency properties of market outcomes, and so on. These topics will remain the bread-and-butter of introductory courses.

Greg Mankiw (2009)

From 2003 to 2005, Gregory Mankiw was the chairman of the Council of Economic Advisers for President George W. Bush. In 2006, he became an economic adviser to Mitt Romney, a role he maintained during Romney's 2012 presidential bid. He is a professor of economics at Harvard and was paid a $1.4m advance to write his best-selling textbook *Principles of Economics*. Economic giant Paul Samuelson once claimed, "Let those who will, write the nation's laws if I can write its textbooks" (quoted in Chandra, 2009). Despite student protests at the narrowness of Mankiw's teaching—in 2011, students walked out of his principles course in protest over his "limited view of economics"

(Concerned Students of Economics 10, 2011)—it is this version of the discipline that has been largely taught in classrooms around the United States. As we will demonstrate throughout this book, Mankiw's unshakeable belief in the efficiency of the market system reflected the dominant trend in the field of economics after the late 1970s.[1]

A standard list of economic goals and priorities would include stable growth, price stability, full employment, and the efficient allocation of resources. Some might even add to this list an environmentally sustainable economy and a reasonably equitable distribution of wealth and income. But the evidence suggests that the post-1970s period in the United States can be characterized as one of instability and inequality relative to the "Golden Age" that preceded it. After the 2008 collapse, critics inside and outside economics accused those dominating the profession for the last three decades of behaving like an "ostrich with its head in the sand," suffering from "groupthink," and promoting "Zombie" economics. While there is some truth to each of these claims, we believe they all miss the central charge.

We will argue that the economists of this era who rose to prominence (like Mankiw) did so not because of their contributions to the standard list of economic goals, but primarily because of their contribution to corporate profits and the wealth of the business class. An efficient, healthy economy shared by all was never a likely outcome of the policies advocated by those who had the power to assert their own interests. And those possessing that power got their way with the help of the economics profession. This period in American history, including the post-2008 years, has been an unqualified success for the American business class. While economics is ostensibly guided by commitments to scientific rigor and objectivity, this boon to business was the predictable result of the specific policy recommendations of those that came to dominate the profession.

How Do "Bad" Economic Ideas Develop?

The ideas of economists and political philosophers, both when they are right and when they are wrong, are more powerful than

---

1 The term "economics" in this book means the academic and professional fields of economics, not trends in the actual economy.

is commonly understood. Indeed, the world is ruled by little else. Practical men, who believe themselves to be quite exempt from any intellectual influences, are usually the slaves of some defunct economist. Madmen in authority, who hear voices in the air, are distilling their frenzy from some academic scribbler of a few years back. I am sure that the power of vested interests is vastly exaggerated compared with the gradual encroachment of ideas ... soon or late, it is ideas, not vested interests, which are dangerous for good or evil.

John Maynard Keynes (1936, p. 383)

Keynes's eloquent account of the importance of economic ideas has been widely used by economists across the ideological spectrum to explain the influence that the profession wields. He suggests that it is the "gradual encroachment of ideas" that influences policy. Keynes also seems to be suggesting that "wrong" or even "evil" ideas of an "academic scribbler" can come to dominate the profession and influence "madmen in authority." Indeed, after the economics profession appeared to fail so miserably during the economic crisis that started in 2008, critics from inside and outside the discipline queued up to point out how wrong (or even evil) economics had become.

If outsiders think the economics profession is a homogeneous discipline where consensus is easily achieved and genuine debate an infrequent visitor, there has been strong criticism of the profession from within, especially since the 2008 economic meltdown. Jeffrey Sachs has been a professor at Columbia and Harvard. He is a special adviser to the UN on its Millennium Development Goals. He has been very critical of recent trends in economics: "What I know about our training, since the early 1980s, the way we train people to think has left them, in mainstream economics and, I would say in mainstream politics, has left them almost unable anymore to distinguish the surface from the underlying reality" (Sachs, 2008). People who would view themselves as slightly further on the fringes of mainstream economics have been even more critical (for a more complete look at economists' opinions on their colleagues' work, see Box 1.1). An important theme of this book is that these internal criticisms were seldom heard, and even more rarely paid attention to, between the late 1970s and the 2008 crisis. Further, there were important limitations to the criticisms of those economists, like Paul Krugman and Joseph Stiglitz, who did manage to make their objections heard.

Academic observers from outside the field of economics have been even more scathing. Akeel Bilgrami, a philosophy professor at Columbia University claimed that

> ... economics is perhaps about the worst offender among disciplines in inuring itself in alternative frameworks of thought and analysis. In fact, I would venture to say that I have never come across a discipline which combines as much extraordinary sophistication and high-powered intelligence with as much drivel. (Bilgrami, 2008)

In the wake of the 2008 economic collapse, even the popular media vilified the profession. Headlines in the *New York Times* argued that

---

Box 1.1   Economists on economics

The 2008 crisis has resulted in some serious soul-searching within economics. Much of the self-criticism revolved around the very narrow nature of what it means to study economics after 1980.

Perry Mehrling, a professor of economics at New York's Columbia University says his graduate students are growing increasingly frustrated by the tendency to "define the discipline by its tools instead of its subject matter ... they find little relationship between the mathematical models in class and the world outside the door" (quoted in Basen, 2011).

Robert J. Shiller, an economist at Yale, claimed that the reason the profession failed to foresee the financial collapse was "groupthink": "Wander too far and you find yourself on the fringe. The pattern is self-replicating. Graduate students who stray too far from the dominant theory and methods seriously reduce their chances of getting an academic job" (quoted in Cohen, 2009).

Willem Buiter, a London School of Economics professor and a former member of the Bank of England monetary policy committee was especially scathing: "The typical graduate macroeconomics and monetary economics training received at Anglo-American universities during the past 30 years or so may have set back by decades serious investigations of aggregate economic behavior and economic policy-relevant understanding. It was a privately and socially costly waste of time and other resources. Most mainstream macroeconomic theoretical innovations since the 1970s ... have turned out to be self-referential, inward-looking distractions at best. Research tended to be motivated

---

academic economists were not sufficiently repentant for their role in creating the economic crash, with headlines like "Ivory Tower Unswayed by Crashing Economy," and "How Did Economists Get It So Wrong?" Other publications were in a more punitive mood. The *Financial Times* wanted to "Sweep Economists Off Their Throne," and *The Atlantic* opted for the corporal "Will Economists Escape a Whipping?" Canada's national newspaper, the *Globe and Mail* weighed in with "Economics Has Met the Enemy, and it is Economics." The fact that it is almost impossible to imagine another area of academics being the subject of such irate headlines underscores both the level of genuine anger at the failings of the profession, but also the fact that Keynes was right in claiming that it had so much influence.

The focus of all these critics is that those dominating the profession won the war of ideas to the detriment of society. How could ideas and

---

by the internal logic, intellectual sunk capital and aesthetic puzzles of established research programs, rather than by a powerful desire to understand how the economy works—let alone how the economy works during times of stress and financial instability. So the economics profession was caught unprepared when the crisis struck" (Buiter, 2009).

James K. Galbraith, an economist at the Lyndon B. Johnson School of Public Affairs at the University of Texas, and long-time critic of orthodox, mainstream economics, was not optimistic about these criticisms leading to any real change in the discipline: "I don't detect any change at all." Academic economists are "like an ostrich with its head in the sand." "It's business as usual," he said "I'm not conscious that there is a fundamental re-examination going on in journals" (quoted in Cohen, 2009).

The most systematic and, perhaps, damning indictment of the state of modern economics can be found in Australian economist James Quiggan's book, *Zombie Economics* (2010). Like Galbraith, he is pessimistic that the flaws in economics that were revealed by the 2008 crisis will lead to any real change in the discipline: "Economists who based their analysis on these ideas contributed to the mistakes that caused the crisis, failed to predict it or even recognize it when it was happening, and had nothing useful to offer as a policy response.

Three years later, however, the ... reanimation process has taken place in the realm of ideas. Theories, factual claims, and policy proposals that seemed dead and buried in the wake of the crisis are now clawing their way through the soft earth, ready to wreak havoc once again" (Quiggan, 2010a).

policies that proved to be such an abject failure come to dominate the economic landscape? Surely, some "academic scribbler" influencing "Madmen in authority" is not an acceptable explanation of the evolution of ideas or policy. Keynes mystified the origin of these ideas and, more importantly, trivialized the means by which they rise to the top. His implication that there is an evolutionary and progressive character to the development of ideas obscures the existing power structure in society. Marx's reflection on an earlier era is a better place to begin if one is looking for a conceptual framework to understand how ideas take hold in society. Marx argued that once the economic system of capitalism became dominant in the nineteenth century, economic debate was

> ... no longer a question, [of] whether this theorem or that was true, but whether it was useful to capital or harmful, expedient or inexpedient, politically dangerous or not. In place of disinterested inquirers, there were hired prize fighters; in place of genuine scientific research, the bad conscience and the evil intent of apologetic. (Marx, 1873, p. 25)

This is not to suggest that Marx's "prize fighters" of intellectual ideas are being dishonest with themselves or the public. Rather, their ideas, in which they no doubt genuinely believe, are promoted, popularized and enacted into policy by those who stand to benefit from them.

Unlike Keynes, who insists that the contest for intellectual dominance is a contest of ideas, Marx argues that it is a contest of power. Economic ideas, and the policies that arise from them, have profoundly different impacts on different groups in society. It is, therefore, in any group's interest to promote those ideas from which it will benefit, while discrediting those that are harmful. The question then becomes, what is the capacity for different groups to promote certain ideas and dismiss others? This depends, most obviously, on the financial, political and institutional resources that they can bring to bear but also on their coherence as a group and their ability to act in concert.

As Marx also suggests, ideas are not formed, disseminated and popularized in a context-free intellectual vacuum. Instead, the ideas that come forward, the extent to which they are believed, and whether they will be adopted as policy are influenced by the social and economic contexts in which they emerge. This could be seen in the fallout from the 2008 crisis. After the economic collapse, there was much more opportunity for critics of the prevailing economic wisdom than was the case prior to the crisis. The ideas of the critics had not changed. Economists like Shiller and Galbraith had been railing against some of the more conservative of the dominant economic ideas, and the policies that stemmed from them, for years without being given a great deal of credence until the crisis. Yet, the lack of real change within economics departments, or in public policy, also demonstrates that it is not only economic conditions that influence ideas. As Quiggan suggested, economic policy that was thoroughly discredited in the eyes of many by the economic crisis still appears to rule the day. This demonstrates that it is not simply economic conditions, broadly speaking, that influence economic ideas, but the way in which those economic conditions affect the material interests of those groups in society that have the capacity to influence the intellectual climate.

The economics profession has a lot to answer for. After the late 1970s, the ideas of influential economists have justified policies that have made the world more prone to economic crisis, remarkably less equal, more polluted and less safe than it might be. We seek to explain why a particular type of economist became so influential, especially from the late 1970s, and demonstrate the damage that their policies have wrought.

Since the 1970s, a dominant group of famous economists have swayed the direction of the discipline, and the policy that it influences, with easily identified distributional consequences. Starting with Milton Friedman, we trace the intellectual history of a common core of economic assumptions and beliefs about using the autonomous individual as the centerpiece for economic analysis, a commitment to formalized modeling, faith in market forces and the failure to recognize power relationships in society. We trace the rise of this dominant trend in the discipline by examining the works of its most famous adherents to demonstrate the limits of the mainstream economists' models and show how implementation of these ideas created the economic context for many of the economic difficulties that we face today. While these economists have helped create an economic policy environment that has proved catastrophic for many, it has also proved remarkably beneficial for the privileged minority, which partly explains why their ideas were greeted with such enthusiasm.

The Book in Brief

Chapter 2 examines how certain ideas came to dominate the discipline itself and the broader policy debate in society. Why do some ideas become accepted, institutionalized and popularized while others are ignored? We argue that economic knowledge is not a Darwinian process where superior ideas overcome their inferior predecessors. Rather, the ideas that dominated the discipline were shaped by a correlated combination of commitments to idealized techniques, methodological individualism and the market. Further, the adoption of certain economic ideas over others has been more a result of the imperatives of the economic environment of the time, and the institutional clout mustered by those who benefit from economic policy, than a battle of academic ideas taking place in a context-free vacuum of abstract intellectual debate. As a result, for over three decades, income, status and Nobel prizes have been the reward for those who created and justified economic policy that has had debilitating effects on the majority of citizens while benefitting a privileged minority.

Chapter 3 provides a concise review of the current economic state of affairs in the United States. This chapter lays out the economic trends that are the result of enacting the economic ideas documented in the rest of the book. The last 35 years have featured stagnating incomes for most Americans alongside large income gains for the rich, creating growing inequality. For the privilege of modest income gains, US families are working longer hours and are subject to worrying environmental conditions. Finally, what limited successes there were in the post-1980 economy were based on the inevitably shaky foundation of household debt, which came crashing down in the 2008 crisis.

Chapter 4 starts our individual case studies with Milton Friedman (Nobel Prize 1976), the godfather of the so-called "conservative counter-revolution" in economics. His writing followed two streams. One was the academic work, sometimes with Edmund Phelps (Nobel Prize 2006). His natural-rate-of-unemployment hypothesis, monetary theory, and views on fiscal policy all contained the message that government should not interfere with the macroeconomy.

The second was his more popular work railing against government regulation and defending the free market. We argue that once you translate the algebra and jargon, Friedman's ideas served the interests of American business at the expense of the rest of society. As with the other economists in this book, we will examine the distributional consequences of Friedman's ideas.

Chapter 5 discusses the works of Gary Becker, James Buchanan, Sam Peltzman, George Stigler and Gordon Tullock, five economists who provided a novel intellectual justification for Friedman's fear of government intervention in the economy. George Stigler (Nobel Prize 1982) is best known for developing the Economic Theory of Regulation, also known as "capture," in which interest groups and other political participants will use the regulatory and coercive powers of government to shape laws and regulations in a way that is beneficial to them, rather than for whom those laws were designed to help.

Becker won the Nobel Prize (1992) for "having extended the domain of microeconomic analysis to a wide range of human behavior and interaction, including nonmarket behavior." Former Treasury Secretary and current Harvard University President Lawrence Summers, claimed it "was the most overdue prize they've ever given." Becker is most famous for applying the assumptions of the rational, maximizing individual to problems that were, prior to Becker, considered outside the realm of economics, like crime, the family, and discrimination. Relevant here is his analysis of interest groups lobbying for government favors.

James Buchanan (Nobel Prize 1986) and Gordon Tullock expanded on this in what became known as "Public Choice" interest group theory, which argues that government intervention leads to waste in the economy. Public choice created the intellectual justification for the elimination of regulations by arguing that the government solution will inevitably be worse than the market failure it was designed to solve. By ignoring corporate economic and political power, public choice introduces a misleading bias into the analysis of how public policies are determined and the appropriate solution to capture.

Robert Lucas (Nobel Prize 1995), Neil Wallace, Thomas Sargent (Nobel Prize 2011), Finn Kydland (Nobel Prize 2004) and Edward Prescott (Nobel Prize 2004) are the subject of Chapter 6. Taken together, these economists advanced a macroeconomic theory that, at its heart, contained two ideas that became very influential in economic policy. The first is that Keynesian fiscal policy was ineffective given the inherent efficiency of markets. The second is that the economy performs best when it is most "flexible." Essentially, this means that the price mechanism is able to fluctuate as freely as possible, which is accomplished in practice by eliminating labor market impediments to downward wage movements, such as minimum wages, favorable union rules, and unemployment benefits. These theories cannot explain the prolonged periods of economic downturn. Critics have ridiculed the interpretation of the Great Depression offered by these economists. Franco Modigliani mocked these economic ideas for implying that, "What happened to the United States in the 1930s was a severe attack of contagious laziness!" (Modigliani, 1977, p. 6). Paul Krugman contemptuously described their explanation of the Depression as the "Great Vacation" (Krugman, 2009e).

Chapter 7 looks at the connection between economics and financial crises. According to the World Bank, there have been 117 systemic banking crises worldwide since the late 1970s (Caprio, 2003). These recurrent crises occurred during a period in which the financial sector became a much larger component of economic activity and there was a decline in regulatory oversight. The ideas of three economists contributed substantially to these trends. Robert C. Merton and Myron S. Scholes (Nobel Prize 1997), or the "Newton of modern finance," developed the formula for opening up the options and derivatives markets. Eugene Fama (Nobel Prize 2013) is famous for the Efficient Market Hypothesis (EMH), which stated that assets are accurately priced and financial bubbles practically, if not entirely, impossible. According to James Crotty, the ideas of these authors led to the light regulatory approach of what he termed the New Financial Architecture (NFA), but they are "based on patently unrealistic assumptions and … no convincing empirical support. Thus, the 'scientific' foundation of the NFA is shockingly weak and its celebratory narrative is a fairy tale" (Crotty, 2009, p. 564). Deregulation of the financial sector and the creation of exotic financial instruments created a very profitable policy environment for the financial sector. It was also directly responsible for the 2008 crisis.

Lawrence Summers and Alan Greenspan are the subjects of Chapter 8. Summers and Greenspan have not garnered economic fame because of their ideas, but because they have translated the ideas of others into public policy. Greenspan was the chairman of the Federal Reserve of the United States from 1987 to 2006. Summers was the deputy secretary of the Treasury until 1999 when he was promoted to secretary of the Treasury in the Clinton administration. He was a professor of economics at Harvard and was president of that university between 2001 and 2006. From 2009 to 2010, he was the director of the Obama Administration's National Economic Council. What have they done in these positions of power? Their policy perspective on the financial sector over which they have ruled, has been, to put it kindly, flexible. They manipulated interest rates and altered regulations to serve American corporate interests at home and abroad, contributing to rising profits, falling wages and one publicly funded financial crisis after another, culminating in the 2008 financial meltdown.

The Conclusion examines the work of two economists, Paul Krugman (Nobel Prize 2008) and Joseph Stiglitz (Nobel Prize 2001), who are perhaps the most famous opponents of neoliberal economics from within the mainstream of the discipline. On one hand, Krugman and Stiglitz demonstrate that economics is not a homogeneous field, in which all scholars toe the neoliberal line. There are important and influential dissenters. On the other hand, the manner in which the academic work of Krugman and Stiglitz relies on mainstream economic methods creates some important problems for their ability to accurately explain the economy since the 1970s. In addition, despite the renown of these authors, even they would have to admit that their suggestions have been largely ignored in the post-1980 world, leaving them increasingly frustrated by the direction of economic policy. Although neoliberal economists do not have a monopoly on economic ideas and there are numerous dissenting voices, from the more mainstream opinions of Krugman and Stiglitz to the more radical theories of Minsky, these alternatives are unlikely to become actual policy unless the influence of business in the political system can be drastically reduced.

2
The Contest of Economic Ideas: Survival of the Richest

Introduction

The evolution of the economic discipline has been portrayed in two very different ways. The first, and probably most popular, explanation is that economic thinking has followed a Darwinian process of survival of the fittest. According to this explanation, ideas are held because they provide the best explanation of the functioning of the economy given the state of the art in the discipline. When a newly minted idea comes along that can better explain the functioning of the economy, the superior idea will be widely adopted. Through this constant replacement of inferior theories with superior alternatives, the frontiers of knowledge are extended. This approach is taken by some of the leading scholars of the history of economic thought, for example Mark Blaug's (1997) *Economic Theory in Retrospect*, perhaps the primary text in the field. According to this view, economic theory advances as intellectual ideas clash in the academic arena and the superior defeat the inferior. Many scholars of the discipline would probably prefer a more gradualist analogy, along the lines of which each new generation of economists stands on the shoulders of giants, but the general notion of the advance of ever better ideas in an always improving discipline is a fairly accurate reflection of this perspective.

The second approach argues that prevailing economic thought is not so much a triumph, no matter how gradual and plodding, of good ideas over bad in the isolated world of the ivory tower. Rather, what is considered "good" or "bad" in terms of which economic ideas are formulated, accepted and adopted, is influenced by attempts to solve the actual economic problems of the day. This is the approach favored by people like Robert Heilbroner (1999) in his seminal book *The Worldly Philosophers* (apparently the second best-selling economics book of all time), which connects the ideas of great economists with their life and times. In the words of John Kenneth Galbraith, "the enemy of the conventional wisdom is not ideas but the march of events" (Galbraith, 2001, p. 24). Perhaps the most famous example that best fits this explanation is that of J.M. Keynes, who formulated a theory on the cause of, and cure for, long-lasting economic stagnation in *The General Theory of Employment, Interest and Money*. The book was published in 1935, when the wealthy capitalist countries were suffering through the decade-long Great Depression, which the economics profession (or to be more precise, the mainstream of economics) could neither explain nor solve. Keynes's theory was not "correct" or "incorrect." The usefulness of what became known as Keynesian economics is still one of the major debates within economics today. However, it did arrive in precisely the right economic context.

We would argue that a more accurate, alternative explanation of what becomes "accepted wisdom" in the discipline is a slightly more complicated process. In keeping with those who have followed on Thomas Kuhn's *Structure of Scientific Revolutions* (1962), we would argue that circumstances play a significant role in the direction of intellectual inquiry. However, it is not narrowly the economic context described in the previous paragraph that defines circumstances. Rather, this more broadly involves three factors.

First, there is an element of truth to the first "advance of academic ideas" approach, but it is less the advance of better ideas over their inferior predecessors than it is the increasing technification of the discipline in its attempt to become the most scientific of the social sciences, marked by the increasing use of mathematics and statistical empirical techniques. Whether this amounts to an advance is more open to debate. The discipline of economics is to be commended for its commitment to seeking chains of reasoning as well as the mathematical and statistical quest for a rigorous understanding of how the world actually works. We will argue, however, that the economists who ascended in the discipline after 1980 did not tether their technical chains to anything that actually resembles a capitalist economy. To borrow a phrase from Anwar Shaikh, in his article "The Poverty of Algebra," "the so-called rigor of their algebra merely disguises the true condition of their theory: rigor mortis" (Shaikh, 1979).

The second factor is the economic context. As already noted, economic ideas are not formulated, accepted and adopted in a vacuum of intellectual debate isolated from the outside world. Rather, as the second approach recognizes, economics (and its conversion into economic policy) does attempt to actually solve economic problems of the day. However, in any given economic context, which ideas will win the debate about what is causing the problem and, therefore, what solution will provide the cure, is not always straightforward. For example, Keynes was not the first economist with a credible theory of the Great Depression. Michal Kalecki's work preceded Keynes, and provided "a more rigorously constructed, coherent, and general system" (Feiwel, 1975). Yet, it was Keynes's ideas that came to dominate the profession and economic policy after World War II, not Kalecki. We would argue that the reason for this is that Kalecki's ideas were based on a class analysis that placed profits at the center of his theory, and contained statements like "The capitalist system is not a 'harmonious' regime, whose purpose is the satisfaction of the needs of its citizens, but an 'antagonistic' regime which is to secure profits for capitalists" (Kalecki, 1991); these ideas were not as palatable to those in a position to make economic policy. The reason that Keynes became a household name while Kalecki was doomed to academic obscurity had less to do with the inherent inferiority of Kalecki's ideas and more that his ideas were more offensive to those with economic and political power.

Third, in relation to the second point, those with economic and political power can influence the dominant economic ideas by using their financial clout to fund institutions that foster and disseminate economic ideas from which they will benefit. Formulating and popularizing economic ideas is not merely an academic exercise. Rather, any set of ideas benefits from financial support, which can facilitate the formulation and dissemination of ideas in a number of ways. Financial support can fund research positions at universities. It can finance research institutes that can solicit and popularize certain ideas over others. It can pay for popularizing these ideas by contributing to book publishing and writing opinion pieces. It can pay to lobby politicians to get ideas turned into policy. This is not to suggest that only ideas backed by the financial clout of the economic elite will ever be heard. Rather, it is to suggest that in the contest of economic ideas, finance, and the institutional capacity that finance creates, makes for a somewhat uneven playing field.

The rest of this chapter will attempt to flesh out how this three-part explanation can explain the evolution of the economics profession since the late 1970s.

Scientific Pretension

Both defenders and critics of the current state of the discipline agree that economists wield considerable influence on the intellectual and policy worlds. Yet, this was not always the case. Prior to World War II, the profession was still in its infancy in the US, and economics did not enjoy the prestige (or perhaps infamy) that it does today. Economists were not frequently sought out to advise on public policy matters, and often when they were, they lacked a "concert of opinion" (Bernstein, 2001, p. 39). This started to change thanks to the contributions of Keynes and the transformation of the discipline during World War II.

Ironically for a discipline associated with analyzing the market mechanism, economics found its feet as a social science under the state-centered decision making of national defense. This was part of a very explicit policy of the American Economics Association (AEA), which wanted economics to be of service to the war effort (Bernstein, 2001, p. 85). It was during World War II and its Cold War aftermath that economics started to develop a "concert of opinion" and a more unified set of tools with which to investigate economic matters. During the war, linear programming was especially valuable to the Navy. The US Department of Defense was also optimistic that the field of game theory could be applied to military situations (Fullbrook, 2005). It was under the Air Force, and its close relationship with the RAND Corporation, that the mathematical solutions of general equilibrium were developed. The Department of Defense publications commended economists Kenneth Arrow and Gerard Debreu for "modeling of conflict and cooperation whether it be [for] combat or procurement contracts or exchange of information among dispersed decision nodes" (Fullbrook, 2005).

The same mathematical rigor was applied by Samuelson to Keynes's theories in the US. Although there was much in Keynes's work that was inimical to formalization, Samuelson succeeded in developing a mathematical "Keynesian" model of the economy that became the "concert of opinion" that was so desired by pre-war economists. However, in restricting Keynes's ideas to a series of malleable equations, Samuelson lost much that was valuable in Keynes. For Samuelson, instability in the capitalist economy, and therefore the need for government stabilization, is caused by real world obstacles to the proper functioning of the market, like wages that are rigid rather than flexible. While this could be used to support the case for Keynesian policy, it also could be, and was, used by more conservative economists to argue that rather than stabilization, a better policy would be to eliminate the rigidities in the economy, by reducing the power of unions or getting rid of employment insurance benefits, for example. What Samuelson lost in his quest for formalization was Keynes's core idea that even when functioning at its best, the market economy was inherently unstable, not because of inconvenient (and perhaps correctable) obstacles, but due to the unpredictable behavior of investors (Smith, 2010, p. 41). Samuelson's formalization involved purging Keynes's more profound critiques of the economic system. Edward Fullbrook described Samuelson's version of Keynes as "like a Henry Miller novel without sex and profanity" (Fullbrook, 2005).

The trend to a more formalized, mathematical profession became even more pronounced after the 1970s. Mathematical rigor has come to be a prerequisite for publication in many of the more prestigious journals and it dominates the training of graduate students at the elite universities. The more important journals, like the *American Economic Review* (*AER*), the flagship journal of the AEA, declared that they would stop publishing in the less than rigorous fields of philosophy and history, which were, unsurprisingly, precisely the areas in which there was the most skepticism about the direction of the discipline. The lack of opportunity to publish in the leading economic journals then created a deterrent for emerging scholars considering pursuing these areas of study. The inability of existing academics in these areas to publish in the supposedly leading journals was also used as proof of their inferiority (Mirowski, 2010). As more focus was being placed on mathematical prowess, students were not being trained to examine actual economic problems or institutions (Hodgson, 2004). One survey of economic graduate students from the "top" US programs found that while 65 percent felt that "being smart in the sense of problem solving" was important to their career success and 57 percent considered "excellent in mathematics" crucial, only 3 percent thought that "having a thorough knowledge of the economy" was beneficial (Klamer & Colander, 1990). This commitment to rigor has served economists well. It has made it the most "scientific" of the social sciences and has created precisely the type of "unified" disciplinary structure that economists had been craving. Economists earn higher salaries than their colleagues in the other social sciences and are more sought after in the public realm from newspapers to the civil service to expert testimony (Fourcade et al., 2015, p. 110). As Richard Freeman wrote in 1999, "[S]ociologists and political scientists have less powerful analytical tools and know less than we do, or so we believe. By scores on the Graduate Record Examination and other criteria, our field attracts students stronger than theirs, and our courses are more mathematically demanding" (Freeman, 1999, p. 141).

Economists' desire to shape their field in a manner that mimics the physical sciences was reflected in the number of physicists migrating into economics. There had been a fairly steady stream of physicists into economics since the turn of the twentieth century, but the number increased considerably after 1980 when the end of the Cold War reduced opportunities in that discipline. The fact that physicists often did not even need to take any economic training to switch academic worlds illustrated the extent to which economics had become a discipline of models (Mirowski, 2010).[1] This would suggest that formalism and rigor in economics have evolved to be an end to themselves rather than a tool to advance the understanding of real-world economic problems. This has not gone unnoticed, even among some of the leading lights of the profession. In 1984, Wassily Leontief, Nobel Prize winner and former president of the AEA stopped writing articles in protest over the abstract theorizing that had come to dominate the discipline. His principle complaint was that those who wanted to study the manner in which the economy really functioned were marginalized and called for a profound rethinking of how economic research was conducted (Smith, 2010, p. 42).

---

1   Many of these physicists were responsible for creating the complicated risk models in the financial sector that were, in part, responsible for the 2008 financial crisis.

According to historian of economics Roger Backhouse, increased rigor introduced a subtle bias into modern economics after the 1970s. Economic conclusions were taken seriously when they were mathematically derived from fully specified assumptions. However, in order to keep the mathematical models tractable, patently false and often misleading simplifications became commonplace. For example, one might reasonably question whether economists actually ever truly believed in the assumptions of perfect competition and individual rational optimization, or whether they were devices employed to permit rigorous analysis of manageable models. In macroeconomics, a number of simplifying assumptions also emerged: people take advantage of all the information available to them, they are infinitely farsighted and they are representative agents (that is, that all people are homogeneous). As was the case with microeconomics, these were not selected because they were in any way deemed to be realistic, but because they facilitated rigor. Yet all of these assumptions introduce a bias towards "conservative" or free market solutions to economic problems (Backhouse, 2005, p. 383; Varoufakis, 2011). So, what appears on the surface to merely be an eminently practical decision to create a rigorous yet manageable model of economic activity tended to produce results that were unintentionally biased against government intervention. The quest for scientific rigor does not inevitably require these kinds of narrow assumptions and much of the economic discipline has moved away from them in its modeling. However, for an influential period during the 1970s and 1980s, these were the commonplace assumptions.

One study examining the incentives that face academic economists argued that although economists are "very honest people who chose their career because they were motivated by noble goals such as the quest for truth," like any other profession they respond to the incentive structures in their jobs (Zingales, 2014, p. 151). For example, because of the obvious requirement of getting published and the central role played in this process by editors of prestigious journals (through selecting referees and even overruling them), if editors are pro-business, then articles are likely to reflect that bias. Although this begs the question of why editors might be pro-business, it would create an incentive for academics to, no doubt unconsciously, tailor their research so that it is more likely to get published. (Luigi Zingales suggests that they might enjoy sitting on corporate boards, but other possibilities could be imagined, from the lucrative fees of the corporate lecture circuit to personal ideology. It could equally be the more hidden bias of assumptions and techniques discussed above.) His litmus test of pro-business bias is the extent to which articles support the current level of executive compensation. Articles that support the current level, or an increase, in executive compensation are considered to have a pro-business bias. Zingales finds that three of the most prestigious economic journals: *Quarterly Journal of Economics, Journal of Political Economy* and *American Economic Review* have a clear pro-business bias, compared to the larger sample of 144 most downloaded articles on the subject from the Social Science Research Network (Zingales, 2014, p. 135).

The pro-free market bias was perhaps more pernicious because it was also deeply hidden. The development of a formalized, mathematical analysis of the economy was very valuable for the profession. It was an important comparative advantage over other social sciences and created the impression that economics was a non-ideological discipline, aimed at providing positive, scientific answers to policy questions. Of course, the absence of politics is much more illusion than reality:

> Even more to the point the rigor and scientific precision that economists claim are characteristic of their discipline serve to silence through the substitution of arguments over ends with those over means, the genuine political debate that has (and will) always surround economic policy formulation as a whole. (Bernstein, 2001, p. 191)

The turn towards a more formal economics, with strict simplifying assumptions, also moved the discipline away from what Robert Heilbroner and Richard Milberg termed macroeconomic foundations. They argue that, ironically, in ignoring the social forces, like power and values, which influence behavior, "for all practical purposes they have eliminated the individual" (Heilbroner & Milberg, 1995, p. 84).

> The development of the human psyche, from the earliest moments of infancy on, takes place through the gradual ingestion and incorporation of the individual's surroundings from its earliest familial influences through its exposure to innumerable influences on other individuals directly or indirectly. Thus the concept of the individual—

the analytical focus of so much conventional social science—appears most clearly in the form of a unique distillation of social influences. In Marx's profound words, the individual appears as "the ensemble of social relations" (Heilbroner & Milberg, 1995, p. 86).

By divorcing the individual from the macrofoundations from which it is formed, economics has forsaken the responsibility for studying the crucial social influences on people's behavior.

Perhaps most important among these neglected macrofoundations is the role of the economic system itself. As Heilbroner and Milberg claim, a discussion of medieval life without acknowledging how it was shaped by the feudal system would be considered a strange omission, yet the nature of the capitalist system is rarely discussed in modern economic enquiry (Heilbroner & Milberg, 1995, p. 6). The economic system in which people currently operate creates a specific class structure in which power is not distributed equally. It creates greater rights and privileges for some than for others. Yet, the underlying social order created by capitalism is not a usual subject of enquiry in mainstream economics. Further, the fact that capitalism is, itself, a social construction, rather than a natural state of affairs, is rarely considered.

Material Interests and Economic Conditions

Economists may revel in arcane mathematical formulas and complex statistical tests but these are rarely purely academic exercises with no bearing on economic reality. Economic theory, and its corresponding policy, does attempt to deal with the prevalent economic conditions. But how the economic "problems" of the day are defined and what the "solutions" to those problems might be is not usually straightforward. It is exceedingly rare for economists to identify an uncontested theory or policy that could be construed as being in the public interest in the sense that it would benefit all of society. Rather, theories or policies tend to benefit some in society at the expense of others. So, the particular economic conditions that are seen as a problem and the specific solutions to that problem will have important distributional effects. This means that the material interests of different groups in society will be differentially impacted by the policies supported by the state of the art in the economic discipline. The corollary of this is that different groups will have a material interest in getting certain economic policies implemented.

Of the differing groups in society, the corporate sector is arguably the most powerful. Corporations are not in the business of producing our goods and services, but in the business of making profits. Without enough profits, they shut down their factories, mines, stores, farms and banks. Without profits, they do not invest in new machines or hire more workers. Maximizing profits is not a matter of morals or ethics for firms, but a condition of survival. The "circuit of capital" demands that businesses first must be concerned with acquiring the least expensive inputs. Second, they must make use of these inputs in a production process that ensures a competitive price in the marketplace. Next, they must be able to market these products in order to be able to sell them. Lower-cost capitalists will drive higher-cost capitalists from the market by reducing prices and having more profits to invest for the next round of production and sales. The firm that is able to introduce techniques that lower costs has profits available to invest in new techniques, which enables it to successfully compete with rivals. Without competitive profits, research and development, investment and advertising all become impossible and the fate of the firm is sealed. This also implies that profits are not only crucial for firms, but also for the economy more generally. When profits are low, firms are unwilling to invest or hire, creating economic malaise. Any explanation of economic conditions that fails to place profitability at the center of the analysis is missing the main story.

Samuel Bowles, David Gordon and Thomas Weisskopf once wrote that profits are the spoils of a three-front war that firms must continuously wage with their workforce, the government, and other companies (especially those from other countries) (Bowles et al., 1986). The conflict with their workers is over containing wages while at the same time convincing them to increase productivity as much as possible. The struggle with the government is over the extent to which the state will impact a firm's bottom line by altering its costs through such things as regulations, taxes, subsidies, or its revenues, through, for example, government purchases. This places the firm in conflict with a wide variety of citizens who expect the government to undertake various profit-constraining activities, from those who pressure the state to implement environmental protection; to those who think that the government has a responsibility to provide for the collective good with respect to health, education and welfare. The third and final front is a battle with other firms to reduce any input costs and increase revenues from product sales. On this front, firms may have an important ally in their national governments, which attempt to tilt the rules of the international economy in favor of their own firms. This can be done by changing trade rules, altering exchange rates, or using military force.

The dominant economic ideas after World War II were very different from those which thrived after 1980. The post-war policy environment was conditioned by the Great Depression of the 1930s, a trauma so grave that it forced a dramatic reconsideration of how the economy functioned. Unemployment rates of over 25 percent, mass poverty and widespread bankruptcy cried out for both an explanation of economic collapse and a remedy to prevent it from happening again. The Keynesian explanation of the Depression appeared to provide both the diagnosis and the cure. The Depression, Keynes argued, was caused by deficient demand. When firms decreased their investment, workers were laid off. Unemployed workers' decreased their spending, reducing sales for firms, cutting profits and forcing further reductions in investments, creating a vicious cycle from which it was difficult to escape. Keynes's cure was to maintain incomes and, therefore, demand, through government job creation. As a sweeping general statement, the dominant post-war macro reflected Keynes's belief that governments could (and should) use fiscal policy—use of the tax and spending powers of government, and monetary policy—the power of the central bank (The Federal Reserve—Fed—in the US) to influence interest rates, to smooth business cycle fluctuations and maintain a low level of unemployment. In addition, the need to maintain consumption created an important justification for government benefits for the unemployed. The double-digit unemployment rates of the Depression also destroyed the facile argument that those without work deserved no financial assistance since those who truly wanted a job could find one. Finally, the collapse of so many firms, especially in the banking industry, created a justification for state regulation to limit the more risky and detrimental activities of companies. The crisis of the Depression could be interpreted as the economic context in which government intervention became acceptable.

We would argue that the post-war intellectual climate within economics was not just down to internal debates among academic scribblers, or the inherent superiority of Keynesian ideas, but the power of different interests in the US to promote certain economic ideas. The very fact that high levels of employment should be an economic goal reflected a different balance of power between groups in the economy. Low unemployment tilts the playing field in wage negotiations in favor of workers and away from business because there are fewer desperate, unemployed laborers with whom the gainfully employed have to compete. In short, when unemployment is low, workers have a stronger hand because they know that they will be harder to replace. In the decades after World War II, tight labor markets (and other pro-worker changes to labor market institutions like the Wagner Act, which made it easier to form unions) did cause a rise in wages during this period. We would argue that it is no coincidence that this was a period in which labor, organized into politically powerful industrial unions, enjoyed much more clout than was the case in the post-1980s economy.

Yet, as we shall see later, Keynesian full employment was not completely antagonistic to profits. The unique characteristics of the post-World War II decades made it possible to have increases in both wage and profits. First, productivity was increasing rapidly because of technological innovation in production. This meant that each worker could produce more in each hour of work. This reduced costs per unit and created the opportunity for wage increases without cutting into profits. It also created the need for a mass market for US products. The second factor was a lack of international competitors for the US after the European economies were decimated during the war, with the result that increased demand by the US workforce was likely to be purchased from US-based companies. Thus, the broad-based income gains that were, in part, due to high employment, played an important role in maintaining profits as well.

Keynesian stabilization policy aimed at maintaining low unemployment was only one of many examples of what was one of the dominant strands of economic thought during this period— identifying areas in which markets fail and prescribing corrective government action, much of which reduced the latitude of firms to pursue profits unhindered. This reflected a balance of power between different groups in society in which labor held greater relative strength than was the case after 1980. However, this is not to say that these policies were antagonistic to business. Business in the US flourished in the 1950s and 1960s, with profit rates that were superior to those even in the boom years after 1980. As we pointed out in the Introduction, there was a remarkably diverse menu of economic ideas, like those of Kalecki, which could have risen to prominence in the wake of the Great Depression and World War II. The fact that it was the ideas of the liberal version of Keynes (as opposed to those either to the "right" or "left") that came to dominate both economic ideas and government policy reflected the balance of power between historically relatively powerful labor and perpetually powerful business.

So, how were the economic problems of the late 1970s defined and who benefitted from the solutions? The conventional story of the downfall of Keynesian economics, with its emphasis on the ability of government to successfully stabilize the macroeconomy, is that it could not cope with stagflation. The late 1970s saw the twin evils of high unemployment and high inflation stalking the US. Traditional Keynesian policy (or to be a bit more precise, the Samuelson variant of Keynes), which focused on manipulating aggregate demand through fiscal and monetary policy, would inevitably exacerbate one of these problems if it attempted to combat the other. Using expansionary policy to alleviate unemployment would stoke the inflationary fires. Attempting to reduce inflationary pressures through contractionary policy would throw people out of work. Keynesian stabilization policy was discredited when it had no answer to the economic dilemmas of the day. This is very much a tale of the limitations of economic theory being shown up by the march of real world events.

There is an element of truth to this story. Traditional Keynesian policy cannot deal simultaneously with inflation and unemployment. Yet it is only a partial truth. Stagflation was a problem, but it was more a symptom than the disease itself. The underlying problem was a decline in corporate profitability and the challenges to capitalist power that had emerged through the 1960s and 1970s. From the end of World War II to roughly the late 1960s, the US corporate world enjoyed strong profits. However, starting around 1965, corporate profits fell precipitously for almost twenty years (Duménil & Lévy, 2004, pp. 24–8). It was this fall in profits that created the economic turmoil in the US. High rates of unemployment, low investment and sluggish economic growth were the inevitable result. Not coincidentally, the anti-inflationary policies that were chosen to get out of the stagflation problem were precisely those that also restored profitability for American business.

The causes of the fall in profits is the subject of much debate in heterodox economic circles (Brenner, 2006; Duménil & Lévy, 2011; Pollin, 2003; Shaikh, 2011), but what is much more universally accepted is that starting around 1980, business and government took active measures to restore profits, creating what became known as "neoliberalism" (Duménil & Lévy, 2012). At the national level, these policies are most closely associated with Ronald Reagan in the US, Margaret Thatcher in the United Kingdom and Brian Mulroney in Canada. Broadly speaking, neoliberalism marked a profound shift in the economic underpinnings of countries, which shifted power to business in several ways (a more detailed account of the economic results of these policies can be found in Chapter 3). First, by abandoning traditional Keynesian demand-side stabilization in favor of monetarist policy aimed at controlling inflation with high interest rates, low levels of unemployment were jettisoned as a policy goal, putting downward pressure on workers' demands. Second, a supply-side program of reducing progressive tax rates (designed to create incentives for investment, savings and work) redistributed after-tax income to the rich. Third, to further reduce costs to firms, the regulatory role of the government was greatly reduced, and where it still existed, traditional bureaucratic regulation was replaced with cost-benefit analysis and market solutions. Finally, the welfare system and labor market were reformed by, among other things, policies reducing the power of unions and making government benefits to the unemployed more miserly. This was euphemistically known as "flexibility," but the distributional effects against labor and for business should be obvious (Jenkins & Eckert, 2000, p. 313). To this list of national policies we could add the international trend to eliminate barriers to trade and financial flows, forcing workers in the US to compete with lower-wage labor in the developing world, while capital was free to find the location in which it could earn the highest return (Duménil & Lévy, 2012).

These neoliberal policies shifted economic risks from either the state or the firm to workers. For example, reduced unemployment benefits transfers the downside risk of economic instability from the government to labor. Similarly, limiting the power of unions reduced workers' job security, making them more likely to face dismissal, moving risk from firms to workers. These changes represented a dramatic reversal of the historical trend of increasing social protection for workers from the vagaries of the labor market. Yet, as John Quiggan pointed out, while workers were expected to shoulder more of the risk in the labor market, risk was being reduced for businesses and their executives. This was most obvious in the massive government bailout of the financial industry which was deemed "too big to fail," but the same socialization of corporate risk was extended to the auto industry as well. Even before the economic collapse, CEOs earned stock options that would yield massive payoffs when the company did well, but would not penalize them when the firm performed poorly (Quiggin, 2010, pp. 16–18).

Most of the economists profiled in this book provided theoretical justification for these policy changes. As Michael Bernstein argued:

> As the Keynesian consensus of the post war era dissolved, and as it was replaced by an increasingly detached social theory that actively condemned governmental activism in the marketplace, the economics profession became less and less an engaged social scientific community and the public service and more and more a mouthpiece for a particular, interest-based agenda ... No longer ministers to statist power, many economists reinvented themselves as privy councillors to private wealth. (Bernstein, 2001, p. 173)

This is not to suggest that economists were "in the pocket" of business. Nor is it suggesting that all of these economists were fundamentally right-wing (although many of them were). Rather, it suggests that of all the economists, and all of the economic ideas that were bandied about, during this period the majority of the ones that rose to prominence—that came to dominate policy and earn disciplinary kudos—were those that favored business (see Box 2.1).

The economists that we discuss below played an important role in legitimizing the neoliberal policies that reversed the profitability decline of the 1970s. This marked an important departure not just for the structure of the economy but also the economics profession,

Box 2.1 An excerpt from "The Social Responsibility of Business is to Increase its Profits," by Milton Friedman, New York Times Magazine, September 13, 1970

When I hear businessmen speak eloquently about the "social responsibilities of business in a free-enterprise system," I am reminded of the wonderful line about the Frenchman who discovered at the age of 70 that he had been speaking prose all his life. The businessmen believe that they are defending free enterprise when they declaim that business is not concerned "merely" with profit but also with promoting desirable "social" ends; that business has a "social conscience" and takes seriously its responsibilities for providing employment, eliminating discrimination, avoiding pollution and whatever else may be the catchwords of the contemporary crop of reformers. In fact they are—or would be if they or anyone else took them seriously—preaching pure and unadulterated socialism. Businessmen who talk this way are unwitting puppets of the intellectual forces that have been undermining the basis of a free society these past decades.

which, as Bernstein pointed out, favored Keynesian policies prior to the 1970s. It also marked an important divergence from the older tradition of classical liberalism, most commonly associated with writers like Adam Smith, which had a strong mistrust of corporate power despite its support of free markets. According to University of Notre Dame economist Philip Mirowski, in contrast to their classical liberal predecessors, a hallmark of neoliberal economics is that "Corporations can do no wrong, or at least they are not to be blamed if they do" (Mirowski, 2009, p. 438). This transformation was not an accidental windfall for the business community, but, rather, was the result of some quite deliberate planning.

Institutional Support

Economists must surely recognize that there is a market for ideas. The choice of research topics, the results of that research, and the dissemination of findings all depend, to some extent, on the financing that is available for different areas of study. Ideas are bought and paid for more than they are "free floating," despite policy intellectuals' frequent claims to the contrary (Jenkins & Eckert, 1989). It was no accident that the dominant ideas in economics reflected the changing sources of institutional support.

In its formative years during and after World War II, various branches of the government—particularly the military—were generous donors to the economics profession. The Navy funded the work of Arrow and Debreu. The Department of Defense, more generally, was another important source of funding for economics research. Finally, the RAND Corporation (which received funding from the Air Force to help US defense policy) provided funding for specific scholars, established "Defense Policy Seminars" at the largest US universities in the 1950s and 1960s, and started a graduate fellowship program in 1965 (Bernstein, 2001, p. 99). These sources of funding fostered a statist discipline that was obviously not adverse to an active role for government.

Yet, the institutional environment in which the economics discipline was emerging was also sensitive to its role during the Cold War. Economic research that hinted at radicalism or was critical of capitalism was not welcomed in a context that was particularly sensitive to anything that might be supportive of the communist cause. Like other areas of society, economics had its own anti-communist purge. This operated, in part, through the passive mechanism of lack of support. Funding for left-wing or radical research was non-existent, making economists interested in career advancement unlikely to follow this path. Yet it was not merely the subtle influence of financial incentives that operated during the Cold War. The more Inquisition-oriented tactics of the McCarthy era were also used. At universities, tenure and promotion were denied for those undertaking radical research. At the Council of Economic Advisers, security checks were performed on graduate students and new employees in case they were ever associated with suspicious characters (Bernstein, 2001, p. 107). There was certainly an explicit attempt to keep anything that looked vaguely Marxist out of the pages of the *American Economic Review* (*AER*). Editor Paul Hoffman rejected a paper that he flagged as worryingly radical in order to stem what he felt would be a torrent of "revised and unrevised Marxism" in the *AER* should the paper be accepted. James Washington Bell, the secretary treasurer of the American Economics Association (AEA) took a more patronizing tone, saying that he was "inclined to believe that any apostle [of Marx] must be mystical and incomprehensible" (quoted in Bernstein, 2001, p. 106).

If it was government that provided the financial resources for the development of the discipline prior to 1970s, business became a much larger force in the post 1970 world. Networks of conservative economists had, of course, been around well before this watershed date, but they were much less influential. Perhaps the most famous was the Mont Pelerin Society, founded at a 1947 conference (in the Swiss resort of Mont Pelerin, of course) and organized by Friedrich Hayek to discuss what he saw as the worrying domination of Keynesian and Marxist planning at the expense of economic freedom. The initial meeting was attended by many economic heavyweights (some of whom will appear in the pages that follow), including Ludwig Von Mises, Milton Friedman and George Stigler. Yet despite Hayek's dream of combating statist ideas with the intellectual superiority of free market economic theory, it is broadly accurate to say that Friedman, Stigler and the rest of their free market colleagues failed to impact policy until the economic crisis of the 1970s.

Essayist Lewis Lapham dates the concerted effort to organize and fund Mont Pelerin-style ideas in the US to a 1971 call to arms called "Attack on the Free Enterprise System," written by Lewis Powell for confidential circulation to the Chamber of Commerce. In it, Powell warned that

> … survival of what we call the free enterprise system lies in organization, in careful long-range planning and implementation, in consistency of action over an indefinite period of years, in the scale of financing available only through joint effort, and in the political power available only through united action and national organizations. (Quoted in Lapham, 2004).

Several now well-known businessmen took up the call including newspaper magnate Richard Mellon Scaife, weapons and chemical manufacturer John Olin, Vicks Chemical's Smith Richardson, beer baron Joseph Coors, and the Koch brothers (one of whom, David, ran as the vice presidential candidate for the Libertarian Party in 1980) who made their money in oil. Coors and Scaife combined to provide the start-up cash for the Heritage Foundation in 1973 and the Koch family financed the Cato Institute in 1977 (Lapham, 2004). These new organizations joined with previously established institutions like the American Enterprise Institute (AEI) in an effort to turn the tide of ideas toward what they would call the "free market." The fact that they received generous financial support and institutional direction from business should also provide some indication of just who would benefit from their economic ideas.

Two sociologists, J. Craig Jenkins and Craig Eckert, who have studied what they call the "new conservative economics," discovered that different institutions specialized in different policy areas. The AEI, for example, was the driving force behind promoting monetarism to combat inflation, fiscal conservatism, and the Government Regulation Program that promoted deregulation. The Heritage Foundation backed the supply-side economic policies of corporate tax reduction and deregulation. The Hoover Institution concentrated on criticizing social welfare programs like social security and income maintenance (Jenkins & Eckert, 2000). This is not to say that all of these organizations were always pulling in the same direction. There are, theoretically, potential conflicts between the balanced budgets advocated by a fiscal conservative and the sharp tax reductions of supply siders. However, despite these differences, a quick comparison of the policies implemented in the neoliberal era and those promoted by these institutions should suffice to demonstrate their remarkable success.

If there remains any doubt about who was directing these institutions or who benefitted from their research and advocacy, a quick glance at their boards of directors should put these to rest. Important business groups like the Business Roundtable, the Chamber of Commerce, and the National Association of Manufacturers cooperated with these institutes and there was considerable cross-pollination of boards. In fact, of the 287 policy directorships in these organizations, 82.5 percent were held by 221 corporate officers and private entrepreneurs (Jenkins & Eckert, 2000, p. 325).

Funding also flowed from the business to these organizations. The Scaife Foundation donated around $20 million to Heritage in the 17-year period between 1985 and 2002. Total donations from business foundations to Heritage totaled $45 million during this period (Backhouse, 2005, p. 380). Of course, individual companies like AIG,

Philip Morris, Lockheed Martin and Exxon Mobile also contributed. The big donor to the AEI (which had grown to be worth $50 million by 2009) was the Bradley Foundation, with lesser contributions from Olin, Scaife and Exxon. The Koch families' money went largely to the Cato Institute to which Scaife and Olin also contributed (Media Matters, n.d.). Even though millions of dollars have been lavished on these organizations to influence the direction of economic policy, in the grand scheme of research foundations, institutions like the AEI are not among the biggest players. For example, the assets of the Ford Foundation were over $9 billion in 2002 compared to the Bradley Foundation's more modest $500 million, while the big recent mover in the conservative foundation world has been the Walton Foundation— established by Walmart founders Sam and Helen Walton—which is focused largely on educational donations, with assets of over $1 billion in 2009 (Media Matters, n.d.). Rather, the success of these organizations was their single-minded use of the funds that they did attract.

Of course, it is also important to get ideas translated into policy. The growing impact of the conservative think tanks during this period is difficult to empirically capture but some scholars have attempted to quantify their influence. Perhaps the best study on this front was conducted by Andrew Rich. He used three measures to assess think-tank influence during the 1990s: a survey of congressional staff and journalists, the number of times they testified before Congress and the number of times they were cited in a newspaper. According to Rich's survey, in 1993 the top five think tanks with the "greatest influence on the formulation of public policy in Washington these days" were Brookings, Heritage, AEI, Progressive Policy Institute and Cato. By 1997, those same institutes occupied the top five positions, but the pecking order had changed in favor of the more conservative organizations. Heritage had moved up to the top spot, with Cato third and AEI fourth (Rich, 2004, p. 81). Sixty-eight percent of the survey respondents claimed that conservative think tanks had a greater influence than liberal think tanks, while only 5 percent argued that liberal think tanks wielded greater influence (Rich, 1997). Rich also found that between 1991 and 1999, conservative think tanks testified before the House or Senate almost one-and-a-half times more often than liberal or centrist organizations (Rich, 2004, p. 94). Conservative think tanks were also "substantively" mentioned in newspapers almost four times more frequently than their non-conservative counterparts during these years (Rich, 2004, pp. 93, 95).

While influencing what constitutes economic common sense can shape the political landscape through changing the ideas of the voting public and policy-making elite, more direct political influence was also helpful for business after 1980. Conservative think tanks have been successful in placing people in a position to advise presidents, particularly those from the Republican Party, increasing the likelihood that economic ideas will be converted into economic policy. Reagan's presidential campaign relied heavily on conservative think tanks to provide intellectual approval for his policies. This was coordinated by Martin Anderson, a senior fellow at the Hoover Institution and key Reagan policy adviser, who believed that gathering a team of intellectuals who would be "co-signing the ideas" of the candidate would dramatically increase his credibility (Abelson, 2009, p. 136). Once in power, the Reagan administration drew heavily from the think tanks that helped formulate his campaign platform. Between 1981 and 1988, nearly two hundred members of conservative think tanks went to work for the Reagan government. Hoover (55), Heritage (36) and AEI (34) were particularly large sources of personnel for the Reagan team (Abelson, 2009, p. 138).

It was during the Reagan years that the Heritage Institute came to prominence as a policy force in Washington. After Reagan was elected in 1980, Heritage presented its report, *Mandate for Leadership*, containing policy proposals cobbled together from its own research and that of other like-minded think tanks, to Edwin Meese III, who commented that the government would "rely heavily on it." By 1982, Edwin Feulner, the head of Heritage, claimed that more that 60 percent of the proposals in the report had been, or would be, adopted. Although it is likely that Feulner was overstating the impact of the document, it did become known as the "bible" of the Reagan administration (Abelson, 2009, p. 139).

Business groups also responded to Powell's 1971 call by organizing themselves more coherently to more clearly express their policy preferences and to coordinate lobbying activity. For example, the Business Roundtable was founded in 1972. Its founding document identified rising wages as a source of declining profits in the early

1970s. Its membership grew through the 1970s so that by 1979, it included nearly seventy of the top one hundred financial and non-financial corporations in the United States. It advocated for reductions in corporate taxes, increasing the retirement age, and cutbacks in environmental legislation. It opposed consumer protection advocated by Ralph Nader and legislation to improve the bargaining power of unions, especially the Labor Law Reform Act of 1978. In March 1981, the Business Roundtable publicly endorsed Ronald Reagan's entire economic program including tight monetary policy, and cuts to taxes, social spending and regulations (Kotz, 2015, p. 72).

A particularly transparent example of the influence of business lobbying on politicians is the American Legislative Exchange Program (ALEC) founded in 1973. ALEC is not really a research and policy organization like those mentioned previously, although it does produce research reports and policy studies. Rather, its main role is to craft "model" bills and resolutions that can be easily turned into law by sympathetic politicians, mostly at the state level. ALEC's funding comes from the by now usual suspects in the business foundation world including Schaife, Coors and Koch, but also draws considerable funding from individual firms. Its list of corporate donors is a virtual who's who of corporate America, from General Motors to Bank of America to Microsoft to McDonald's. Donor firms acquire veto power of the wording in the legislation cooked up by ALEC (Nichols, 2011). In one year alone (1999–2000), ALEC claims to have introduced a remarkable 3,100 individual pieces of legislation. Its recent activities include: the Automatic Income Tax Reduction Act, which would provide an automatic biennial tax rate decrease; the Public-Private Fair Competition Act, which would establish whether state agencies compete "unfairly" with the private sector, and the anti-union Right to Work Act, which removes employee's obligation to pay union dues (Rogers & Dresser, 2011). ALEC's bill pipeline was not confined to these areas, but extended to writing legislation on the environment, public schools, and health care. ALEC bills have been successfully adopted, sometimes word for word, at the state level. One might claim that this was politics "by business, for business," rather than any romantic, inclusive notions of "the people."

Business could certainly consider its institute money well spent in terms of economic output. Influential books like Milton Friedman's

Free to Choose were published. A positive deluge of newsletters and ready-for-print newspaper op-ed pieces from institutes like the Heritage Foundation and the AEI promoted neoliberal economic ideas on a wide variety of topics. Talking points were produced for sympathetic media figures like Bill O'Reilly (Lapham, 2004). In the words of Backhouse, "Funding to liberal causes has been as large, if not larger, but it has been less narrowly focused on achieving specific goals" (Backhouse, 2005, p. 381).

Conclusion

The story of how economic ideas evolve over time is not a simple one. It is not just that superior ideas overtake more primitive ones. Nor is it a matter of real-world events providing the counter-evidence to force a reconsideration of the dominant economic ideas of the day. Rather, economic evolution has been the result of a combination of forces. First, the discipline itself has (perhaps unconsciously) created a conservative, free market bias with the particular assumptions and methods that it has chosen to employ in its quest for rigor. Second, economic ideas have evolved since the 1970s in a manner that supported neoliberal policies that have restored business profits after their decline prior to the mid-1980s. Third, it was no accident that economic theory developed in this way. The US business community invested in organizations that created and disseminated research that supported these neoliberal changes. According to University of Chicago Professor Richard Posner, "modern economics is, on the one hand, very mathematical, and, on the other, very skeptical about government and very credulous about the self-regulating properties of markets" (Cassidy, 2010c). Although the economists who developed the ideas that justified this direction in the discipline were no doubt often doing so ostensibly to improve the lot of all of society, the next chapter will demonstrate that the results of the neoliberal era unambiguously favored a particular subsection of society: the business class.

3
The Consequences of Economic Ideas

There's class warfare, all right, but it's my class, the rich class, that's making war, and we're winning. (Warren Buffett, 2006, quoted in Stein, 2006)

Introduction

The last chapter suggested that three separate but interrelated factors contributed to a neoliberal or conservative bent to economic policy after about 1980. The bulk of this book is devoted to putting names to these abstract economic ideas by looking at the particular theories and affiliations of the most famous economists of this generation. However, before we get into the esoteric world of economic theory, it is worthwhile to provide a bit of evidence of the economic conditions that have been wrought by neoliberal economic ideas. Remember that neoliberal economic ideas came to prominence during a period of economic malaise, particularly in the US (and other Anglo economies), but felt around the world. The promise of these economic ideas was that they would lead America (and the other countries that followed this advice) out of stagflation and back to prosperity. The actual result could be much better described as tremendous prosperity for a minority, and long-term stagnation for the rest. This is true not only in terms of the most obvious measures, like income, but is also true in terms of important non-income components of economic well-being like economic stability, job security and a clean environment.

The US: Neoliberal Decline

In the previous chapter, we asserted that neoliberal economic policy was very good for profits and helped business in the US bounce back from the doldrums of the 1970s. Figure 3.1 shows data on the profit rate for the US. The graph shows clearly that the profit rate declined through the 1970s and then recovered after the early 1980s. This was, of course, part of the promise of neoliberal economic ideas. Their policies were aimed at restoring profits, although they were often not particularly explicit about this goal. Yet, these policies were not only supposed to increase profits, they were also supposed to deliver benefits much more broadly to the population at large. It is here that the effects of neoliberal policy diverge so dramatically from its promise.

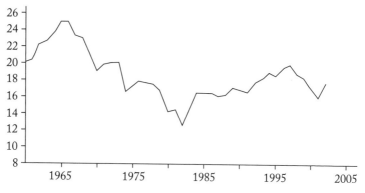

Figure 3.1   US profit rate, percent

Source: Duménil & Lévy, 2005.

The partial restoration of profitability did not quite bring the US back to the halcyon days of economic growth that existed prior to 1970. In his defense of all things Keynesian, *Keynes: The Return of the Master* (2009), Robert Skidelsky provides a telling contrast in world growth rates. Average annual global economic growth prior to 1973 was 4.8 percent. Between 1980 and 2009, this rate had fallen to 3.2 percent. The US followed a similar pattern. From 1950 to 1973, real economic growth averaged 4.2 percent per year. From 1980 to 2007, this dropped to 3 percent (Bureau of Economic Analysis, 2012). So, even by this broad measure of economic success, the neoliberal policies in vogue after 1980 were not as successful as the more interventionist policies enacted following World War II.

The US: Growth Through Exploitation

The economy looks even worse when we examine where the gains from that more limited growth actually went. Total income made in the economy is divided up between different groups in society. One of the most obvious divisions is between profits and what is paid to workers. During the "Golden Age" prior to 1980, the gains were shared between profits and wages, in part because the labor market context, like lower unemployment and higher unionization, created a more even balance of power between employers and employees. As productivity increased, wages increased at roughly the same rate. When neoliberal policies started to be introduced after 1980, the gains from production started to go far more to profits than to wages and benefits for workers.

Some of the architects of these policies were quite frank about their goals. In the UK, Alan Budd, professor of economics at the London Business School and chief economic adviser to Margaret Thatcher, described in astonishingly candid terms what occurred during the 1980s, stating that contractionary monetary policy and neoliberal fiscal policy were seen by the Thatcher government as

> ... a very good way to raise unemployment. And raising unemployment was an extremely desirable way of reducing the strength of the working classes. ... What was engineered—in Marxist terms—was a crisis of capitalism which re-created the reserve army of labor, and has allowed the capitalist to make high profits ever since. (Cohen, 2003)

Reflecting on American workers' lack of willingness to bargain or strike for higher wages, and the higher profits that resulted from this trend, Federal Reserve Chairman Alan Greenspan referred to them as "traumatized" (quoted in Perelman, 2011, p. 48), even after unemployment fell in the US through the 1990s:

> Increases in hourly compensation ... have continued to fall far short of what they would have been had historical relationships between compensation gains and the degree of labor market tightness held ... As I see it, heightened job insecurity explains a significant part of the restraint on compensation and the consequent muted price inflation ... The continued reluctance of workers to leave their jobs to seek other employment as the labor market has tightened provides further evidence of such concern, as does the tendency toward longer

labor union contracts. The low level of work stoppages of recent years also attests to concern about job security ... The continued decline in the state of the private workforce in labor unions has likely made wages more responsive to market forces ... Owing in part to the subdued behavior of wages, profits and rates of return on capital has risen to high levels. (Greenspan, 1997)

There are a number of ways to measure the impact of neoliberal policies on the power of workers in the labor market. The percentage of the workforce that was unionized declined steadily during this period. Another, related, measure is the willingness and ability of workers to go on strike to back their demands for higher wages and better working conditions. Between 1966 and 1974, there was an average of 352 work stoppages involving at least a thousand workers, per year. After 1981, workers became much less militant. In the decade of the 2000s, the most strike-filled year was 2000 in which there were only 39 large walkouts. In 2009, there were five (Perelman, 2011, p. 49). Even in the low unemployment years prior to 2008, workers in the US were cowed into passivity; after the economic collapse, they were even quieter.

The lack of power for workers in the neoliberal labor market had predictable effects on the distribution of income between profits and wages. According to economist Lester Thurow, US real per capita GDP rose 36 per cent from 1973 to 1995, yet the real hourly wages of non-supervisory workers declined by 14 per cent (1996, p. 2). Joel Rogers, director of the Center on Wisconsin Strategy, calculated that if wages had tracked productivity since 1980 as they had after World War II, "median family income in the U.S. would be about $20,000 higher today than it is" (Tasini, 2006). Even during the economic boom period from 2001 to 2006, workers did not gain nearly as handsomely as business. Wages and salaries grew at a modest 1.9 percent per year after adjusting for inflation during this period, while corporate profits after inflation increased by 12.8 percent annually. As a result, in 2006, wages and salaries made up a smaller percentage of total national income (51.6 percent) than at any point in the past 77 years. Even if benefits, like health care, are tacked on to wages to calculate overall compensation, the broad trends remain the same. Overall compensation increased at 2.5 percent a year after inflation, a much slower rate than is usually the case during economic booms, so that it stood at 64 percent of national income in 2006, the second lowest it has been since 1968 (the lowest was 1997) (Aron-Dine & Shapiro, 2007, pp. 1–2).

The growth of corporate profits relative to worker compensation is also reflected in a growing inequality between the very rich and the rest of society. Figure 3.2 shows that between 1967 and 2009, the share of total income that was earned by the wealthiest 20 percent of the population increased from 44 percent to 50 percent, the other 80 percent of the population took home a lower share of income. The real gains have come at the very top of the income spectrum. In fact, the higher up the income spectrum, the larger the gains during this period. The top 5 percent of earners saw their share of income increase from 17 to 22 percent. According to inequality experts Thomas Piketty and Emmanuel Saez, between 1973 and 2000, the average income of the bottom 90% of US taxpayers fell by 7%. Incomes of the top 1% rose by 148%, the top 0.1 % by 343%, and extremely well off in the top .01% rose by an amazing 599% (Piketty & Saez, 2003). CEO compensation has followed this trend. In 1965, the average pay of the CEOs at the top 350 US firms (ranked by sales) stood at about 20 times the average compensation of their workers. Figure 3.3 shows that this ratio increased steadily, but fairly slowly until about 1990, when it exploded

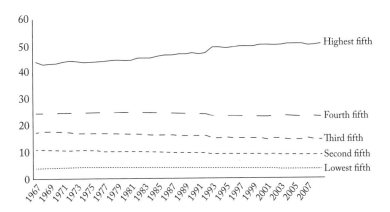

Figure 3.2   US share of income by quintile

Source: US Census Bureau, Current Population Survey, Annual Social and Economic Supplements.

to around 400 times in the late 1990s. Despite some moderation since those heady days for business bigwigs, CEOs take home over 200 times the compensation of their average worker (Mishel, 2012).

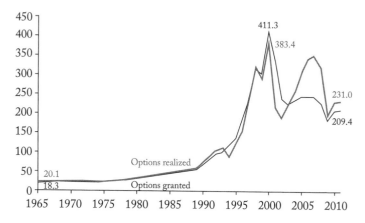

Figure 3.3   US ratio of CEO to worker compensation: 1965–2010

Source: Mishel, 2012.

The distribution of wealth in the US has been even more unequal than the distribution of income. For example, in 2009, the top 10 percent of earners earned 47 percent of the income. However, this pales in comparison to the 73 percent of the net worth (all assets minus all liabilities) held by the top 10 percent. Somewhat surprisingly, this inequality in wealth has worsened after the 2008 economic crisis. While discussions about a declining stock market and a poorly performing business sector might have provided the impression that the rich were a bit hard done by after 2008, the decline in the value of the housing market was much more severe, which has a larger impact on families with less wealth, since their major asset is usually a home. As a result, between 2007 and 2009, the wealthiest 20 percent of households saw their wealth decline by 16 percent, on average, per year. The bottom 80 percent (the rest of the population) had reductions in wealth of 25 percent annually in this period (Allegretto, 2011, p. 3). The average wealth of the top 1 percent of the population stood at 225 times the median in 2009, up from 125 in 1962, and the highest ratio in history (Allegretto, 2011, p. 7).

Box 3.1   The raging Cajun

Stagnating wages and growing inequality were an inevitable result of economic policy that transferred power away from labor and to business in an effort to restore profitability in the US. The only silver lining for most working families was that after the mid-1990s, unemployment was very low, so getting a job (no matter how poorly paid) was easier than it had been, and their wealth was increasing courtesy of rising housing values. The economic crisis of 2008 wiped out both of those positives, as unemployment jumped to 10 percent and the bottom fell out of the housing market. Former Clinton political strategist James Carville, the man credited with the perplexingly famous catchphrase "It's the economy stupid," was appalled by the lack of concern for the vanishing wealth of the middle class (a precarious situation that his candidate did a great deal to create) in elite policy circles after the 2008 crash:

> ... the recent economic crisis left the average American family in 2010 with no more wealth than in the early 1990s, erasing almost two decades of accumulated prosperity.
> It is a depressing state of affairs when about two-thirds of our fellow citizens are caught in an economic trap that is wrecking their lives financially and emotionally.
> And the reaction to all of this has been limp at best ... The point here is that we are reading the most significant economic story of our time and its effect on the psyche of the people who should know better is minimal.
> The big scandal in America is that our middle class is shrinking, and no one seems to care. Maybe someone somewhere somehow should consider doing something else.

James Carville, "What if the rich lost 40% of their wealth?",
CNN.com, June 14, 2012

The growing disparity in incomes and, therefore, ability to consume, was not lost on Citigroup. In a 2005 note to its investors, it described the US (along with Canada and the UK) as a "Plutonomy—an economy powered by the wealthy." In a plutonomy, income and consumption are so unevenly skewed toward the richest that there is really no such thing as an average "US consumer." Rather, there are two very distinct types of people, the very small group of elite at the top and the rest. According to Citigroup analysts, successful companies will be those that market to the rich, whose income and wealth were rapidly expanding, in contrast to firms that serviced the stagnant income of the poor. Their advice to investors was to concentrate on luxury brands, including Porsche, Hermes, Bulgari and Burberry (Kapur et al., 2005).

The Condition of the US Family:
I Owe My Soul to the Company Store

"You work three jobs? ... Uniquely American, isn't it? I mean, that is fantastic that you're doing that."

> President George W. Bush to a divorced mother
> of three in Omaha, Nebraska in 2005

The trends in income and wealth inequality would be troublesome even if worker compensation was growing at a reasonable rate, but at least in that case workers could console themselves that they might be falling further behind the executive class, but at least they were improving their lot over time. However, gains for labor have been very modest and have only been possible by sacrificing other, non-work, activities. By the mid-2000s, it was not uncommon for men to work more than 60 hours a week and women to work more than 50. A growing number of people took on two or three jobs. All told, by the 2000s, the typical American worker worked more than 2,200 hours a year—350 hours more than the average European worked, more hours even than the traditionally industrious Japanese. It was many more hours than the typical American middle-class family had worked in 1979—500 hours longer, a full 12 weeks more. Americans now sleep between one and two hours less than they did in the 1960s (Reich, 2010, p. 86). According to the Brookings Institution, what increase in incomes there were for the median American family were the result of increased hours worked, which went up by 26 percent between 1975 and 2009, mostly as a result of women doubling the hours of paid employment that they put in during this period (Greenstone & Looney, 2011).

Yet, even increased hours at work have not alleviated the income stagnation for the American family. Higher expenses have eroded the increase in incomes that longer work days made possible. Elizabeth Warren argues that the cost of two cars, health insurance, mortgage payments, day care, and other necessities meant that a two-income

---

Box 3.2   Were-wolf hunger

Writing during an earlier period of capitalist development, Karl Marx was concerned that, in the absence of counter-acting tendencies, like increased power for labor, companies might well literally work their employees to death. He wrote in *Capital* that

> ... in its blind unrestrainable passion, its were-wolf hunger for surplus-labour, capital oversteps not only the moral but even the merely physical maximum bounds of the working-day. It usurps the time for growth, development, and healthy maintenance of the body. It steals the time required for the consumption of fresh air and sunlight ... Capital cares nothing for the length of life of labour-power. (Marx, 1889, p. 250)

---

family in 2006 had $1,500 less discretionary income than their single-income counterparts of the previous generation (Warren, 2006). It is true that some of them bought houses beyond their means, but by Warren's account they were not suckered into luxury consumption, but desperate to maintain their historical standard of living.

With workers facing stagnant or falling real wages, longer hours and increasing economic fragility, borrowing became an increasingly attractive option. Companies found that extending credit was a lucrative addition to their usual business of profiting by actually producing goods and services. Households found themselves trapped in a vicious cycle of growing debt, of two very different types. Mortgage debt was induced by the dream of home ownership coupled with historically very low interest rates, meaning that high debt could be justified by lower debt payments. The second type of debt, like that on credit cards or payday loans, carried punitive interest rates, resulting in much higher payments per dollar of debt. Overall debt levels began to rise rapidly around the mid 1980s, when it stood at about 60 percent of income. By 2007, the ratio of total debt to personal disposable income topped out at 138 percent before falling slightly to 128 percent in 2009 (Allegretto, 2011, p. 21). Even the reduced interest payments on debt made possible by low interest rates could not compensate for the overall increase in debt. The US household debt-servicing ratio, the percent of income spent on debt payments, hovered between 11 and 12 percent from early 1980 to 2000. However, after 2000 that ratio increased steadily, to 14 percent in 2008 (Shaikh, 2010). While the US population, in general, was falling further in debt, this was disproportionately true for workers. In 2007, 86 percent of families in which the head of the household was working for someone else carried debt in the US, compared to 77 percent of all families. A larger percentage of working-class families (54 percent) also carried some credit card debt relative to the general population (46 percent) (Baragar & Chernomas, 2012). Debt to finance consumption is a widespread feature of the economic reality for US workers in the twenty-first century. In return, a larger portion of the money wage is now handed over to the financial sector through the increasingly habitual interest (including mortgage) payments of households.

US Instability

Stagnant wages and growing debt were problems not only for the increasingly stressed and overworked individuals that suffered under the post-1980 economic structure. Those same conditions also sowed the seeds for the economic collapse of 2008 in the wake of the mortgage market meltdown. For many analysts, the crisis itself was caused by the collapse of the housing market but this is an incomplete explanation for two reasons. First, the collapse of the housing market was, in part, driven by the low household incomes. US workers facing stagnant real wages and the longest work week in the industrialized world resorted to borrowing to maintain their consumption, including their homes. Business found it profitable to extend extraordinary levels of credit to households as a complement to increasing profitability in the sphere of production. In addition to firms traditionally involved in lending like banks, other companies, from supermarkets to car makers, jumped on the creditor bandwagon. The result was a dramatic increase in worker indebtedness and the instability that would inevitably follow when those bills came due. The first sign of the impending crisis was triggered by highly indebted households contracting their spending. The resulting reduction in sales created excess fixed capital capacity for business, which responded with a rapid decline in investment. The financial crisis that erupted in 2008 contributed to the decline in investment as expectations for future profitability collapsed and credit contracted.[1]

Second, the housing market and subsequent financial collapse were the result of the deregulatory policies that were a crucial part of the post-1980s policy environment.[2] This was not some external "shock" to the economic system, but a result of the profit-seeking behavior of firms in a deregulated industry in the context of stagnant household incomes. The entire tragic episode can essentially be summarized in a few sentences. Loans were being made to increasingly risky customers, on increasingly speculative terms. Worse, the banks that made the loans earned income through commissions, as opposed to the more traditional method of having the loan repaid, because they sold the mortgages on to others in bundled securities. As families started to default on what they thought was going to be their dream home, the banks and investment firms that had purchased mortgage-backed securities found themselves holding badly overvalued assets (Hudson, 2009).

However, a more complete explanation would have to explain why these loans were being made. Much of the fragility in the US mortgage market stemmed from the expansion of subprime mortgages. A subprime mortgage is granted to applicants whose credit rating is too poor to qualify for a conventional loan. Because these applicants are higher risk than more creditworthy customers, the interest payments charged by lenders were correspondingly higher. While in retrospect offering expensive loans to marginal borrowers seems like a recipe for disaster for lender and borrower alike, it was being done in a broadly favorable economic climate. US monetary policy created a prolonged period of historically low interest rates, making debt more attractive and creating a long-term increase in the value of housing. House prices increased by 51 percent between 2000 and 2005, which was twice

---

1   For a more complete discussion of how the structure of the US economy created the 2008 crisis see Kotz, 2009; McDonough et al., 2010; McNally, 2010; Duménil & Lévy, 2011 and Varoufakis, 2011. For a more general explanation on the role of money and monetary policy on economic stability, see Lavoie et al., 2010.

2   For more on the role of finance in the economic crisis, especially the role of the rise of new financial instruments and speculative investments, see Minsky, 1986; Spotton Visano, 2006; Crotty, 2009; Martin, 2011).

the growth of the next best five-year period for the previous thirty years (Getter et al., 2007, p. 1). As long as housing prices continued to increase, a borrowers' growing wealth would compensate for their rising mortgage payments and lenders would have a valuable asset in the event that the borrower defaulted on their mortgage and the lender foreclosed. In this environment, the value of subprime mortgage loans increased from $160 billion in 2001 to $600 billion in 2006.

However, subprime mortgage loans, which were outside of federal regulatory oversight, contained an average mortgage debt payment-to-income ratio of 40 percent, well above federal guidelines (Getter et al., 2007). As the subprime market expanded, increasingly marginal borrowers were enticed with increasingly suspect interest schemes. For example, an adjustable rate mortgage offers a low "teaser" interest rate for the first couple of years, and then increases to above market rates for the rest of the payback period. An interest-only mortgage delays the payment on the principle for a specified period of time, allowing the borrower to only pay the interest costs. After this period, of course, the compressed payments on the principle greatly increase the monthly payments. Because the total payments for these kinds of subprime mortgages were considerably higher than a conventional mortgage, they were very profitable as long as they were repaid. Precisely because these subprime mortgages were more lucrative than their conventional counterparts, people that would have often qualified for conventional loans were given subprimes. Of course, the higher payments increased the likelihood that they would default. This problem was exacerbated by the flexible interest rates on many of these loans. When interest rates started to rise in 2007, mortgages that were barely manageable for many people became impossible. The default rate on subprime mortgages increased from 10 percent in 2004 to 17 percent in 2007 (Mortgage Bankers Association, 2007). As people began to default and fewer buyers were looking for homes in a higher interest rate environment, housing values began to sag. The decline in housing values piled on the financial distress for many families, since often the amount of their mortgage exceeded the now-decreased value of their home.

The economic crisis of 2008 was not an unexpected shock to an otherwise stable system. Rather, the crisis in the housing mortgage market and the economic crisis that followed were fostered by limited income gains for families who took on increasing debt loads to purchase housing and other consumer goods. Firms in a deregulated lending industry profited handsomely from extending increasingly large loans to increasingly marginal borrowers. From this perspective, the economic crisis of 2008 was born in the labor market and deregulatory policies that were hallmarks of neoliberal economic policy.

The US Environment

It is not only the cold, hard world of income and consumption that has turned against most Americans since the 1980s. In terms of the more difficult to quantify, but nevertheless important, areas of social protection there has been a remarkable turn for the worse. Post-1980 economic policy, with its stress on supply-side solutions, resulted in a withdrawal of state regulatory oversight in both specific industries, like the financial sector, accounting and the media, and protective regulation, like the environment and worker safety. Governments employed a number of crafty tactics to reduce their regulatory role without the drastic, and perhaps politically unpopular, step of eliminating an entire agency. Especially during the Republican presidencies of Reagan and George W. Bush, agencies were seeded with executive-level appointees who did not have a strong commitment to protective regulation, creating a much more collaborative approach with business. In addition, budgets were slashed to make monitoring and enforcement increasingly difficult. This resulted in a dramatic decline in both the willingness and ability to uphold regulatory rules. Between 1981 and 1984, the budgets of regulatory agencies in the United States fell by 11 percent overall. To focus on the pollution example specifically, the Environmental Protection Agency's (EPA) budget fell by 35 percent. The staff of the EPA was reduced from 14,075 to 10,392. Its referrals to the Justice Department for the prosecution of violators fell by 84 percent and the number of enforcement orders fell by 33 percent (Blyth, 2002, pp. 181–5).

The whittling away of the regulatory state did not end in the mid-1980s. After inflation, the EPA's budget fell 25 percent between 2004 and 2009 (Union of Concerned Scientists, 2008, p. 19). In 2010, The President's Cancer Panel pointed out that, although every year between one and two thousand new chemicals are created and introduced into industrial processes, "only a few hundred of the more than 80,000 chemicals in use in the United States have been tested for safety." The Panel also criticized US regulatory oversight of chemicals, which it argued was hindered by a lengthy list of impediments, including "inadequate funding and insufficient staffing," "weak laws and regulations, and undue industry influence" (Reuben, 2010, p. ii). The EPA monitors chemicals under the Toxic Substances Control Act (TSCA). But it did not require companies to perform toxicity tests (in fact, it discouraged them, because if the tests were positive the company must report it). The EPA required the testing of only 1 percent of commercial chemicals in the late 2000s, regulated only five and has not attempted to ban one since 1991 (Reuben, 2010, p. 22).

Assessing overall pollution statistics is difficult because they are very heavily impacted by changes in industrial structure and swings in economic activity. Countries that produce more services and less manufacturing will use less energy and have lower emissions. When economies boom, energy use and pollution will increase, all else being equal, since more is being produced. Despite these difficulties, there is little question that the US (and its North American neighbor, Canada) is a ravenous energy user, even compared to countries that have comparable standards of living like Sweden and Germany (see Table 3.1). Although the US did manage to reduce its amount of energy use per capita during the boom times between 1997 and 2007, its overall energy use continued to increase. Further, part of the reason for the decrease in US energy use was not due to any active energy use strategy but because of the decline in manufacturing taking place in the country. It is no coincidence that the big mover in energy use per person, China, saw a rapid increase in manufacturing exports to the US during this period. A very similar story could be told about CO_2 emissions (see Table 3.2). The US (along with Canada) emits far more CO_2 pollution than other wealthy nations like Sweden and Germany. Its emissions have been declining, although not as much as Sweden or Germany, and much of this decline is due to the changing industrial structure in the US, which is increasingly buying its manufacturing goods from Third World locations like China.

The US not only makes a disproportionate contribution to global problems, like climate change, it also has a number of more local environmental hazards. Further, environmental problems are not distributed evenly across income groups. It is most often the less affluent members of the working class that live in hazardous proximity to environmental dangers. Louisiana is the poorest state in the union. It is also famously home to "Cancer Alley," a 150-mile stretch between Baton Rouge and New Orleans that contains 150 petrochemical and chemical facilities, and as its name suggests, has the highest cancer mortality rate in the US (Katz, 2012, p. 102). Another study ranked the environmental hazards from a wide variety of industrial sources in 368 communities in Massachusetts. All but one of the 15 most "intensively burdened towns" had an average household income of under $40,000. There was also a pronounced racial gradient. Only 20 towns in Massachusetts had a non-white population of over 15 percent. Yet of these 20 towns, nine were among the 15 most burdened. The study concludes that "the communities most heavily burdened with environmentally hazardous industrial facilities and sites are overwhelmingly low-income towns and/or communities of color" (Faber & Krieg, 2002, p. 286).

Table 3.1   Energy use per capita

	Tonnes of oil equivalent per person, 2009	*Percent change, 1997–2007*
Canada	7.53	+2.6
US	7.03	−1.3
Sweden	4.88	−2.8
Germany	3.89	−4.3
China	1.70	+68.1
India	0.58	+23.4

Source: International Energy Agency.

Table 3.2 CO_2 emissions per capita

	Tonnes per person, 2009	*Percent change, 1996–2006*
Canada	15.43	+5.8
US	16.90	−2.5
Sweden	4.48	−18.2
Germany	9.16	−13.0
China	5.13	+67.0
India	1.37	+28.8

Source: International Energy Agency.

US Exceptionalism: It Doesn't Have To Be Like This

While other nations have faced the same global economic context, they have not adopted the neoliberal package with the same fervor as the US. Interestingly, the countries that have taken a more skeptical approach to neoliberal economic policy have performed better than the US in many ways.

The World Economic Forum (WEF) is a Geneva-based foundation whose annual meeting of chief executives and political leaders, held in Davos, Switzerland is a gathering of the truly rich and powerful. The WEF is funded by a thousand corporations, each of which has annual revenues of more than $1 billion. Every year, the WEF produces its *Global Competitiveness Report*, which ranks the competitiveness of the world's economies. The top ten countries of World Economic Forum Growth Competitiveness Index Rankings for 2011 in rank order were: Switzerland, Sweden, Singapore, the US, Germany, Japan, Finland, the Netherlands, Denmark and Canada (Schwab, 2010, p. 15). What was most interesting about this list was how many of these countries have strong rules that explicitly resist the neoliberal economic policy agenda by using government intervention to regulate industry, strengthen the power of workers in the labor market, and redistribute incomes. This is not a one-year anomaly, European countries that have been more cautious about neoliberal policy than the US (especially the Nordic nations) have fared well in the WEF competitiveness rankings year after year. In 2005, the report lauded these nations for the quality of their public institutions, budget surpluses, low levels of corruption and high degree of technological innovation. Although these states had high taxes and a strict regulatory framework, they were characterized as having "excellent macroeconomic management overall," according to Augusto Lopez-Claros, chief economist at the WEF:

Integrity and efficiency in the use of public resources means there is money for investing in education, in public health, in state-of-the-art infrastructure, all of which contributes to boost productivity. Highly trained labor forces, in turn, adopt new technologies with enthusiasm or, as happens often in the Nordics, are themselves in the forefront of technological innovations. In many ways the

Nordics have entered virtuous circles where various factors reinforce each other to make them among the most competitive economies in the world, with world class institutions and some of the highest levels of per capita income in the world. (Lopez-Carlos, 2005)

Recall that the main, stated objective of neoliberal policy was to restore the economy to glowing health after the doldrums of the 1970s. We have seen that in terms of economic growth, the period after 1980 was not as strong as the pre-1970 period. Importantly, growth was also not unambiguously superior to countries that pursued other, less austere, regimes. Table 3.3 compares the economic growth of the US to a few of the nations that have resisted neoliberal economic policies for different time periods. The table only contains data up to 2008, so it does not include the disastrous economic impact of the post-2008 economic crisis, which hit the US particularly hard, so this presents the best possible case for the US and its neoliberal policies. Yet, whether we take the longer-term period from 1980 to 2008 or the supposed boom period of the early 2000s, the US does not really outperform these other nations. The neoliberal economists that came to dominate the discipline argued that policies to increase workers' power in the labor market or redistribute income were luxuries that would slow economic growth. Yet, research has shown that this theorized trade-off between equality and efficiency does not exist. A 2002 OECD report concluded that there is no evidence that equality affects GDP "one way or another" (Arjona et al., 2002, p. 28). Neoliberal economic policy, with all of its attendant inequalities, wage stagnation and decreased social mobility, does not produce higher growth rates than nations that do not impose these maladies on themselves.

Table 3.3   Economic growth: percent change in real GDP per capita, PPP

	1980–2008	*1990–2008*	*2000–08*
Denmark	64.21	34.14	7.80
Germany	62.18	30.58	11.61
Sweden	68.44	39.61	17.68
United States	68.80	35.00	8.75

Source: Calculated from OECD StatExtracts—GDP per head, US$, constant prices, constant PPPs.

The US cannot claim a great advantage over other nations when it comes to economic growth, but the score is more unambiguous on social measures. Unfortunately for the US, its record shows that it is unambiguously inferior. In a nation that celebrates the "rags to riches" story of social mobility, where anyone can be president, the difference between a son's income and his father's in the US was the third lowest of twelve OECD nations, behind only Italy and the UK (another neoliberal paragon) in 2010. Three of the top four socially mobile nations, as measured by the intergenerational difference in income between a father and his son, were Denmark, Norway and Finland (OECD, 2010, p. 185). According to the report, "redistributive and income support policies are associated with greater intergenerational social mobility" (OECD, 2010, p. 184). Tables 3.4 and 3.5 show that in more social democratic economies, like Sweden, which have followed a very different macroeconomic model, there is more equality and less poverty while still maintaining a competitive and vibrant economy. Table 3.4 shows the percentage of the population that has incomes below the poverty line. Table 3.5 uses the Gini coefficient to measure inequality. A Gini of zero would represent complete equality, where every person in the country received the same income. A Gini of 1 would represent complete inequality, where one person received the entire income in a nation. So, the closer the Gini is to zero the more equal the income distribution in a country.

The US also scores very poorly in terms of social justice. In 2011, the OECD report on social justice ranked the US 27 out of 31 countries, ahead of only Greece, Chile, Mexico and Turkey. (OECD, 2011, p. 8). The score was compiled by looking at how well counties fared on six measures: poverty prevention, access to education, labor market inclusion, social cohesion and non-discrimination, health, and inter-generational justice. The US didn't rate very highly on any of these measures. Its best ranking was a modest 16th in both labor market inclusion and social cohesion. It was a particular laggard (29th) in the area of poverty, which the OECD described as "alarming" (OECD, 2011, p. 7).

The top five places in the social justice ranking went to Iceland, Norway, Denmark, Sweden and Finland. Further, the World Health Organization (WHO) Commission on Social Determinants of Health argued that "Nordic countries, for example, have followed policies that encouraged equality of benefits and services, full employment, gender equity and low levels of social exclusion." This, said the Commission, "is an outstanding example of what needs to be done everywhere." According to Sir Michael Marmot, the Commission Chair, health policy needs to focus on "creating the conditions for people to be empowered, to have freedom to lead flourishing lives" (WHO, 2008). You might call it the triumph of the Nords.

Table 3.4   Poverty rates before and after taxes and transfers: total population

Country	Mid-1980s		Mid-2000s	
	Before	*After*	*Before*	*After*
Sweden	26%	3%	27%	5%
United States	26%	18%	26%	17%

Note: The poverty rate is defined as 50 percent of the current median income.

Source: OECD StatExtracts Income Distribution—Poverty.

Table 3.5   Gini coefficients before and after taxes and transfers: total population

Country	Mid-1980s		Mid-2000s	
	Before	*After*	*Before*	*After*
Sweden	0.4	0.2	0.43	0.23
United States	0.4	0.34	0.46	0.38

Source: OECD StatExtracts Income Distribution Inequality.

Conclusion

It is not accurate to say that the economic hard times were a result of the 2008 crisis. In the US prior to 2008, businesses, and the rich people who own them, did very well but the rest of the nation suffered through what passed for an economic recovery after the malaise of the 1970s. Inequality increased and wages stagnated. Families worked longer hours and fell further in debt. A more accurate statement would be that even during the boom period, the spoils of economic growth were going to a very few people who were already very well to do, while everyone else either gained very little or were actually worse off. Moreover, the very neoliberal policies that created this inequality and income stagnation played a crucial role in weakening the economy so that it was susceptible to crisis. This catalogue of failure is the legacy of the economists surveyed in this book and of those who implemented their policies.

4
Milton Friedman: The Godfather of the Age of Instability and Inequality

Introduction

Milton Friedman died on November 16, 2006 at the age of 94. When people pass away, they are usually feted with hyperbolic praise, but Friedman's posthumous accolades were remarkable even by the standards of the most glowing of obituaries. *The Economist* described him as "the most influential economist of the second half of the 20th century ... possibly of all of it" (*The Economist*, 2006a). Fed Chair Alan Greenspan said "There are many Nobel Prize winners in economics, but few have achieved the mythical status of Milton Friedman" (Formaini, 2002). One of the most transcendent assessments came from a conservative finance professor at the University of Chicago, John H. Corchane, who claimed that "he was in part responsible for ending inflation, giving us 20 years of growth and lifting six billion people out of poverty" (Waldie, 2008). Even well-known liberal Paul Krugman conceded that "I regard him as a great economist and a great man" (Krugman, 2007e).

Friedman is most closely associated with the University of Chicago, where he spent most of his career. In fact the term "the Chicago School" of economics has come to describe not only the economics department at Chicago but also a certain kind of economist, particularly inclined to follow in Friedman's footsteps. Not coincidentally, there is considerable overlap between the two. His influence in Chicago was such that after his death the economics department named a prestigious research institute in his honor: the Milton Friedman Institute for Research in Economics (in 2011 it was merged with the Becker Center on Chicago Price Theory to create the Becker Friedman Institute for Research in Economics).

Yet, it would be a gross understatement to claim that Friedman had a few critics. Naomi Klein's bestseller *The Shock Doctrine* (2008) singled out Friedman as the chief villain among the rogue's gallery of the economics profession. An entire chapter of her book is dedicated to Friedman and the Chicago School's association with the brutal Chilean dictator Augusto Pinochet and other bits of nastiness in Latin America. Another book, *Not So Free to Choose* (Rayack, 1987) (a take on Friedman's famous *Free to Choose*) is entirely dedicated to demonstrating that Friedman played fast and loose with real-world evidence in order to defend the indefensible consequences of his economic policies. After the economic crisis of 2008, self-declared centrist and MIT economic legend Paul Samuelson crowed, "today we see how utterly mistaken was the Milton Friedman notion that a market system can regulate itself" (Samuelson, 2009). Joan Robinson of Cambridge University offered what perhaps, to a Friedman supporter, would be the most unkind cut of all, stating that "insofar as he offers an intelligible theory, it is made up of elements borrowed from Keynes" (Robinson, 1971, p. 87). Krugman also moderated his "great man" eulogy with "Friedman was wrong on some issues, and sometimes seemed less than honest with his readers" (Krugman, 2007e).

Although there is considerable debate about whether his ideas were effective or desirable, there is much less controversy about whether they were influential. In the words of Krugman:

> A number of economists played important roles in the great revival of classical economics between 1950 and 2000, but none was as influential as Milton Friedman ... By the century's end, classical economics had regained much though by no means all of its former dominion, and Friedman deserves much of the credit. (Krugman, 2007e)

Most scholars see Friedman as working in two very different spheres: academic and policy. His more academic work revolved around his macroeconomic theories on the permanent income hypothesis and adaptive expectations. It was in this area that he received the Nobel Prize in 1976 "for his achievements in the fields of consumption analysis, monetary history and theory and for his demonstration of the complexity of stabilization policy" (Nobelprize.org, 1976). His public policy pronouncements were a relentless assault on what he saw to be iron-fisted governmental interference with the liberty of the free market. According to Krugman, "there was Friedman the economist's economist, who wrote technical, more or less apolitical analyses of consumer behavior and inflation ... [and the] looser, sometimes questionable logic of his pronouncements as a public intellectual" (Krugman, 2007e).

So, there are three opinions on how to interpret Friedman's legacy. One preposterously suggests that he was responsible for lifting 6 billion (almost everyone on earth) from poverty. The second portrays him as a rigorous academic economist whose enthusiasm for the free market led him to abandon his lofty academic principles while tilting at the windmills of government intervention in the realm of public debate. And a third holds him responsible for his contribution to the instability, inefficiency and inequality that characterized the past 35 years or so of US economic history. We will argue that, of these options, the third comes closest to the truth. Although Friedman's academic ideas were dressed up in the impressive rigor that was so attractive to the economic discipline, there was very little to distinguish it from his more policy-oriented ideas, Krugman's claims notwithstanding. They were all part and parcel of the same project: to remove business-constraining government from the economic realm. Despite Friedman's claims about the broadly distributed benefits of these ideas, in practice they had the impact of contributing significantly to the 35-year ascendance of the business class and the concomitant economic problems that we summarized in Chapter 3.

Friedman's Macroeconomics or the Big Picture

The Great Depression, like most other periods of severe unemployment, was produced by government mismanagement rather than by any inherent instability of the private economy. (Milton Friedman, 1962, p. 38)

Friedman's theoretical macroeconomic world rests on three interrelated ideas: the significance of how much money is in circulation, which is the responsibility of the state (monetarism), the theory that workers and firms form their expectations of wages and prices based on their past experience with inflation or deflation (adaptive expectations), and the idea that an economy has a rate of unemployment to which it will tend in the long run (the natural rate of unemployment).

The interrelationship between these concepts can be seen in Friedman's explanation of the Great Depression of the 1930s. According to Friedman (and Anna Schwartz, the co-author of *A Monetary History of the United States*), the root cause of the Great Depression (rebranded as the Great Contraction in Friedman and Schwartz) was a decline in the money supply. The basic story is that when banks failed in the US, the reduction in the money supply caused prices to fall—deflation (Friedman & Schwartz, 1963). The downside of falling prices is difficult to explain to people for whom it is a rarely experienced phenomenon. Recent economic history is characterized almost exclusively by some level of inflation, with deflation only rearing its head under extreme economic duress, and even then, only for very brief periods of time. However, Friedman's adaptive expectations theory implied that deflation can lead to economic collapse.

The fundamental problem with deflation, according to Friedman, was that it sent out the wrong signal to workers in the labor market. Friedman (and co-author Edmund Phelps of Columbia University) argue that workers know their exact nominal wage because they can see their paycheck, but they suffer what economists call "money illusion" because they form their expectations about price changes based on past price behavior, when prices were higher. This leads them to believe that the purchasing power of their wages (their real wage) has gone down when their nominal wages drop, but, in fact, it has not because prices are also falling (Gordon, 1979 [1976]; Modigliani, 1977). Soured on the labor market by this apparent decline in real wages, workers chose to quit their jobs in large number. Friedman's theory of the Great Depression was summarized by economist John Harvey of Texas Christian University:

> Workers, not realizing because of money illusion that the cost of living has declined (and that firms' offer is therefore not unreasonable), quit their jobs. And that, apparently, is how unemployment rose to 25% in the 1930s: the money supply fell, lowering prices, leading firms to offer lower wages, and causing workers to voluntarily quit their jobs! (Harvey, 2012)

There are a few important implications of this interpretation of the Depression (and other, similar but less catastrophic downturns). First, unemployment was voluntary. Workers became unemployed because they quit their jobs or reduced their work hours, thinking that their real wage had declined. This is very much a vision of the labor market characterized by voluntary decisions by workers. If they think that their wages are falling below an acceptable level, they simply choose not to work. A second implication is that government was responsible for the economic crisis. While it was private for-profit bank failures that led to the decline in the money supply, "the Federal Reserve system forced or permitted a sharp reduction in the monetary base," so that the quantity of money fell by one-third (Friedman, 1968). For Friedman, it was the government's job to bail out the economy by providing enough money to avoid deflation so that workers wouldn't suffer from money illusion—an example of Robinson's view of Friedman relying on Keynes. (For critics, it is ironic that Friedman—the great free market advocate—proposed a statist solution to the Great Depression.) Government inaction and confused, self-destructive workers caused the Great Depression. Third, Friedman and Schwartz presented an interpretation on the causes of the Depression to rival Keynes's once dominant theory that the economic failure was brought on by a decline in demand. While Keynes argued that depressions could not be rectified by monetary policy alone, but required the strong action of fiscal policy, along with a long list of regulations, including restrictions on trade, Friedman's theory implied that intrusive government action to stimulate demand and regulate the economy was unnecessary. The only tonic necessary was sensible monetary policy.

The same theoretical constructs can be used to explain why the monetary authority should not use active monetary policy to lower the unemployment rate. According to Friedman, there exists a "natural" rate of unemployment in the labor market that will result in wages rising at a "normal" rate. Expansionary monetary policy can push employment above the natural rate by decreasing interest rates, which will encourage investment and consumption causing employment and output to increase. For Friedman, this increase in employment can only be temporary and at the price of increased inflation. In the short run, each individual firm will be under the impression that the increase in general demand is an increase in demand particular to its product and respond by producing more and selling at a higher price. It also means that the firm is willing to pay higher nominal wages to attract labor. As long as employers think that the increase in price of their product is greater than the nominal wage increases, they will think that their profits are increasing and be willing to hire more workers and produce more output. Workers see this increased nominal wage and, under the money illusion, falsely see it as increase in their real wage since they base their price expectations on lower past prices rather than the new higher ones, so they are willing to work more in response to the increased demand for their labor (Friedman, 1976). Of course, this positive impact on output and employment is only temporary. As workers come to realize that the price level is rising along with their nominal wages, they will incorporate this new information into their bargaining and ask for higher nominal wage increases. Firms will also realize that what they took for an increase in their own price is, in fact, a general price increase. Firms will then reduce their output and workers will reduce their supply of labor, returning the economy to the "natural" rate of unemployment but at a higher price level. So, in the long term, expansionary monetary policy will only increase the price level (Friedman, 1968). As a result, monetary policy should create a stable level of inflation, not attempt to influence employment or output: "Money matters a great deal for the development of nominal magnitudes, but not over the long run for real magnitudes" (Friedman & Heller, 1969, p. 47). The general conclusion is that "fine tuning has been oversold" (Friedman & Heller, 1969, p. 46).

An active fiscal policy is even less palatable for Friedman. The Keynesian fiscal prescription for a recession is for the government to run a deficit. Since this requires government borrowing, Friedman argued that it would force up interest rates by increasing the demand for loans. The increased interest rate would then cause a decrease in private-sector activity. Keynesian stabilization policy is actually counter-productive. Deficit spending is designed to stimulate the economy, but it causes the contraction of the private sector. The opposite is true when the government runs a surplus: interest rates fall and the private sector expands (Friedman & Heller, 1969, pp. 51–3). This creates a kind of stabilization policy nihilism for Friedman. Changes in aggregate demand through either monetary or fiscal policy have no long-term impact on output or employment. Any expansion of the economy beyond Friedman's natural rate will, over the long term, only result in higher inflation, not higher output or employment.

Friedman is careful to point out that the natural rate is not "immutable or unchangeable," but is determined by economic structures in things like the labor market and the degree of competition or monopoly. For example, the natural rate of unemployment is increased by "legal minimum wage rates ... and the strength of labor unions" (Friedman, 1968, p. 9). He blamed the stagflation of the 1970s in the US on an increase in the natural rate because of the entry of more marginally employed workers, like women and teenagers, and the increase in "assistance to unemployed persons" (Friedman, 1976, p. 273). Lowering the non-inflationary level of unemployment can only be done by improving these "real" elements of the economy like eliminating unions, unemployment insurance and minimum wages, not with a Keynesian stabilization policy.

Friedman's Macro: What's Wrong

There are a number of problems with Friedman's version of the macroeconomy. These are not merely the careless mistakes of an economist without a particular predisposition to certain kinds of economic policies. Rather, they create precisely the kind of systematic bias in the economy that tilted so many of the economic rules in favor of the corporate world. Who gains and who loses from Friedman's macroeconomic world can be seen by looking at the nature of unemployment and policy implications of the natural rate.

The preceding section demonstrated that, for Friedman, changes in employment are caused by workers' decisions about how much they are willing to work for any given real wage. Unemployment increases during a recession because the lower perceived real wage makes people less willing to work. It is this mechanism that causes unemployment to increase during a recession. This generates the highly counter-intuitive implication that in recessions workers quit their jobs in high numbers. It also implies that the rate at which firms lay off workers should not change in economic downturns. Neither of these implications stands up to even casual empirical scrutiny. In fact, voluntary quits in the US actually decline during recessions while layoffs by firms increase— fairly intuitive facts that run directly counter to Friedman's theory of the macroeconomy (Gordon, 1979 [1976], p. 274). If they were not taken so seriously in the economic world, these conclusions would be laughable and they certainly fail on any test of common sense or empirical support.

Box 4.1   Myopic paddling

It was not only Friedman's counter-intuitive claim that unemployment was voluntary, even in an economic downturn, which failed to represent the real world particularly accurately. The Friedman-Phelps characterization of job search under adaptive expectations must also look a little unfamiliar to most workers. According to Northwestern University economist Robert Gordon:

> The lack of reality in the standard new microeconomics model is vividly illustrated in Phelps's well known "island parable", in which individual firms are represented by separate islands lacking any inter-island communications link. Since the employee does not learn instantaneously of wage rates on other islands, but rather gains the information only after a slow trip by raft … if a firm offers lower wages because of a lack of demand some workers quit on the assumption that their situation is unique, boarding their rafts to sample wage offers on other islands. Only after several inter-island voyages do they realize that the recession-induced decline in demand is universal and that they will be no better off in a new job than in the original firm.

Workers do not really behave like this. For example, modern communications make it possible for workers to search for alternative employment "without any prior need to quit … Real world employees are not nearly as mindless as the parable suggests" (Gordon, 1979 [1976], pp. 273–4).

The insistence on voluntary unemployment also reflects Friedman's misplaced belief that all factors of production have equal clout. In Friedman's theory, workers have the luxury to reduce their hours of work or stay home altogether when they think that their real wages are declining. While this might be true for a fortunate few, this interpretation of the labor market does not accord particularly well with most people's experience. Most workers have little option but to sell their labor on the market. They own no other productive resources and have little cash set aside to voluntarily reduce their labor hours. Employees' lack of power in the labor market is especially great during economic downturns when unemployment is higher. It is this rising unemployment, and the resulting reduction in worker's power that causes the reduction in wages. This suggests a very different cause and effect than that proposed by Friedman. According to Friedman, it is the perception of falling real wages that causes workers to withdraw their services from the labor market, causing unemployment. In reality, it is unemployment caused by involuntary layoffs that causes the decline in real wages.

While conceptualizing unemployment as voluntary puts a false positive veneer on people being out of work, the concept of the natural rate of unemployment surreptitiously tilted the labor market in favor of corporations in two ways. First, Friedman insisted that policy makers "cannot know what the natural rate is" (Friedman, 1968, p. 10), and should therefore, avoid using full employment stabilization policy for fear of pushing the unemployment rate below the natural rate and sparking inflation. This was important in the context of the post-1970s economy, when US firms were attempting to reduce their labor costs as one means of restoring profitability. When unemployment rates soared during the 1980s, in part because of very tight monetary policy, the concept of the natural rate was used to justify prolonged periods of high unemployment in the cause of inflationary discipline to the out of work citizenry. Essentially, the natural rate was taken to be whatever the unemployment rate was at the time (Palley, 2006). High unemployment rates, which lasted until the mid-1990s, were one of the factors that created stagnating wages for workers, as described in Chapter 3.

Second, the "real" economic factors that would cause the natural rate to be higher were precisely those that favored workers in the labor market. While Friedman identified a number of policies outside the labor market that would increase the natural rate, like increased corporate concentration, it was labor market policy, particularly policies that protected workers, which he targeted repeatedly as being problematic. According to Friedman, labor unions, unemployment benefits and minimum wages all push up workers' earnings making more unemployment necessary to combat inflation. Economist Robert Pollin suggests that the "natural rate" is really a social phenomenon measuring the class strength of working people: "class conflict is the specter haunting the analysis of the natural rate" (Pollin, 1998). This is nicely demonstrated in a paper by Robert Gordon, which estimated the natural rate (it came to be called the NAIRU—non-accelerating inflation rate of unemployment) decline in the US between the 1960s and the 1990s. He speculated that

> ... the late 1960s were a time of labor militancy, relatively strong unions, a relatively high minimum wage and a marked increase in labor's share in national income. The 1990s have been a time of labor peace, relatively weak unions, a relatively low minimum wage and a slight decline in labor's income share. (Gordon, 1997, p. 30)

In the language of the natural rate, limiting the strength of working people will create lower inflation and higher levels of employment.

The US economy since the 1980s does provide a handy natural experiment to test the distributional impact of Friedman's policies to improve the natural rate. Since 1980, the US has enacted many of Friedman's natural rate-decreasing policies. Income supports to the poor have been reduced, unionization rates have fallen and tax rates on the rich have dropped. As Chapter 3 documented, the result has been a dramatic increase in inequality between rich and poor in the US since 1980. Even among the relatively wealthy, the big after-tax income gains have gone to the very upper echelons of the income distribution. These trends are no coincidence given the fact that wages have not kept pace with productivity in the US.

Countries that have the kind of policies that Friedman argues should increase the natural rate, like Sweden, have fared no worse in terms of its macroeconomic performance than countries, like the US. Most workers in Sweden are unionized, the unemployment insurance benefits are far more generous and the tax system transfers far more income from rich to poor. Yet, as we showed in Chapter 3, these countries rank at the very top of the World Economic Forum (WEF) competitiveness ranking and fare as well as the US in terms of economic growth.

Friedman's macroeconomic approach also directs attention away from theories (like those of Keynes) that suggest capitalist economies have a tendency to stagnation and towards the idea that problems are caused by interventions in the market like government and unions. If not for their ideological usefulness, dressed up as they are in the language and technique of the mainstream economist, his ideas would not pass either predictive tests or the test of logic. Friedman's macroeconomic ideas provided considerable intellectual justification for abandoning labor market protection for workers and Keynesian full employment policies. These changes resulted in income stagnation for workers, greater inequality, and more instability after the 1970s, but also resulted in a restoration of profitability.

Friedman's Microeconomics: Market Fundamentalism

The overarching theme behind all of Friedman's work, but which is particularly explicit in his more public policy writing in microeconomics, is that an economy based on the market will float along happily on the waves of progress, while one hampered by the lead weight of government will sink like a stone. This is based on two complementary propositions. First, that the market delivers results that are superior to any other institutional arrangement. We might call this the "government is unnecessary" proposition. Second, that even when the results of the market are not completely satisfactory, any intervention by the government to rectify the situation will result in an inferior, rather than superior outcome. We might call this the "government is harmful" proposition. The market is superior to the state with respect to the provision of goods and services because it is competitive, driven by the need to respond to the demand of consumers for low-cost, high-quality goods and services. The state has no such competitive incentive structure and so it will produce less efficiently.

Government is Unnecessary

While the market is not perfect, and will inevitably have a few bad apples lurking in the barrel, according to Friedman, "on the whole, market competition, when it is permitted to work, protects the consumer better than do the alternative government mechanisms that have been increasingly superimposed on the market" (Friedman & Friedman, 1990, p. 223). His answer to the question "who protects the consumer?" is the competition of the market. Offering poor service, substandard fare, or dangerous products is tantamount to business suicide in a market in which firms eagerly compete for customers.

Only by selling superior goods at reasonable prices will businesses attract the custom necessary to thrive in the cut-throat world of the free market: "It is in the self-interest of the businessman to serve the consumer" (Friedman & Friedman, 1990, p. 223).

For those that argue that the consumer needs to be protected by government in situations where the purchasing decision is fraught with complexity or potential safety issues, Friedman argues that this is better done through the private sector. While many purchases, like consumer electronics, are a bit complicated for the average person to wrap their head around, the private sector has developed mechanisms to protect the purchaser. Department stores, with reputations to protect, will carefully screen out poor merchandise. Further, the importance of branding for large firms makes it unlikely that they would compromise their expensively assembled and carefully cultivated brand with shoddy products. Finally, "Still another device is the private testing organization ... For the consumer there are private organizations like ... Consumer Reports" to which consumers can turn to determine product quality (Friedman & Friedman, 1990, p. 224).

His belief in the disciplinary mechanism of the market and sovereignty of the consumer is perhaps nowhere better, and more controversially, displayed than when he argued against any professional licensing arrangement, including physicians. According to Friedman, anyone should be able to set out their shingle as a doctor and the iron laws of demand and supply should soon separate the skilled surgeon from the butchering hacker: "Insofar as he [the doctor] harms only his patient, that is simply a question of voluntary contract and exchange between patient and physician. On this score there is no ground for intervention" (Friedman, 1962, p. 147). Doctors of poor quality will soon find themselves without any patients and be forced out of the profession. Further, government intervention is unnecessary in health insurance since "the costs of ordinary medical care are well within the means of most American families. Private insurance arrangements are available to meet the contingency of an unusually large expense" (Friedman & Friedman, 1990, p. 115). Not only will competition ensure a safe and cost-effective supply of medical services, there is no case for anything other than a privatized health care system. Consumer protection merely requires competition. If this is true in the complicated world of medicine, it must also hold in other areas like drugs, food and other areas of consumer safety.

Friedman uses the same logic of voluntary exchange and competition to argue that the labor market produces efficient and fair results. The answer to the question "Who protects the worker?" is not unions or government regulation, but other employers: "Their demand for his services makes it in the self-interest of his own employer to pay him the full value of his work" (Friedman & Friedman, 1990, p. 246). For Friedman, the labor market is not characterized by an unequal power relationship between employer and employee, but is a voluntary exchange between equals. This is nicely demonstrated by his insistence on the symmetrical possibility of exploitation in the labor market: "An employer is protected from exploitation by his employees by the existence of other workers whom he can hire" (Friedman & Friedman, 1990, p. 246).

For Friedman, a market economy, characterized by economic freedom, will likely have the pleasant side-effect of greater income equality, but equality should not be a driving principle of economic policy. The essence of this argument is that inequality, and the incentives that go with it, are crucial in sending the right signals to economic actors. Jobs that are valued by society should pay well in order to attract more people to that field. As long as people have a reasonable opportunity to succeed, defined by having very few state-imposed limits on what they can do to make money, then equality of outcome is not particularly important.

> The liberal will therefore distinguish sharply between equality of rights and equality of opportunity, on the one hand, and material equality or equality of outcome on the other. He may welcome the fact that a free society in fact tends toward greater material equality than any other yet tried. But he will regard this as a desirable by-product of a free society, not its major justification. (Friedman, 1962, p. 195)

Government is Harmful

While Friedman concedes that there will be occasions where the free market does not function perfectly, he finds that government intervention to correct for these rare problems is likely to do more harm than good. This is true in virtually any situation, from intervention in the price of products, to regulatory attempts to ensure consumer safety. Returning to the example of medicine, Friedman argues that government-imposed requirement for doctors to receive a certain level of training (like any kind of mandatory professional standards, from requiring that welders receive some sort of certification of their competence, to having lawyers pass the bar) is little more than a barrier to enter the industry, reducing competition and, therefore, forcing up the price to the consumer with artificially created restrictions of supply. Freidman claims that "licensure has reduced both the quantity and quality of medical practice" (Friedman, 1962, p. 158).

Friedman makes much the same claim for any intervention in the market. Regulatory agencies designed to protect the consumer are not only unnecessary, but also actually injurious. The FDA "has done more harm by retarding progress in the production and distribution of valuable drugs than it has done good by preventing the distribution of harmful of ineffective drugs" (Friedman & Friedman, 1990, p. 206). Similar concerns are expressed about the Consumer Products Safety Commission (CPSC) and the Environmental Protection Agency (EPA). The general point is that the increase in costs necessary to meet what will inevitably be an overly fussy and bureaucratic precautionary apparatus will create burdens that far outweigh any slight gains in improved safety.

Part of the reason for government's lack of success in improving the outcomes of the market is that its regulatory apparatus would be "captured" by the very business interests that it was developed to oversee. In an argument that, not coincidentally, was adopted and refined by the public choice school which is discussed in Chapter 5, Friedman argued that, "the natural history of government intervention" (Friedman & Friedman, 1990, p. 201) followed a very predictable path: a problem with the free market gives rise to a popular movement pressuring the government for intervention, resulting in the passage of some law. The reformers turn to some new cause and the truly interested parties (the firms in the industry) go to work to ensure that the laws are used in their benefit: "In the end the effects are precisely the opposite of the objectives of the reformers ... (Friedman & Friedman, 1990, p. 201).

We will return to the problems with the idea of regulatory capture in Chapter 5, but for now we will merely comment that although in the US, especially after the 1980s, the business class certainly captured the regulatory apparatus of the state, there is nothing inevitable in this outcome. Nor is the Friedman solution to capture, having no regulation, particularly helpful.

Predictably, Friedman is also very dismissive of the results in industries that feature public ownership or substantial government intervention. In contrasting the organizations, like the Post Office, that Americans find most wretched, with those, like consumer electronics, that they find most satisfactory, Freidman concludes, "the shoddy products are all produced by government or government-regulated industries" (Friedman & Friedman, 1990, p. 192). Returning to the health care example, government-provided universal health insurance, as is practiced in countries like Canada, would not decrease medical costs, "at least until someone can find some example of an activity that is conducted more economically by government than by private enterprise" (Friedman & Friedman, 1990, p. 115).

The general conclusion is that, for Friedman, freedom of exchange, narrowly defined as the lack of coercion, is a fundamental right to be championed as an end to itself. Conveniently, this important freedom is also instrumental in providing the greatest level of broadly distributed material benefits. The prosperity generated by individual self-interest in a competitive market, however, can be jeopardized by unwarranted interference with the market:

> The United States has continued to progress; its citizens have become better fed, better clothed, better housed, and better transported; class and social distinctions have narrowed; minority groups have become less disadvantaged; popular culture has advanced by leaps and bounds. All this has been the product of the initiative and drive of individuals co-operating through the free market. Government measures have hampered not helped this development. We have been able to afford and surmount these measures only because of the extraordinary fecundity of the market. The invisible hand has been more potent for progress than the visible hand for retrogression. (Friedman, 1962, pp. 199–200)

Friedman's Microeconomics: What's Wrong

Friedman's animosity to regulation is based on the claim that it is competition, not the government, which produces the best economic results. A complete accounting of the economic debate that rages around Friedman's claims in all of these areas is beyond the scope of this work, but it would be fair to say that his assertions are far from established fact. In this section, we will provide a few specific examples, in the consumer market, and in innovation, which should cast considerable doubt on Friedman's insistence that it is the private sector that is the wind that fills the economy's sails while the government is nothing but dead weight.

Turning first to the consumer market, Friedman contends that government oversight is unnecessary and harmful. Yet in a study of several industries, the very private testing organization that he put forward as a more desirable substitute for government regulation, *Consumer Report* (*CR*), declared that decreased regulation had resulted in markets with large price increases, worse product choice and reduced safety. Its conclusion was that, on balance, consumers have lost ground since deregulation began in the telephone, banking, electricity, television and airline industries. Overall consumer prices often fell after deregulation, but they were falling for decades before, typically at a faster rate. There has been a decrease in consumer choice in the airline, banking and television industries, where fewer companies control a larger share of the market than prior to deregulation. Banking has been a disaster, with 1,600 bank failures in the United States, even before the financial crash of 2008 with its massive and growing cost to taxpayers. Deregulated airlines have given customers more connections, delays, cramped seats and uncomfortable planes. According to *CR*, the marketplace has become more adversarial toward consumers. The absence of strict rules has inspired aggressive tactics and enabled sellers to gain disproportionate power over buyers. *CR* recommended more regulation and vigorous anti-trust enforcement in order to protect consumers from increasingly rapacious business practices (*Consumer Reports*, 2002).

Perhaps the best example of Friedman's insistence that the private sector is universally superior to government is in the area of health care. This is an industry in which consumers are poorly equipped to determine for themselves what care they need, creating considerable asymmetry between the expert provider of health care services and the less informed patient. When a physician recommends surgery, prescribes a drug, or requires a test, few patients are sufficiently confident of their medical knowledge to go against their doctor's orders. In a private, for-profit health system, this creates ample opportunity for what is called "supply-induced demand"—the idea that health care providers are in a position to have consumers use more services than they might genuinely need. Friedman downplays the problems that this will create for the consumer in the market for health, as he does with any other market with this type of difficulty, yet in health care, public or non-profit provision has been found to be superior to the private, for-profit sector.

While the debate about the merits of a public vs. a private system continues to rage, it is very inconvenient for Friedman's position that the US, which relies most heavily on a private health care system, has the highest costs and the worst health indicators among the wealthy nations. US life expectancy is 79.6 years. According to the 2010 United Nations Human Development Index, this places it behind 28 other countries, following Greece and Liechtenstein and just above Costa Rica, Portugal and Cuba. In terms of mortality rates for children under five, it ranks a worrying 46th, just behind the UAE and above Chile (United Nations, 2011). In 2015, the US spent 17 percent of its GDP on health care. This is the highest of the 35 countries in the Organization of Economic Cooperation and Development (OECD) by a considerable margin. The country ranked second, Switzerland, spent 11.5 percent and the OECD average was a much more modest 9 percent. The combined level of public and private health care spending per person is also much higher in the US than any other country. The US spent $9,451 per person, while the second highest nation, again Switzerland, spent only $6,935 and the OECD average was $3,740 (OECD, 2016).

These broad measures, suggesting that the private health system in the US produces worse health results at a greater cost, are reinforced by more direct evidence from health insurance. The overhead cost of administrating a private, multi-payer system is generally much larger than a single-payer public system. In the US, this waste has been estimated at $400 billion (Freeman, 2009; see also Congressional

Budget Office, 2011). Further, in 2007, prior to the Obama administration's reform of US health care under the Affordable Care Act (ACA), about 15–16 percent of the US population (over 40 million people) did not have insurance, putting the lie to Friedman's claim about its affordability (DeNavas-Walt et al., 2008).

Contrary to Friedman's claims, for-profit health care delivery is more expensive without delivering better care. Medicare spending per capita (adjusted for health characteristics) in communities with for-profit hospitals ($5,172) was higher and increasing faster compared to communities with non-profit hospitals ($4,440) in 1995 (Silverman, et al., 1999; see also Woolhandler & Himmelstein, 1997). A study by Alan Sager and Deborah Socolar of the Boston University School of Public Health estimated that in the US "one-half of health spending goes to clinical and administrative waste, excess prices, and theft" (Sager & Socolar, 2005, p. ii).

Despite the higher costs, quality of care is not superior in for-profit health facilities. Studies on patients as diverse as those suffering from heart attacks (Shen, 2002) to those who need dialysis facilities (Garg et al., 1999; Devereaux et al., 2002) show that mortality rates were higher in for-profit care. One of the dialysis studies estimated that as many as 2,500 deaths each year may be due to treatment at profit, as opposed to non-profit facilities (Devereaux et al., 2002). Patient surveys also fail to reveal a preference for care in for-profit systems. In the 1990s, people in the US reported much lower satisfaction with their health care systems than did Canadians, Western Europeans and the Japanese (Isaacson, 1993). A 2005 survey of six wealthy nations found that "the US often stands out for inefficient care and errors" (Schoen et al., 2005). A massive survey of 82,583 Medicare patients in 182 health plans found that non-profit health plans scored higher than for-profit on measures of overall quality, access to care and customer service (Landon et al., 2001). In sum, in a review of some 150 studies comparing access, quality and cost effectiveness between the two ownership models in health care, 18 found that for-profit centers were better, 88 determined that non-profits were superior and 43 concluded that there was no real difference (Vaillancourt & Linder, 2003).

The point here is that health care is but one example of Friedman's remarkable and erroneous insistence that competition will protect the consumer and that government intervention can only worsen the situation. It is not true in the market for health care, nor is it true in many other markets that suffer from any number of market imperfections, of which the information asymmetry in health care is merely one of many. The accompanying box demonstrates similar flaws in Friedman's logic in the areas of food safety. In these circumstances, government intervention can actually produce superior results.

**Box 4.2   An excerpt from Paul Krugman's "Fear of Eating,"
New York Times, May 21, 2007**

Yesterday I did something risky: I ate a salad.

These are anxious days at the lunch table. For all you know, there may be E. coli on your spinach, salmonella in your peanut butter and melamine in your pet's food and, because it was in the feed, in your chicken sandwich.

The economic case for having the government enforce rules on food safety seems overwhelming. Consumers have no way of knowing whether the food they eat is contaminated, and in this case what you don't know can hurt or even kill you. But there are some people who refuse to accept that case, because it's ideologically inconvenient.

I blame the food safety crisis on Milton Friedman, who called for the abolition of both the food and the drug sides of the F.D.A. What would protect the public from dangerous or ineffective drugs? "It's in the self-interest of pharmaceutical companies not to have these bad things," he insisted in a 1999 interview. He would presumably have applied the same logic to food safety (as he did to airline safety): regardless of circumstances, you can always trust the private sector to police itself.

O.K., I'm not saying that Mr. Friedman directly caused tainted spinach and poisonous peanut butter. But he did help to make our food less safe, by legitimizing what the historian Rick Perlstein calls "E. coli conservatives": ideologues who won't accept even the most compelling case for government regulation.

Earlier this month the administration named, you guessed it, a "food safety czar." But the food safety crisis isn't caused by the arrangement of the boxes on the organization chart. It's caused by the dominance within our government of a literally sickening ideology.

For Friedman, the economy is not a place where some groups have power over others. Health care is not an arena in which often desperate and less than fully informed patients seek the advice of expert physicians. Rather, consumers of medical care can evaluate the advice offered by doctors and make informed treatment choices.

Similarly, for Friedman, firms and their workers are merely equally powerful owners of different factors of production and earn income that is "different in form but not in substance" (Friedman & Friedman, 1990, p. 20). One owns capital, the other labor and they negotiate a labor contract between them on mutually beneficial terms. The labor market is not a place of power and inequality, where employers are at a considerable advantage over their employees. Ignoring the differences in power between different forms of income serves two important, interrelated purposes. First, it provides a justification for income disparity in a society. If certain groups in society earn a great deal more than others, it is not because of power relationships, and the institutional rules that support them, that favor one group over another but rather, it is because those at the more affluent end of the income scale deserve their reward for their skill and effort. According to Friedman, "accumulation of wealth was the most readily available measure of performance" (Friedman & Friedman, 1990, p. 133). Second, it justifies labor market policy that does nothing to redress the power imbalance in the labor market. There is no need for unions, minimum wages, or social insurance programs in Friedman's account of the labor market. Friedman hides the actual power relationships in the labor market behind the impersonal and merit-based guise of the market mechanism. The policy implications of his labor market theories, which are reflected in his supposedly neutral ideas of the natural rate, very much favor those who do very well by being on the employing side of the labor market. Of course, there is evidence from the past about the effect of unregulated markets. Before the interventions of the regulatory state were introduced, the title of Upton Sinclair's famous book *The Jungle* (first published in 1906) was an apt description of the effects of the free market in food on consumers and workers alike. The age of regulation was the response to the ravages of the free market on workers, citizens and consumers.

Friedman's claim that our material progress is the product of private-sector innovation in spite of the drag of the government is also dangerously misleading. A major theme in much of Lester Thurow's work has been the necessity of recognizing market failure with respect to long-term investment by business. In *The Future of Capitalism* (1996), he argued that private firms will not invest sufficiently in R&D for two reasons. First, the investment is likely to create greater social benefits than narrow private returns for the company. Second, firms tend to have short-term time horizons. Since the return to basic, as opposed to applied, science is both longer term and more uncertain, it is extremely unlikely that private firms could afford to undertake this type of research. Because governments tend to be more indifferent as to who reaps the benefits from investments in R&D, nor is it focused on its own profit, it plays an essential role in long-term investment in capitalist economies.

Tangible evidence on the important role of the state in innovation can be found by a quick glance at some of the everyday products that owe their existence to government funding. Maxipads, Deet bug repellent, permanent-press cotton, shrink-proof wool, the soybean ink used in *USA Today*, disposable diapers, frozen foods and lactose-free milk were all invented by the Agricultural Research Service of the US government (Rawe, 2004, p. 68). US federal funding was also directly responsible for the cross-country railroad, the exploration of space, atomic energy, the Internet, the Global Positioning System (GPS), lasers, computers, magnetic resonance imaging (MRI), Teflon and other advanced materials and composites, communications satellites, jet aircraft, microwave ovens, solar-electric cells, modems, semiconductors, storm windows, genetic medicine and biotechnology (Office of Science and Technology Policy, 2000).

Both economic theory and historical evidence suggests that there are holes in the claim that it is the private sector alone that is responsible for our economic dynamism. Government has been a crucial contributor to the technological advances in our economy. Further, many of these state-funded innovations have gone on to contribute substantially to the profits of private-sector firms (Mazzucato, 2013). In this one area, Friedman's economic perspective actually does severe damage to the interests of the business class. Without government, innovation, productivity and economic growth would suffer dramatically.

Friedman's commitment to profits is laid bare in his discussion of corporate concentration. According to Robert Van Horn of the University of Rhode Island, traditional conservatives, like Henry Simons, were greatly suspicious of the corporate world, especially when firms became sufficiently large that they reduced competition. Simons saw "monopoly in all its forms, including 'gigantic corporations' and 'other agencies for price control,' as 'the great enemy of democracy'"

(Van Horn, 2011, p. 1527). However, Friedman was more amenable to corporate concentration than his traditional conservative ancestors, arguing that even industries with a few, large firms would function in much the same manner as if it were competitive (Van Horn, 2011, p. 1544). Friedman makes a distinction between problematic monopoly power that is caused by government mandate—with the exception of patents, of which he approves (Friedman, 1962, p. 127)—and more acceptable monopoly power caused by the "natural" functioning of the market. This is an interesting, and, some would argue contradictory, position for a man whose theories rely so heavily on competition to protect the consumer and worker.

Conclusion: Friedman and Profits

Friedman has a legitimate claim to be the most influential economist of the post-war period. Friedman, and the people that implemented his ideas, quite literally changed the world. His academic contributions to macroeconomic theory that earned him the Nobel Prize and his public policy recommendations were increasing influential after 1980. While many, like his eminent critic Krugman, separate his academic macroeconomics from his public policy work in microeconomics, this distinction is misleading. Friedman's business-friendly ideology, which has been so widely adopted by governments, is remarkably consistent whether you examine his more theoretical work or his policy pronouncements. What Friedman describes as the free market is desirable and any intervention in that market, impeding the actions of firms, is harmful.

Friedman's macroeconomic theory rejects the Keynesian anti-recession policy of deficit spending and low interest rates to maintain full employment. Moreover, he argues that a low-inflation, high-employment economy is fostered by things like low unionization rates and meager unemployment insurance benefits. Following Friedman's desired macroeconomic structure exacerbates the power imbalance to the benefit of firms and detriment of workers. Full employment, strong unions and higher unemployment insurance benefits all create more power for workers in the labor market, going some small way to redressing the inherent power imbalance between firms and their employees.

Friedman's animosity toward government regulation may make the world a place so dangerous that fellow economist Krugman is frightened of eating a salad, but this has some real benefits for many firms. Most obviously, reduced regulatory oversight will decrease the compliance costs for firms. Less obviously, to the extent that firms' taxes fund regulatory agencies, reducing government spending on monitoring and enforcement will increase the after-tax income of business. This is consistent with many of Friedman's other policy recommendations, like abolishing corporate income tax (1962, p. 132).

Reducing government provision of goods and services has a similarly one sided distributional impact. By definition, government provision reduces the scope of opportunities for business profit. In the US, the private, for-profit health insurance industry earned a healthy $10–15 billion profit each year in the late 2000s (Freeman, 2009). When the government provides health insurance, as it does in Canada, there is one less industry in the economy in which private-sector profits can be made. This uneven accounting is not isolated to the health insurance industry. It is true every time that the government provides any services, from energy to jails. Conversely, when government is removed, this opens up avenues for firms to profit. Friedman advocates for broad-based privatization including education, especially at the post-secondary level (1962, p. 99).

Friedman argues that these policies will lead to faster economic growth, greater prosperity, less unemployment, more affordable products and better consumer safety. However, none of these claims can be empirically demonstrated. Rather, what these policies very predictably do is shift the broad policy terrain to greatly favor business.

5
The Deregulationists:
Public Choice and Private Gain

Introduction

In Chapter 4, we focused on a single author whose ideas, we argue, contained much of the intellectual ammunition for the revolution in economic policy that transformed the US after 1980. In this chapter, rather than focusing on one particular author, we will analyze a school of thought, under whose umbrella many famous economists sheltered. In different ways, all of these authors refined and advanced Friedman's ideas on the problems of government regulation of the free market. Between the 1970s and 1990s, proponents of what came to be known as "Public Choice" sought to apply the techniques and assumptions that had become commonplace in economics to the political system (which explains the alternative name of "rational choice in politics"). The authors surveyed in this chapter, the most famous in this tradition, argue that this method allows them to examine the political world in a positive, scientific manner, rather than the romantic, normative fashion that economists had previously used to study public policy.

Three University of Chicago economists—George Stigler, Sam Peltzman and Gary Becker—all made forays into developing an economic theory of political behavior using the assumptions of rational choice. Although all three were known for a variety of contributions in other areas, for the purposes of this chapter, it is their work in forging an intellectual attack on government regulation that is relevant. Stigler received his PhD at Chicago, like Friedman who he claims was a major influence (Stigler, 1982). Also like Friedman, Stigler was a member of the Mont Pelerin Society whose goal was to save the free market from the clutches of government. Stigler moved from university to university before settling back in Chicago in 1958. He received the Nobel Prize in 1982 "for his seminal studies of industrial structures, functioning of markets and causes and effects of public regulation," but in this context it is his work on regulation that is most relevant. In his obituary in the *New York Times*, Stigler was described as a pro-business conservative, albeit one who maintained his intellectual independence (Passell, 1991).

Becker graduated from Chicago's PhD program in 1955 and joined Columbia University before returning to Chicago in 1970. He claimed that his decision to leave Columbia was, at least in part, caused by what he perceived to be the intimidation of free inquiry at Columbia during the student movements of the late 1960s (Becker, 1992). Again, Friedman had a profound impact. Becker described him as "by far the greatest living teacher I have ever had" (Becker, 2009, p. 141). Becker is renowned for applying the tools of microeconomics, especially the assumption of individual, maximizing rationality, to non-market activities such as discrimination, education, crime and politics. He was awarded the Nobel Prize in 1992 "for having extended the domain of microeconomic analysis to a wide range of human behavior and interaction, including nonmarket behavior." He also received the US Presidential Medal of Freedom, the highest civilian award in the US, from President Bush in 2007 (University of Chicago, 2007). Like Stigler, Becker was an unabashed opponent of what he viewed as government's unwarranted intervention in the economy. In his final column in a regular series for *Business Week*, he wrote, "my first few economics courses taught me the power of competition, markets, and incentives," and the "debilitating effects of onerous regulations in investment, employment, and prices." (Becker, 2004). Also like Stigler, Becker was a member of conservative, free market think tanks. He was part of the Mt. Pelerin Society, and he joined the Hoover Institution, where he was one of the eight Hoover Fellows on the Defense Policy Board that, according to the *Chicago Tribune*, played "an influential role in pushing the Bush administration toward an invasion of Iraq" (Stanford University, 2001; Hedges, 2002).

Rounding out the Chicago trio, Peltzman also earned his doctorate at Chicago, graduating in 1965. Like Stigler, after some early career voyaging, he landed back at Chicago, joining the School of Business in 1973. Peltzman is most famous for his research pointing to the flaws in the regulation of specific industries, like pharmaceuticals and automobiles. However, the article that we will focus on most prominently in this chapter is his advancement of Stigler's theory of regulation in his article, "Toward a More General Theory of Regulation."

The two economists most closely associated with public choice are James Buchanan (who won a Nobel Prize in 1986 for his work in this area) and Gordon Tullock (who controversially did not).

Buchanan viewed himself as a champion of the people, railing against the elite institutions that constrain their freedom. Buchanan claimed that his resentment of the elite came from personal experience during World War II, where he was scorned by those from exclusive Northeastern universities like Harvard and Yale: "I went to midshipman's school in New York. It's a long story, but there was a lot of obvious discrimination against all of us who went to small southern colleges, despite our records" (Warsh, 1993, p. 94). This sense of being an outsider in the elitist world continued throughout his academic career, though Buchanan overcame this aversion to attend graduate school at the University of Chicago. He described himself as a "libertarian socialist" on entering the school, but had a road to Damascus-style conversion to dedicated free marketeer while taking Frank Knight's course in price theory (Buchanan, 1999a, p. 15). On graduating in 1948, Buchanan bounced around several universities but he is most closely associated with his time at Virginia and George Mason universities, where the school of public choice put down institutional roots. Perhaps part of the reason that he felt himself to be on the outside of economics is that he has been very critical of the discipline's turn toward formalized modeling and abstract theorizing, a trend that has turned economists into, in Buchanan's words, "ideological eunuchs." He lamented current economics' lack of interest in the real issues of economic policy while focusing on more irrelevant, abstract concerns: "They seem to get their kicks from the discovery of proofs of propositions relevant only for their own fantasy lands" (Warsh, 1993, p. 96).

Buchanan claimed that he avoided any requests to lend his name to policies or causes. He would "sign no petitions, join no political organizations, advise no party, serve no lobbying effort" (Buchanan, 1992, pp. 105–6). Yet, according to one biography, Buchanan has been "involved, directly or indirectly, in nearly every significant skirmish of the American tax revolt, from Propositions 1 and 13 in California, in

1973 and 1978, to Proposition 2 1/2 in Massachusetts, to Proposition 6 in Michigan, to the Balanced Budget Amendment" (Warsh, 1993, p. 94).

Buchanan's objection to government and his sense of being an outsider has been carried on by his graduate students. Paul Craig Roberts, one of Buchanan's students, argued that academics in the public choice tradition were excluded from jobs in top schools and had to settle for second-choice careers in policy circles, many in the Reagan administration during the 1980s, but also in think tanks like the Heritage Foundation and Cato Institute. Roberts, himself, settled in the Reagan White House where he was instrumental in crafting the 1981 tax cuts (Warsh, 1993, p. 95).

Tullock, Buchanan's slightly less influential partner in public choice, is an obvious addition to a book about economics but a more controversial inclusion in a book about economists. Tullock only took one course in economics. His academic credentials come from a law degree in 1947 from the University of Chicago, famous for its heritage of resident Chicago School economists like Henry Simons (Tullock's only formal economics instructor) and Ronald Coase. The Faculty of Law also had a close relationship with economics department members like George Stigler and Gary Becker.

After serving as a practicing lawyer, working for the Foreign Service, and teaching at the University of North Carolina, Tullock joined Buchanan at the University of Virginia in 1962. His own sense of being an outsider in the economics profession was no doubt reinforced when Tullock was denied promotion to full professor (three times) at the University of Virginia. This feeling was probably cemented in 1986, when his co-author and co-founder Buchanan was awarded the Nobel (surely going some way to dispelling Buchanan's portrayal of himself as an outsider in the profession), but Tullock's name was not included. In what could be interpreted as either gross hubris or an unanticipated slight, Tullock claimed that he was under the impression that he was going to be given the Nobel right up to the unfortunate October morning when the award went to only one of the Buchanan–Tullock tandem (Warsh, 1993, p. 98).

Like Becker, Tullock applied conventional economic assumptions to non-economic topics such as civil wars (Tullock, 1974) and, even more surprisingly, animals (Tullock, 1971). However, his most famous contributions were his research in the area of public choice, which will be documented below, and his stewardship of the institutions in which public choice was centered. The journal that became the flagship of public choice, appropriately named *Public Choice*, was started out by Tullock under the slightly less catchy title, *Papers on Non-Market Decision Making*. According to one biographer, Tullock kept a remarkably tight rein on the journal's content, often acting as sole reviewer for submissions. In what must have been an incredibly heavy workload, he "read every manuscript submitted to his journal and made decisions unilaterally to reject, ask the author to revise and resubmit, or to accept it for publication" (Shughart & Tollison, 2015, p. 5). Further, he would tailor the stringency of the acceptance criteria to encourage areas that he felt were particularly interesting as well as fledgling academics, fundamentally altering the landscape of public choice through his editorial control. It is interesting that *Public Choice* gained the wide acceptance it did given these less than commonly accepted editorial practices and Tullock's own penchant for more descriptive work compared to the mathematical formality and statistical modeling of most economic journals.

Tullock also founded the Center for Public Choice, the academic home of *Public Choice*. After he resigned (as did Ronald Coase for similar reasons) in protest over Virginia's academic slap in the face, he and Buchanan (who had also resigned in protest from Virginia) joined forces at the Virginia Polytechnic Institute (now Virginia Tech) to form the Center in 1969. In 1983, Tullock, Buchanan and the Center packed up and moved en masse to George Mason University.

Perhaps part of the reason for the success of the Center is that it has been able to count on funding from some very wealthy backers. In the years between 2010 and 2015, the Center received donations from many of the usual contributors discussed earlier in the book, including the Scaife Foundation, Koch Foundation, Whole Foods, President Reagan's chair of the Federal Trade Commission and budget director, Jim Miller III, and the Earhart Foundation, which has also funded think tanks that attempted to discredit global warming and anti-affirmative action campaigns at universities (Center for Study of Public Choice, 2014). Not coincidentally, George Mason also hosts the Mercatus Center, an economic think tank started with money from the Koch Foundation, which is still represented on its Board of Directors.

The Center describes itself as the "world's premier university source of market oriented ideas." It traces its intellectual ancestry to scholars such as "Friedrich A. Hayek, Elinor Ostrom, Douglass North, James Buchanan and Vernon Smith" (Mercatus Center, 2016). Mercatus has been described as, "the most powerful think tank you've never hear of," by *the New Yorker* (Mayer, 2010). According to a *Wall Street Journal* article, when George W. Bush took office in 2001, his administration asked for a list of regulations that needed to be eliminated or changed. Mercatus submitted an impressive list of 44, 14 of which ended up on Bush's ultimate "hit list" of 23, an impressive record of persuasion for any lobby group (Davis, 2004).

These pioneers in applying the world of rational choice to the political realm blazed a new trail in economics. They have created a lasting institutional legacy by founding the now-established field of public choice. However, as the biographies above suggest, and the analysis below will demonstrate, their ideas were not ideologically neutral, nor was it likely they were intended to be. Their ideas provided much of the intellectual justification for the decline in the protective role played by government.

Rational Choice in Politics: The Theory

The starting point of public choice is that the assumptions and methods that have served economics, particularly microeconomics, so well when economists study markets should not be abandoned when they turn to study the political system. Public choice is the study of collective behavior in that it analyzes the formation of group action in the public sector and how policy outcomes will be determined. However, its analytics in this area are based on the economic assumptions of methodological individualism in the sense that "separate individuals are separate individuals and, as such, are likely to have different aims and purposes for the results of collective action" (Buchanan & Tullock 1999 [1962], pp. 6–7). Generally, actors are believed to behave rationally in the political system (Green & Shapiro, 1996). They will undertake an action only when the marginal benefits of doing so are anticipated to outweigh the marginal costs. Becker illustrates the general assumptions of public choice writers: "Political equilibrium has the property that all groups maximize their incomes by spending their optimal amount on political pressure, given the productivity of their expenditures, and the behavior of other groups" (Becker, 1983, p. 372).

According to public choice authors, the use of microeconomic assumptions creates a theory of government that improves on previous normative assertions about what government should do. Public choice brands itself as a theory of "collective choice that is in some respects analogous to the orthodox economic theory of markets" that has "a limited claim as the only positive social science" (Buchanan & Tullock 1999[1962], p. 17). James Buchanan has suggested that public choice theory be interpreted as "politics without romance"(Buchanan, 1999b). What public choice scholars are suggesting is that prior to their contributions, while the market had been subject to stern positive tests that identified numerous cases of market failure, the world of politics had been treated as idealized realm, not subject to the same rigorous scrutiny. As a result, government intervention was often proposed as a remedy for the shortcomings of the market. By subjecting government to the same kind of examination to which the market had been put, public choice authors argue that it is possible that government failure is at least as common as market failure (Sandmo, 1990). Government intervention needs to pass two hurdles. The first is to discover a case in which markets fail. The second is to demonstrate that government intervention can actually improve on the market failure. As Becker spelled out explicitly in an article in the late 1950s, "it may be preferable not to regulate economic monopolies and to suffer their bad effects than regulate them and suffer the effects of political imperfections" (Becker, 1958, p. 109). Public choice's contribution is the introduction of this second hurdle, which it sees as a correction of the earlier scientific record, requiring a certain pragmatism in comparing alternative politicized institutional structures.

An early, influential example attempted to explain how regulation of industry emerged in a democracy (Stigler, 1971, 1974; Peltzman, 1976; Becker, 1983, 1985). In general, this theory begins with the assumption that the political world is populated by three types of rational actors: politicians, voters, and those that join interest groups. Politicians are motivated through self-interest. While the specific utility function of the politician has been the subject of some debate, a common assumption has been that politicians act as though they maximize votes. The politician can either attract votes by enacting policies favored by the voters or using interest groups' money to "purchase" votes through advertising and other information-influencing methods.

Interest groups of producers and consumers seek to convince politicians to grant them favorable policies in exchange for the provision of votes and money, the two things politicians need to get elected. As rational actors, members of interest groups will engage in these activities only if the expected benefits outweigh the costs. The big problem that faces any interest group is that the benefits from political activity, such as protective regulation or pollution-free air, are non-excludable. This means that any individual will benefit from interest group success whether they contribute to the interest group or not. This is the famous "free rider" problem in which individuals will refuse to contribute to a non-excludable good because they cannot be prevented from benefiting from it. Of course, the problem with free riding is that if everyone does it, there is less chance of interest group success, which has a cost to the individual. In this cost-benefit calculation, producer groups have inherent advantages over consumer groups because they are both smaller and better organized through pre-existing institutions like industry associations. The increasing costs that consumers face from any increase in prices from government intervention that benefits firms (like a price floor or tariff) will only be a small burden for each individual person and they will be spread over very large numbers. Producers, by contrast, are fewer in number and each individual business would stand to benefit substantially from regulatory favors. The differing costs and benefits facing these two groups explain the differing amount that they are willing and able to spend on influencing the political system for or against regulation. As Peltzman (1976) was able to stress, however, the producer group will not entirely capture the policy process as long as the consumer is able to influence the politician to some extent.

The last group specified in this theory is the voters. The "instrumental" model of voting assumes that people will vote to maximize their rational self-interest (for example, Peltzman, 1976;

Becker, 1983; Sjoblom, 1985).[1] Since one voter's ability to influence an electoral outcome is infinitesimal, the gains from voting are small. When gathering information is costly, a rational voter will expend little time or energy in this process, allowing his or her perception of self-interest to be swayed by the easily accessible information provided by politicians and interest groups (Tullock, 1967). People's voting patterns under the instrumental model have been succinctly, if somewhat bombastically, summarized as "they vote their interest, as best such interest is perceived to be through the fog of rational ignorance, stupidity, persuasion and lies" (Rowley, 2012, p. 43).

The individual actors in the political system are assumed to act in the same rational fashion as individuals in a market context. The only difference is that the benefits and costs of the political system are different from those that exist in the market and so people's rational, maximizing behavior will reflect that difference. The most obvious and crucial distinction is that it is entirely rational for voters to remain ignorant in the political system but to be much more fully informed when making market decisions, because the benefits of the infinitesimal influence on an election are much smaller than the benefits of actually purchasing something in the market. Public choice interest group theory treats the political system as a market in which favorable policies go to those with the highest demand. Although it is assumed that an informed, one-issue vote on a transfer from the voters/taxpayers to firms would invariably fail, the political system rarely offers either one-issue or well-informed voting. Instead, issues are bundled into platforms at election time and voters are "rationally" poorly informed. In this context, interest group expenditures, and their ability to influence voter decisions through information provision, become a crucial factor in political outcomes. While it is true that producers have more influence than consumers in the political system, this is due to their "advantage as a small group with a large per capita stake over the large group with more diffused interests" (Peltzman,

---

[1] There is also an "expressive" theory of voting in which people derive utility from the act of voting for a certain democratic result without the expectation that their vote will actually make that result come to pass. The authors compare this motivation to that of cheering for a team at a sports event. See Brennan & Lomasky, 1994; Brennan & Hamlin, 1998; Copeland & Laband, 2002; Laband et al., 2009.

1976, p. 212). For public choice writers, the ability to influence decisions, or power, in the political system is analogous to demand in the market. One of the basic claims that results from public choice theory is that good government policies, most of which would result in smaller government, will be in short supply in a democracy because of the rational ignorance of the voters.

The assumption in this theory is that government intervention makes consumers worse off than they would be in a free market. This assumption is made more explicit in the public choice ideas of capture and rent seeking, which were introduced in our discussion of Friedman. "Capture" refers to the virtually inevitable tendency of government regulation to be taken over by the industry it is designed to oversee. Stigler applies the by now familiar idea of rationally poorly informed voters losing out to very determined special interests to argue that "as a rule, regulation is acquired by the industry and is designed and operated primarily for its benefit" (Stigler, 1971). According to Stigler, industry will often seek rules that restrict entry of competing firms rather than direct subsidies, because the latter can get diluted by new firms seeking to grab their share of the cash. For Stigler, examples abound, from licensing requirements in industries, like dentistry and physicians, to restrictions on imported oil. Even regulation brought in with the best of intentions will be turned to the benefit of the industry it was designed to constrain. For example, the seemingly reasonable weight restrictions on "motor trucking," in place to protect wear and tear on roads, varies by state according to the strength of the rail lobby, which opposes trucking, and the supportive farming lobby. Where truck competes most closely with train, for example, the powerful rail lobby successfully limited the weight that trucks were allowed to carry (Stigler, 1971, p. 10).

The incentive for regulatory capture is that government intervention can provide substantial benefits to firms. Rent is income earned above what would normally be necessary to attract resources to a particular employment or investment. While it is possible to apply this idea to a number of circumstances, such as the very high incomes of professional athletes when their next best alternative employment would likely pay them a fraction of their sporting income, a great deal of public choice writing has focused on the extra income stemming from favorable government legislation. Part of the reason for the focus on the government is the idea that in market environments, rents tend to be eroded as either firms or workers flood into lucrative sectors, which forces prices down (Buchanan, 1980, p. 5). It is only where barriers to entry exist that this natural tendency will be blocked, creating an incentive for firms to seek out government legislation to prohibit entry. The costly activity of convincing government to provide this protection, akin to the "royal monopoly privilege" of the mercantilist days of old, is termed "rent seeking" (Buchanan, 1980, pp. 7–9). By diverting business activity away from productive investments and toward wasteful lobbying activity, rent seeking creates an additional cost of government intervention beyond the usually counted items of raising tax revenue and regulatory compliance (Krueger, 1974; Tullock, 1967, 1980, p. 17). The conclusion of both capture and rent seeking is that even when the government gets involved for the most noble of reasons, the almost inevitable outcome is that it will produce a worse outcome than if the market was left to its own devices.

The tendency of rent seeking to expand the size of government is exacerbated by the incentive structure inside the bureaucracy. Again, using the hallmark public choice tactic of applying the assumptions of rational maximization to a political context, Tullock assumed that pursuing bureaucrats' own interests would most likely involve maximizing their incomes, promotions and other personal rewards. Within the incentive structure of a government bureaucracy, these rewards can be obtained by commanding an ever larger government agency. The individual bureaucratic goal would naturally lead to an "over-expanded" government, creating a vicious cycle of inefficiency, further agency growth and more inefficiency (Tullock, 1965, p. 177; Thompson, 2008).

A society that realizes the political system will inevitably produce harmful government intervention has an incentive to design constitutional rules that constrain state activity. Buchanan and Tullock argue in favor of restrictive rules that inhibit the ability of the state to interfere in "human and property rights" (Buchanan & Tullock, 1999 [1962], p. 64). Unfortunately, as far as these public choice authors are concerned, many Western democracies, including the US, have abandoned these constitutional restrictions, resulting in an undesirable increase in the government's ability to create severe gains or losses for individuals. It would, therefore, be wise policy to place renewed restraints on the legislative power of governments by creating voting procedures that make it more difficult to pass new intrusive rules (Buchanan & Tullock, 1999 [1962], p. 210).

These constitutional recommendations are one example of Buchanan and Tullock's general solution to the problems of government, which is simply to have less government. They cast a fond eye back to the early days of American political economy, when the government represented a much smaller portion of the economy: "In an era when the whole of governmental activity was sharply limited ... the relative absence of organized special interests is readily explainable" (Buchanan & Tullock, 1999 [1962], p. 206). Writing in his regular column for *Businessweek*, Becker made similar recommendations, arguing that the only way to reduce undesirable business influence on government was to "eliminate many of the regulations affecting economic activity" (Becker, 1994, p. 18).

Although public choice authors claim to bring a positive, scientific approach to what, they argue, had previously been the overly romantic view of government, it is surely no coincidence that Buchanan and Tullock are strongly personally opposed to state intervention of almost any sort. When asked what the "optimal" size of government would be, Buchanan responded, "Several people have tried to estimate this and they come out with figures like government spending at 15% of GDP. In the modern world it has gone to 40% or above. So we are way beyond the optimal, and that is easier to say than what the optimum is" (Buchanan, 2001). Predictably, Buchanan opposed any policy that expanded the size of government, including the fiscal stimulus package used to ease the US out of the deep recession of 2008: "we have made no progress toward putting limits on political leaders, who act out their natural proclivities without any basic understanding of what makes capitalism work" (Conway, 2009). This is a specific example of Buchanan's long-standing animosity towards Keynesian intervention (a topic to which we will turn later in the book), based on its tendency to increase the role of government. His menu of social ills to be laid on the doorstep of big government, and its inflation-causing tendencies, is surprisingly varied, including

... a generalized erosion in public and private manners, increasingly liberalized attitudes toward sexual activities, a declining vitality of the Puritan work ethic, deterioration in product quality, explosion of the welfare rolls, widespread corruption in both the private and the governmental sector, and, finally, observed increases in the alienation of voters from the political process. (Buchanan, 1999c, p. 67)

For Tullock, the interesting exception to this small government role is the military: "if you look at governmental agencies, they are too big for everything. Except possibly the army. The army has very pronounced economies of scale, you can't really get too big" (Tullock, 2003).

In addition to his work on interest groups, Becker has also extended the assumptions of economic rationality to crime. In keeping with Becker's research agenda to apply commonly used economic tools and assumptions to novel areas, his work on crime rests on the theory that breaking or obeying the law is a rational calculation of costs and benefits: "a person commits an offense if the expected utility to him exceeds the utility he could get by using his time and other resources at other activities" (Becker, 1968). This economic approach allowed Becker to make a number of proposals designed to deter crime by increasing its costs and reducing its benefits. For example, increases in legal income or an increase in "'law abidingness' due to 'education'" would reduce crime. Also in keeping with conventional economic approaches, Becker's theory suggests that there is an optimal level of punishment for criminals that would deter criminal behavior and minimize social harm from crime. Further, the extent to which violators will invest in conviction-avoiding activities will depend on their income. Because criminal activity is based on costs and benefits, high-income earners will devote considerable resources to such things as good lawyers or legal appeals to reduce the probability of incarceration "because the cost in lost income is very high to them" (Becker, 1968, p. 195). Of course, the converse is true of low-income earners, who will spend more energy avoiding fines than prison because their foregone time is worth less to them (Becker, 1968, p. 196). The implication is that, even for similar offenses, the rich should be fined and the poor imprisoned. Becker's claim for his approach is that it delivers predictions and policy prescriptions that follow logically from the starting assumptions.

While an economic theory of crime may seem like a bit of a diversion in a chapter on the merits (or lack thereof) of regulation, Becker's approach has been applied to white-collar crime, which often involves firms (or those that make decisions within them) violating their governing regulations. In the late 1980s and early 1990s, the US Sentencing Commission released three draft reports on corporate crime. The final draft was considerably different than the first. In the first draft, the Commission recommended a dramatic increase in the fines that had previously been levied on violating firms. However, strong corporate opposition was successful in getting these penalties substantially reduced by the final draft (Etzioni, 1993, p. 150). In addition to reducing punishments, the Commission provided a list of extenuating circumstances that would further reduce the penalties, including a "lack of knowledge by management, prompt reporting, and recognition and acceptance of the criminal act" (Etzioni, 1993, p. 151). The economists on the Commission advocated strongly for lower corporate fines. According to sociologist Amitai Etzioni, the "pro-business" ideology of these economists led them to both focus solely on the economic costs and benefits of crime, as Becker emphasized, and recommend very low penalties. The economists on the Commission followed Becker's theoretical recommendation that the costs of a fine should be high enough to deter activity. However, a crucial part of the deterrence effect is not only the fine for violation, but the likelihood of being detected. One of the economists on the Commission, Jeffrey Parker, argued for fines based on a detection rate of about one out of ten or twenty. However, actual detection rates of about one in fifty are probably more realistic, which would require fines five times as large as would be implied by Parker's detection estimate (Etzioni, 1993, p. 152). Indeed, the approach of the economists was so profoundly at odds with the rest of the Commission that they were relieved of their duties.

The rational choice approach to politics exemplified by public choice has garnered considerable acclaim for taking economic assumptions and techniques out of their usual realm and into politics. While some scholars of public choice claim that the alleged anti-government bias in public choice is inaccurate (Ginsburg, 2002, p. 1148), it is certainly true that its most famous founders developed a theory of government failure that reflected their personal beliefs about the shortcomings of the state. Public choice scholars have been very successful in developing a theory that has gained considerable traction inside and outside the discipline. However, they may have been less successful in developing a reasonable theory of how government actually works.

Rational Choice in Politics: What are the Problems?

Critics of applying the economic methods of rational choice to the political world have pointed out several problems, which, taken together, demonstrate that public choice misrepresents how the political system actually works. Rational choice politics, at least as practiced, by Tullock, Buchanan, Becker, Peltzman and Stigler, takes a theory of government with profound normative implications and presents it as a positive, value-free science. The very starting assumption of individual maximization in the political system does not appear to paint a very accurate picture of politicians' or voters' actual motivations. The theory of rent seeking and capture misrepresents the winners and losers from regulation and, therefore, mistakes who is actually in favor of regulation and who is opposed. Becker's analysis of white-collar crime justifies lax enforcement and toothless regulations. Finally, by locating the source of political influence in the differing costs and benefits facing interest groups, it mistakes where the actual source of political influence lies.

Anti-government Bias

While the rational choice approach to politics portrays itself as a positive, scientific approach to studying government, in practice it reflects a thinly veiled distaste of the state by the founders of the discipline. The anti-government bias is nicely demonstrated in the discussion about rent seeking. Theoretically, rent seeking could apply to any "unproductive" use of funds to create high profits. For scholars like Buchanan and Tullock, however, in practice rents are generated almost exclusively by the government. The public choice founders did not, for example, focus on the extensive list of business activities that could, by most definitions, be considered unproductive activity such as advertising, public relations, financial speculation, and the many non-governmental restrictions on entry. In their tribute to Tullock, economists William Shughart II and Robert Tollison argue that when money is spent on lawyers and lobbyists to create governmentally restricted markets, such as cabbies spending money to ensure that the taxi-licensing system remains in place:

> ... those resources could have been deployed in other, more socially productive activities, such as negotiating private contracts or designing effective advertising campaigns that arguably reduce transaction costs, increase economic efficiency and thereby expand the nation's wealth. (Shughart & Tollison, 2015, p. 14)

The default assumption by these scholars is that even something as obviously unproductive as most advertising, which seeks to manipulate consumer preferences and foster dissatisfaction with people's existing lifestyle, actually improves economic efficiency by providing people with better, objective information. Further, the assumption that the free market, without government intervention, is a natural and efficient state of affairs, so that deviations will decrease overall economic welfare is, in itself, a strong assertion.

The anti-government criticism of public choice is not new. As early as the 1970s, critics were arguing that some public choice theorists' policy recommendations were biased, with "a consistent non-interventionist, anti-administration, and a conservative bent" (DeGregori, 1974, p. 211). Twenty years later, another author could still remark that "the Virginia School of public choice was launched as a needed corrective to the theory of market failure, but has developed into a one-sided attack on government" (Udehn, 1996, p. 195; see also Scaff & Ingram, 1987; Honderich, 1996; Carpenter & Moss, 2014, p. 10). The policy conclusion that runs from this asymmetry in public choice is that rent seeking and capture are primarily caused by government and that the obvious solution is to shrink the size of the state. However, it discounts or ignores the many "unproductive" activities that occur in the everyday activities of private-sector firms. While public choice criticizes the conventional theory of promoting an idealized version of state remedies for the failures of the market, it puts forward an idealized version of the market that will always appear superior to the imperfections of the state (Novak, 2014, p. 46).

Assumption of Rational Self-interest

There are also problems with the foundational assumption of public choice: that people behave in a rationally self-interested manner in the political system. For example, in Tullock or Becker's work, the motive of self-interested politicians is to get elected. While there is obviously some degree of truth in this assumption, a theory that rests on this as the exclusive, or even driving, motive of political behavior ignores the very real prospect that politicians act along ideological lines, or even what they perceive to be the public good. One study investigated the extent to which self-interest could accurately predict voting behavior by the US Senate on coal strip-mining regulation. It found that voting was significantly influenced by altruistic or ideological factors such as genuine concern for the public good (Kalt & Zupan, 1984).

The self-interested voter, no matter how well informed, is also a problem for public choice theory. This assumption fares poorly in empirical studies that have attempted to determine whether people actually vote in this manner, leading one study to claim that "our main finding is that ideology is the most consistently important determinant of public opinion on a number of major economic policy issues, and objective measures of material self-interest are the least important" (Blinder & Krueger, 2004, p. 329). This study is not alone. According to Harvard's Gar Orren, "the single most compelling and counterintuitive discovery of research on political attitudes and behavior over the last thirty years is how weak an influence self-interest actually exerts" (Orren, 1988, p. 24). Studies of voting behavior found that people are more likely to vote ideologically than for their individual economic self-interest and will vote for an incumbent if the economy as a whole is doing well rather than if they are individually doing well (Wright, 1993; see also Mansbridge, 1990; Renwick Monroe, 1991; Green & Shapiro, 1996).

Basing a theory of politics on faulty assumptions has important consequences for policy. Buchanan claims that the goal of public choice is to "channel the self-serving behavior of participants towards the common good in a manner that comes as close as possible to that described for us by Adam Smith with respect to the economic order" (Buchanan, 1978, p. 17). However, if the starting assumption of individual maximization is incorrect, then the policy recommendations that focus on privatization and a minimal state will also be wrong (Petracca, 1991). According to Harvard's Amartya Sen, the assumption of individual rationality renders public choice unable to address the most pressing issues, from poverty to environmental preservation, which must consider people's social values and engage in a public discussion of what is best for the welfare of all society (Sen, 1995; see also Barry, 1984; Mitchell & Munger, 1991).

The assumption of individual maximization also creates a nasty little inconsistency for public choice theory. The public choice "paradox of voting" is that if one rationally weighs the costs and benefits of actually turning up to vote from a purely self-interested standpoint, no one should actually cast a ballot. This is because the benefit of voting is the chance of influencing the election in the voter's desired direction, which is absurdly small. If there are any costs (gas or time, for example) to voting, people should stay away from the polls. In fact, the voter has a greater chance of being killed on the way to the polling station than influencing the election (Pressman, 2004, p. 6). Yet people actually do turn up to vote and in quite large numbers. Public choice scholars have attempted to theorize away this inconsistency by resorting to an explanation for this turnout that rests on people having a "taste," for voting (Brennan & Hamlin, 1998), or that they do so out of a sense of duty, but these are tautological defeats for the crucial rationality assumption (Ginsburg, 2002, p. 1147). Rational choice authors claimed that the individual maximizing assumption is realistic because it assumes that people behave in politics as they do in the rest of their lives. Yet, people and politicians do not appear to behave in this narrow, self-interested manner. In fact, many political actions consider something broader, such as the public good, or ideological beliefs.

Who Benefits from Regulation?

The theories of capture and rent seeking do contain some important truths regarding the influence that firms have on specific regulations. It is certainly true that the firms subject to government oversight have a large interest in channeling the rules in their favor. To take one particular example that fits well with capture theory, the tobacco industry is heavily regulated for what most people would construe as a reasonable public health motive. Tired of fighting rearguard actions against interventionist legislation, Philip Morris embarked on its Regulatory Strategy Project, with the long-term goal of creating regulation with a set of core principles protecting the rights of tobacco companies, including preventing the Food and Drug Administration (FDA) from altering cigarette design, removing nicotine as an ingredient, interfering with marketing, or otherwise infringing on the "rights" of adult Americans to smoke. This wish list was successfully passed into law in 2009. In addition to these constraints on regulation, the bill "grandfathered" existing tobacco products and created impediments to the development of new substitutes, even if they were safer than current cigarettes. This last provision favored Philip Morris at the expense of new entrants to the industry and its competitors that had been developing precisely these kinds of cigarette substitutes. Such was the influence of Philip Morris in developing the regulation to suit its own needs that it became known as the "Marlboro Protection Act" (Potter, 2010, pp. 213–14) Capture theory is useful in specific cases where firms use regulation to improve their competitive position.

However, as economists George Akerlof and Robert Shiller argue in their book, *Phishing for Phools*, much of the evidence presented in support of regulatory capture is of the "man bites dog" variety, which highlights the exception that validates the theory and ignores the more frequent "dog bites man" story where regulation actually fulfills the function for which it was intended (Akerlof & Shiller, 2015, p. 144). Akerlof and Shiller favor the more nuanced idea that regulation does actually impose constraints on firms in the service of the public good (unlike capture theory), but that business interests do have influence over their formulation and operation. Further, even if regulations are subject to corporate influence, to argue that we should do away with regulation because it is flawed would be like implying "that because spouses, children and friends are often troublesome, we should never get married, never become parents, and have no friends" (Akerlof & Shiller, 2015, p. 145). Returning to the days before regulation, in which there was no requirement for drugs to demonstrate their safety or effectiveness, for example, would seem to be a step backward. Similarly, removing all regulatory oversight on cigarettes would not seem to be the ideal solution in Philip Morris example. In fact, the unregulated free market solution has already been tried and found detrimental to human health.

This is not to say that firms do not have undue influence over the regulations that govern them, from food and drug industry influence at the FDA, to chemical industry influence at the EPA, to financial industry influence over the Security and Exchange Commission (SEC). Businesses have become so active in influencing the activities of regulatory agencies that one study argues that it is the "modus operandi of at least a large proportion of corporations in the United States" (Bohme et al., 2005, p. 338). For example, the Occupational Safety and Health Administration (OSHA) works in very close collaboration with industry. An agreement between the agency and the industry trade association, the American Chemistry Council (ACC), states that one of its goals is to "provide expertise in the development of training and education program for OSHA's Voluntary Protection Program evaluators and Responsible Care auditors" (Davis, 2007, p. 386). A study examining nutrition-related health problems in the United States found that much of the blame could be traced to the fact that the "food industry seems to exert a big influence on the development of food policies" (Dubois, 2006, p. 138).

Yet, in these examples, capture theory is less useful because while the firms have influence over public policy, they use their rent-seeking funds to seek precisely the small government that public choice authors prefer, but argue firms do not desire. For example, business successfully lobbied the Department of Labor under President Bush for changes in the way toxins were measured in the workplace, making it more difficult for the OSHA to find them harmful to workers (Leonnig, 2008, p. A01). Similarly, the President's Cancer Panel's conclusion about the regulation of chemicals in the US was that "as a result of regulatory weaknesses and a powerful lobby, the chemicals industry operates virtually unfettered by regulation or accountability for harm its products may cause" (Reuben, 2010, p. 23). A court challenge from industry forced OSHA to scrap a 1979 ruling that set the standard for benzene, a known carcinogen, at one part per million (ppm), rolling the requirements back to 10 ppm. This was despite 1989 and 2005 studies that found that Chinese workers exposed to benzene were statistically more likely to develop bone marrow cancer, lung cancer and leukemia, even for those with exposure levels between "6 to 10 ppm" (Davis, 2007, pp. 384–6). One survey discovered that 42 per cent of EPA scientists knew of instances where "commercial interests have inappropriately induced the reversal or withdrawal of EPA scientific conclusions or decisions through political intervention" (Union of Concerned Scientists, 2008, p. 23). In response to industry pressure, the National Toxicology Program (NTP) delayed listing fiberglass insulation for nearly six years, and removed saccharin from its *Report on Carcinogens* (Huff, 2007, p. 109). The list of products over which regulatory oversight was delayed or prevented altogether includes (but is by no means limited to) benzene, vinyl chloride, lead, asbestos, Vioxx and arsenic (Bohme et al., 2005; Michaels, 2008; Pearce, 2008).

In all of these cases, the decline in regulation sought and received by firms has left the general public worse off. These costs and benefits of regulation are the opposite of those theorized by public choice theory, which argues that firms will gain and consumers will lose. Stigler argued in his tellingly titled article, "Why have the socialists been winning," that the burdensome growth of government was due to "the use of public power to increase the incomes of particular groups in society" (Stigler, 1986). According to Becker, decreasing government intervention may occur because government programs must be paid for through taxes, which inevitably create a drag on the economy. While interest groups have a large incentive to influence political outcomes in order to increase their favorable policies from the state, this will be limited by the voting public if the costs become too large (Becker, 1983). While this has some intuitive appeal, it reverses the actual groups that are for and against regulation. The history of interest group activity after 1980 is not that the general public has lobbied vociferously for reduced government oversight against the wishes of protected firms, but that firms have engaged in a concerted effort to reduce regulations, mostly against the wishes of the rest of the population. Rather than consumers benefitting from decreased regulatory activity opposed by firms, as public choice suggests, people are harmed by the decreased regulation desired by firms. Since the 1980s, the regulatory agencies that have been set up to shield people have become increasingly dominated by the corporations that they are supposed to be overseeing. However, in contrast to public choice assertions, firms have not used this influence to bolster regulatory protection but to weaken or dismantle regulation. Corporate success in this endeavor has meant that our food, environment and workplaces are increasingly unregulated, to the detriment of the general public.

Enforcing Regulations

Becker's approach to white-collar crime has important implications for regulations, which like other laws, are only as strong as the monitoring and enforcement that accompanies them. As we have seen, while Becker is in favor of imprisoning poor offenders, he prefers fines for higher-income miscreants. In order to keep firms, and the wealthy individuals who make business decisions, on the regulatory straight and narrow, Becker advocates a fine equal to the gain from the crime adjusted for the likelihood of detection, which he argues would eliminate the incentive to commit crime. In addressing corporate crime, this logic has a certain appeal. When the costs of violation are greater than the benefits, profit-maximizing firms are unlikely to break the law. However, in practice, the Becker approach is unlikely to act as an effective deterrent because it is likely to result in punishments that are too low, creating a permissive environment for white-collar crime. Given the very low detection rates for corporate crime, the fine would have to be extraordinarily large to act as a meaningful deterrent. Etzioni admitted that his own estimate of detection rates, one out of fifty for white-collar crimes, was inevitably wildly speculative; detection rates are inherently "very difficult to establish," since they require knowledge of the number of times violations occur but are not caught (Etzioni, 1993, p. 152). The one-in-fifty detection ratio may be optimistic for many regulations. On average, state-run OSHA enforcement could only inspect each workplace once every 55 years (McQuiston et al., 1998; Weil, 1996). In Chapter 3 we demonstrated how the neoliberal policy of cutting funding to regulatory agencies, like the EPA, compromised their ability to detect violations. The obvious solution to this problem would be a dramatic increase in monitoring activity by the state to detect non-compliance. In fact, criminology research suggests increased monitoring would be more effective than severe penalties. The reason for this is that people do not, generally, want to be caught violating rules and so frequent inspections, even without large penalties, can often be an effective deterrent (Dukes et al., 2014, p. 318). However, for Becker and many other public choice theorists, increased monitoring falls afoul of the desire to maintain a small state, especially as it pertains to regulating firms.

With low detection rates, to act as a meaningful deterrent fines would have to be so high that they would be almost impossible to levy on a firm without inducing bankruptcy, or at least considerable financial stress. Fines this injurious to firms are unlikely to be levied. Perhaps this explains the seemingly low fines levied by OSHA in the 1990s. The average federal fine for a "serious" violation in 1995 was $763, and the maximum fine was only around $7,000 (Weil, 1996; McQuiston et al., 1998). In the book *Too Big to Fail*, law professor Brandon Garrett chronicles the pattern of negotiation and compromise that prosecutors settle for when faced with the well-financed legal departments of corporations. According to Garrett, despite the headline-grabbing initial penalties, many are greatly reduced, and high-level employees get off without any penalty at all (Garrett, 2014). While Garrett focuses on finance as the source of corporate power in the legal system, economist David Gordon points to the structural necessity of creating a profitable economic environment as a determining factor in monitoring and fine levels (Gordon, 1971; see also Nickerson, 1983). Given the negative impact that steep fines would have on firms, they are unlikely to be levied on a systematic basis. In fact, the likely result of Becker's approach to crime is precisely the low-detection, low-fine environment that benefits business, and has been put in place increasingly since the 1980s.

Becker's insistence of fines as the most appropriate penalty for corporate crime explicitly rejects one alternative deterrent and fails to even consider another. Becker explicitly rejects prison time for high-income earners, based on the logic that they will undertake more actions to avoid jail than a fine, making conviction more difficult. The implication that this would make almost all jail terms in essence debtors' prisons, limited to low-income offenders for whom fines are not an appropriate penalty, might be objectionable in and of itself to some. However, the converse of Becker's own logic is that jail time appears to be a severe prospect for high-income earners and might act an impressive deterrent, not, it should be pointed out, because of the elimination of freedom it entails but because of the lack of ability to earn their impressive salaries. And Becker fails to consider the option of nationalizing businesses that commit offenses. This would obviously provide a fairly substantial deterrent and would not suffer from the problem of putting the firm out of business that plagues large fines. However, given Becker's distrust of government and support of private enterprise, it is likely safe to assume that he would not support this alternative.

The Source of Business Influence in Politics

Finally, rational or public choice misrepresents the source of influence wielded by firms in the political system. Recall that the explanation rests on the differing costs and benefits facing actors in the political system. A small number of firms stand to benefit substantially from regulation, while a large group of consumers are individually harmed a small amount. Firms then have a large incentive to invest in lobbying, while individuals will have much less desire to mount a counter-campaign. Conceivably, any group with a similar size and vested interest would also wield the same sort of influence in the political system. The idea from which public choice authors are carefully distancing themselves is that business, as a class (or interest group in public choice language), has an inherent political advantage in the capitalist system based on its ownership and control of the productive capacity in society. Instead, political outcomes are determined by the costs and benefits facing rational actors (Hudson, 2002; see also Atkinson, 1983).

In fact, some public choice authors have been clear about setting up their theory as a superior alternative to radical explanations of politics. Robert Tollison claimed, "the confusion with Marxist theory is more apparent than real" (Tollison, 1982, p. 591), because outcomes are not determined by the power of classes or interests but by the costs and benefits facing the individuals that belong to those interests. Buchanan and Tullock, "reject any theory or conception of the collectivity which embodies the exploitation of a ruled by a ruling class" (Buchanan & Tullock, 1999 [1962], p. 17). Becker echoed this sentiment when he claimed that the differing costs and benefits facing individuals in a group, far more than the "production relations emphasized by Marx, explain the prominence in political life of economic pressure groups" (Becker, 1983, p. 388). In public choice, access to favorable policies does not depend on whether a group is either capital or labor. In fact, both capital and labor, or specific subsections of these two broad interests (industry groups and unions, for example), can develop significant political clout. In the rational choice theory of politics, the corporate world is able to win favorable treatment solely because of its large "demand" for favorable policies, compared with the opposing "demand" of the taxpayers or consumers.

The sort of radical theory that rational choice capture theory tries to supplant was developed in the 1960s. It had in common with public choice a desire to subject regulation to a more rigorous accounting, but it located the source of corporate influence not in the relatively favorable costs and benefits for firms and their industry groups but, in the tradition of Marx and Veblen, in the more pervasive power of business as class (Kolko, 1963; Weinsten, 1968; Sklar, 1988). These works explored the regulatory push of the progressive period in US history, which spawned agencies like the FDA and the anti-trust Federal Trade Commission (FTC). The common theme of these studies was that, from the outset of the drive for regulation in the early 1900s, "class conscious" members of the business elite were able to co-opt the process so that the legislative regime legitimized modern capitalism, which did involve a certain degree of ceding to public pressure demanding some constraints on the most odious activities of firms, but in a manner that was controlled and acceptable to business (Berk, 1991; Novak, 2014). They did so with the financial power at their disposal, their ability to provide plum jobs for regulators and the requirement of framing regulations in a manner that would maintain a profitable environment for firms.

These radical theories also offer a more plausible explanation for government regulatory trends over the last 35 years. What public choice lacks, or deliberately avoids, is a theory that acknowledges the uniquely powerful position of firms in the capitalist economy due to their financial clout and the necessity of creating a profitable policy environment conducive to private-sector investment (Udehn, 1996, p. 204). A more robust theory of government intervention would be able to explain, for example, why firms would request and receive the changes to policy instigated by the American Legislative Exchange Program (ALEC) discussed in Chapter 2, the cuts to social regulation listed in Chapter 3, and the deregulation of consumer protections and food safety covered in Chapter 4. As we saw in Chapter 3, all of these deregulatory changes were part of a broad effort to restore the profits of firms that had fallen through the 1970s.

It is difficult to see how public choice theory's focus on differing costs and benefits in the political system could explain the transformation in corporate support for government intervention in the post-war period. According to economist David Kotz, business in the US, and the interest groups that represented it, such as the Committee for Economic Development (CED) were broadly supportive of a post-World War II compact resting on the pillars of collective bargaining, Keynesian stabilization of the business cycle and government social welfare programs (Kotz, 2015, p. 54). However, by the late 1970s, rising labor costs, the expansion of the state into social regulation such as the environment, and growing international competition combined to create an economic environment that convinced firms that a dramatic restructuring needed to occur. Their response was outlined and coordinated by organizations such as the Business Roundtable. The Roundtable's position papers and lobbying efforts insisted that "excessive government regulation" was to blame for the low productivity growth in the 1970s (Kotz, 2015, p. 70). A public choice explanation of this transformation would have to rely on a change in the costs and benefits of business rent-seeking behavior, which is difficult to imagine. A more plausible interpretation is that in a period of economic decline caused by falling profits, firms have a greater incentive to shed costs including those that stem from regulation. Further, governments are more likely to take these requests seriously in a context of declining profits and investment than they are when profits and investment are high.

Conclusion: Deregulation and Profits

The rational choice approach to politics, a cornerstone of public choice, has enjoyed a meteoric rise as an economic field. From a few dedicated scholars toiling away in the academic margins in the 1960s, public choice has become a respected field in the discipline. Applying commonplace economic tools to politics followed a general trend of using economic methods to analyze what were previously considered non-economic subjects like crime, discrimination and family dynamics. Its most famous practitioners, like Tullock and Buchanan, argue that the application of economic assumptions and techniques to the political system allow for a more rigorous, scientific examination of outcomes of the state. They contrast this approach with what they describe as the less analytic theories of government that took for granted that intervention would be welfare improving.

However, the portrayal of rational choice as a more positive, less normative approach to analyzing government masks a fairly transparent political agenda by the scholars investigated in this chapter. Buchanan, Stigler, Becker and Tullock all view government intervention in the economy as a deleterious force, constraining the free market. Unsurprisingly, their positive approaches yield results that fairly uniformly find evidence of government failure. The policy implications that follow from the research by these authors are clear. Since rent seeking and capture are only possible because of government intervention, reducing government is the solution.

Interestingly, the supporters and opponents of regulation are the opposite of those predicted by these authors. While the ideas of capture and rent seeking do accurately reflect a very small subsection of regulatory activity, and can nicely explain policies like the smoking example used earlier and when industries seek protection from international trade, they are more problematic when addressing most regulations. For most other regulations, it is the regulated firms that are staunchly opposed and devote their considerable political influence, not to reinforcing or redirecting the regulations, as these authors have suggested, but to eliminating or minimizing state interference. On the other hand, the general public is broadly supportive of these policies. Perhaps this is because the public understands the costs and benefits of regulation better than these public choice authors. The public is often better protected with regulation than without, while the activity of firms is often constrained. The deregulatory history of the US since 1980 has not been the triumph of the citizen over the wishes of the firm, but the exact opposite. Further, these founders of rational choice in politics deliberately set their theory up as a superior alternative to a class-based explanation of political influence. Yet a more radical theory that understands that power in the political system does not come from differing costs and benefits facing interest groups, but from the structural power of business in a capitalist economy, can much better explain the deregulatory trends since 1980.

It is, perhaps, no coincidence that the rise of the economic approach to politics has occurred precisely when firms engaged in a massive political and economic effort to reduce the regulatory "burden" of the state in a successful effort to reduce their costs and restore profits after the 1970s. As a theory of government failure, public choice aligned nicely with Ronald Reagan's famous claim that "government is not the solution to our problem; government is the problem" (Reagan, 1981). The institutions of public choice, from university departments to research institutes, have benefited from corporate funding. The public choice policy prescriptions of these authors align very nicely with the desire of firms to shed governmental regulation and transfer economic decisions from the state to the market (Wright, 1993).

6
The Great Vacation: Rational Expectations and Real Business Cycles

Introduction

Wage slavery can be a grind. The top-down, command-and-control style of most employment fails to give many workers a sense of fulfillment during the time that they spend in their cubicle or at the assembly line. Yet, for most people, unemployment is something to be avoided. A choice between earning an income with a job, no matter how unpleasant, or doing without a weekly pay packet altogether, is really no choice at all. The economists in this chapter, however, view a job as something that many people can take or leave. In fact, it is people's willingness to give up their employment when wages drop that is the hallmark of a school of macroeconomics that rose to prominence in the 1970s and 1980s.

As we saw in Chapter 4, Friedman's macroeconomic research attempted to call into question the Keynesian explanation for the cause of, and cure for, economic fluctuations and the devastating unemployment that inevitably accompanies them. As was the case with the public choice authors in Chapter 5 who picked up and refined Friedman's microeconomic contempt for regulation, subsequent macroeconomic theorists have advanced Friedman's incomplete attack on Keynesian policy. Like Chapter 5, this chapter will look at the work of what might be termed the founding, or at the very least, most famous, proponents of what became an influential economic school of thought: Robert Lucas, Thomas Sargent, Neil Wallace, Finn Kydland and Edward Prescott.

If Milton Friedman could make a claim to being the most influential economist since Keynes, Lucas has been dubbed the only slightly less prestigious, most influential macroeconomist of the last quarter of the twentieth century (Fischer, 1996; Hall, 1996). Like so many of the authors discussed in these pages, Lucas received his PhD from the University of Chicago, graduating in 1964. When asked which economists had the most influence on his work, Lucas responded that Friedman was a "great teacher," whose ideas forced students to rethink their whole social philosophy (Lucas, 1996; Snowdon & Vane, 2005, p. 274). After graduating from Chicago, he joined Carnegie Mellon University, but such is the gravitational pull that the University of Chicago economics department exerts on its former students that Lucas returned to the department in 1975. He was awarded the Nobel Prize "for having developed and applied the hypothesis of rational expectations, and thereby having transformed macroeconomic analysis and deepened our understanding of economic policy" (The Royal Swedish Academy of Sciences, 1995). As we shall see, the manner in which rational expectations transformed economics was to, "throw the Keynesian paradigm off its pedestal" (De Vroey, 2001, p. 127).

Lucas has been fairly unpredictable in his public pronouncements on economic policy. His parents were advocates of the New Deal, which apparently influenced his decision to vote for Barack Obama against John McCain in 2008, based primarily on "the racist history" of the US (Jenkins, 2011). He also described himself as "never going to be anywhere near the far-right end of the spectrum for Chicago" (Klamer, 1984). On the other hand, his other policy pronouncements do seem to put Lucas more squarely in the free market camp. Lucas was not very keen on Obama as a president, claiming that he was "caught by surprise by how far left the guy is" (Jenkins, 2011). In addition, despite stating that McCain "didn't have a clue about the economy" (Jenkins, 2011), Lucas signed a 2008 petition supporting McCain's economic policy and another in 2012 backing Mitt Romney. He has also signed single-issue petitions opposing "anti-sweatshop" legislation and in favour of moving social security toward individually owned accounts (Klein & Daza, 2013). In a 2012 interview, he stated his opposition to socialized medicine and high marginal tax rates on the rich (Klein & Daza, 2013). In terms of long-term growth policy, he argued that the lesson from countries like Taiwan, Korea and Japan are that "conservative, pro-market, pro-business" policies lead to economic success. Africa's sub-par performance, on the other hand, was due to "too much socialist influence" (Snowdon & Vane, 1998, p. 135).

Lucas was a friend of Neil Wallace while the two were completing their PhD programs at Chicago. Like Lucas, Wallace graduated in 1964. He is mostly associated with his time at the University of Minnesota, where he spent thirty years between 1964 and 1994. He moved to Pennsylvania State University in 1997, after a brief stint at the University of Miami. Wallace is best known for his work with Thomas Sargent. The two are considered founders of the new classical school that revolutionized macroeconomics. Although Wallace has an impressive array of awards to his name, including Distinguished Fellow at the American Economic Association and a Fellow at the American Academy of Arts and Sciences, it is probably fair to say that he does not enjoy quite the same celebrity as Sargent.

Thomas Sargent received his PhD in 1968 from Harvard University. After a stint in the US Army and a very brief period at the University of Pennsylvania, Sargent settled in with Wallace at the University of Minnesota from 1975 to 1987. Since then he has bounced around from the University of Chicago to Stanford University to his current post as the William Berkley Professor of Economics at New York University. Along with Chris Sims, in 2011 Sargent was awarded the Nobel Prize for "their empirical research on cause and effect in the macroeconomy." That less than enlightening synopsis of Sargent's research, which really could probably describe most modern macroeconomics, hides Sargent and Wallace's influence, which, as we shall see, revolutionized macroeconomics through the adoption of rational expectations and equilibrium models that appealed to economists because of their theoretical consistency with microeconomic assumptions about the economy.

Sargent is, in some ways, cagier than Lucas about where he stands on economic issues. He is insulted by people who call him a "non-Keynesian" or "right wing" (Sommer, 2011a), arguing that he, and his work, are not political, but technical (Klamer, 1984, p. 62). He declares himself a long-time Democrat and maintains that government needs to play a role in economic affairs (Sommer, 2011b). He claims both Friedman and the prominent Keynesian economist James Tobin as major influences (Klamer, 1984, p. 62). On the other hand, outside observers have placed him firmly in the "free market" camp and there seems to be considerable evidence for this (Cowen, 2011). Sargent is a Senior Fellow at the Hoover Institution, a think tank known for its conservative orientation that promotes personal and economic liberty and limited government (Hoover Institution, 2016). Sargent has argued that the higher unemployment rates in Europe compared to the US can be explained by the generous European system of unemployment benefits and has expressed concern that recent increases in the social safety net in the US will lead to higher persistent unemployment (Sargent, 2010).[1] While Sargent views his work as non-political, we will see that it certainly has political implications.

Lucas was also a good friend of Ed Prescott, who received his PhD in 1967 from Carnegie Mellon. After graduation, Prescott taught at the University of Pennsylvania until 1971 before returning to Carnegie Mellon, where he stayed until 1980. He then joined the "freshwater" home of rational expectations, the University of Minnesota, for over twenty years before moving to Arizona State University in 2003. In 2004, Prescott won the Nobel Prize in Economics for his work with Finn Kydland on "dynamic macroeconomics: the time consistency of economic policy and the driving forces behind business cycles."

Prescott is more forthcoming about where he stands politically than Sargent. He claims that although he went through high school as a Fabian socialist, the ideological blinkers worn by his fellow students at Swarthmore College cured him of his socialist leanings. He generally favors economic policy that promotes "individual responsibility and decentralized arrangements" as opposed to "paternalistic statism" (Klein et al., 2013b). Prescott has presented at the Cato Institute, one of the think tanks highlighted in Chapter 2, which is "dedicated to the principles of individual liberty, limited government, free markets and peace" (Cato Institute, 2016), on how private accounts in Social Security could boost GDP and increase the incentive to work. In 2009, he signed an open letter to Barack Obama that was sponsored

---

1   Sargent does not argue that generous unemployment benefits will always create unemployment. If the labor market functions so that spells of unemployment do not reduce lifetime income substantially, generous benefits can lower unemployment. However, he argues that since the 1970s, losing a job has meant an increased drop in human capital during the non-work period, so the negative impact of longer unemployment spells caused by generous unemployment insurance has increased.

by Cato opposing the post-crisis economic stimulus package in the American Recovery and Reinvestment Act (Cato Institute, 2009) and supported Mitt Romney for president in 2012 (Klein et al., 2013b). He claims that the slow growth in the US economy since 2007 was due to an "explosion in federal regulation, intervention and subsidies," including, but not limited to Obamacare, high corporate tax rates and "numerous antibusiness National Labor Relations Board decisions" (Prescott & Ohanian, 2014). He also argued that Americans work more than Europeans because of the incentive of lower tax rates in the US (Prescott, 2004). In perhaps his most controversial public pronouncement, he claimed that "it is an established scientific fact that monetary policy has had virtually no effect on output and employment in the U.S. since the formation of the Fed" (Appelbaum, 2014). As we shall see, this statement is far from an "established fact," but it is an inevitable conclusion from Kydland and Prescott's theory.

Finn Kydland is a rare non-American in this book. He grew up in a small town in Norway and was the only person in his elementary school to complete high school. He lists Lucas as one of his major academic influences and completed his PhD at Carnegie Mellon in 1973 under Prescott. After briefly returning to Norway, Kydland returned to Carnegie Mellon in 1978 where he stayed until 2004 when he moved to the University of California Santa Barbara.

Kydland does not like offering policy opinions. He even refuses to be drawn out when interviewers have sought out his political views. However, he has been classified by others as leaning toward free market policies (Klein et al., 2013c). Like Sargent, Kydland was a National Scholar at the conservative Hoover Institution. He is also a member of the Copenhagen Consensus Center (CCC), "a think tank that researches the smartest solutions for the world's biggest problems, advising policy makers and philanthropists how to spend their money most effectively" (CCC, 2016). Its founder and president is the controversial environmentalist Bjorn Lomborg, author of the *Skeptical Environmentalist*, which argued that the world should not be attempting to reduce greenhouse gas emissions. In 2009, Kydland contributed to a report for the CCC proposing that world leaders should focus on geo-engineering as a solution to climate change in the near term, rather than mandating cuts in greenhouse gas emissions (Eilperin, 2009).

Rational Expectations and the Real Business Cycle: The Theory

One of the most apparently damaging blows to the Keynesian prescription of counter-cyclical policy might not appear, at first glance, to be the knockout punch that it became. Much of the traditional justification for Keynesian policy was provided by macroeconomic models in which people's response to policy changes was predictable. For example, if governments increased spending in the economy, firms would respond with a predictable increase in investment to meet that demand. This permitted a macroeconomic model to predict what would happen to the economy in response to a specific policy change. The now-famous Lucas Critique of Keynesian policy started from the premise of rational expectations. As we saw in Chapter 4, Friedman applied the Adaptive Expectations Hypothesis (AEH)— that people base their expectations on past truths. The flaw with this assumption is that it does not allow people the very real tendency to use current information in their decisions. The Rational Expectations Hypothesis (REH) corrected this perceived shortcoming by modeling behavior that allowed actors to use up-to-date information as well as past events. Workers can read the newspaper, listen to the radio, these days go online, rather than only using the past as a guide. In economic language, agents make the best use of information available to them. If rational expectations are correct, then people will take the policy change into consideration when making their decisions. Since it is virtually impossible for the economic modeler to predict how people will respond to the policy change, it is impossible to accurately determine how the economy will react.

To take one example from Lucas, one possible counter-cyclical policy during a recession might be an investment tax credit. The goal of this policy is induce investment by firms to stimulate the economy. In order to do this, the government needs to know how much investment is expected to increase with a change in taxes. However, even if there is ample econometric work specifying a relationship between tax rates and investment based on past changes, it is not valid to assume that firms will respond in an identical manner to future tax changes. This is especially true if, as should be the case for an expansionary policy, the tax cut is temporary, in which case the modeler would have to know how firm decisions would respond to a change in policy of uncertain duration, a difficult task indeed (Lucas, 1976; for more on Lucas's rational expectations, see Lucas, 1972, 1973; Lucas & Sargent, 1981). The conclusion is that it is beyond the ability of economic models to accurately predict the consequences of "arbitrary" policy decisions.

In addition to creating uncertainty surrounding counter-cyclical policy intervention, rational expectations became an important component of a theory of business cycles that came to prominence in the 1970s and 1980s. These models had several key components that combined to offer up a theory of economic fluctuations that provided an alternative to the Keynesian demand-based explanation. In addition to rational expectations, these macro models applied the assumptions that firms maximize profits and individuals maximize utility, which was pleasingly consistent to many economists, because it aligned macroeconomic theorizing more closely with the assumptions that were deemed to be standard in micro. The authors highlighted in this chapter viewed the economy as perfectly competitive, where no firm or worker had sufficient market power to influence the price. The economy was also characterized by flexible wages and prices that adjust instantly in response to changes in supply and demand. For example, if the demand for labor falls and firms are willing to hire less people at existing wages, the surplus of workers will cause wages to fall. The decline in wages then increases the number of workers that firms will be willing to hire and decreases the number of workers willing to supply labor in that market. As a result of falling wages, the surplus of labor is eliminated and markets will rapidly tend to an equilibrium in which supply equals demand. The assertion of flexibility and equilibrium, a hallmark of classical economists, helped name this school of thought the "new classicals"[2] (Lucas, 1972; Sargent, 1979; Snowdon & Vane, 2005, p. 219).

Astute readers will be slightly perplexed about how an equilibrium theory, in which demand equals supply in all markets, can explain business cycles. After all, if wages adjust instantly so that the

---

2   Although there are some differences between RBC and the new classical school surrounding whether monetary policy is ever effective, they have enough in common that RBC was branded "new classical mark II" by one expert on the history of economics (Snowdon & Vane, 2005, p. 294).

number of jobs in the labor market equals the number of job seekers, involuntary unemployment, the hallmark of a downturn, is non-existent. Real Business Cycle (RBC) authors explain this through changes in productivity, wages and the amount that people want to work. In RBC theory, business cycles originate with random shocks, or large fluctuations, in the rate of technological change (Kydland & Prescott, 1982). These shocks could be caused by a number of events like (un)favorable weather in agriculture, large changes in energy prices, major social upheavals, or damaging government policies, but the most likely are changes in productivity, due to say, a change in technology. While these events are genuinely diverse, they are all external "shocks" to the stable economy that originate outside the normal functioning of the economic system. That is, RBC theory does not trace the source of the productivity change to any predictable or inherent tendencies in the economic system toward downturns, as we attempted to do in Chapter 2's discussion of the 2008 crisis. RBC authors suggest that the rate of technological advance in society has considerable variation, meaning that there are booms, with rapid adoption of innovations, and slowdowns, where technology advance is stagnant. Prescott demonstrated that there is considerable pro-cyclical variation in the "Solow residual," a measure that attempts to calculate the effects of technological change by taking the difference between the percentage change in outputs and the percentage change in inputs. For example, if there has been no increase in the amount of capital and labor inputs used in production but output increases, the assumption behind the Solow residual is that the output increase must be due to technological improvements (Prescott, 1986). Kydland and Prescott estimated that changes in the Solow residual could account for about 70 percent of the variation in output in the US post-war period (Kydland & Prescott, 1991). When positive technology shocks occur, then labor productivity will increase. In competitive labor markets, the increase in productivity will cause an increase in real wages.

In an effort to move beyond a technological explanation of productivity shocks, Prescott (and co-author Ellen McGratten) turned to government policy as a source of instability. They explained the very slow recovery after the 2008 crisis as a shock in productivity rather than the standard explanation of ailing credit institutions, indebted households and jobless workers. Given the absence of an obvious technology shock during this period, Prescott and McGratten argued that the post-2008 malaise was caused by the escalating costs incurred by businesses to comply with regulations and the tax costs of paying for the workers at regulatory agencies. They interpret these rising costs as a decline in productivity (McGratten & Prescott, 2012).

The second hallmark of RBC theory is that workers respond to changes in real wages through "intertemporal" changes in labor supply, which means that people will work more when wages are high so that they can work less when wages are low (Lucas & Rapping, 1969; Kydland & Prescott, 1982; Mankiw, 1989; Snowdon & Vane, 2005, p. 340). Economic fluctuations are caused by employees changing the number of hours they work in response to the changes in real wages that stem from temporary productivity shocks. When an adverse technology shock occurs and wages fall, workers will reduce the amount they want to work, creating a recession. Workers make up for this income decline by working longer hours when positive technology shocks increase wages. In explaining the Great Depression, Prescott claims that, "market hours fall, reducing output … and more time is allocated to leisure" (Prescott, 1999, p. 26). In this theory, unemployment is voluntary. In labor market equilibrium, the number of workers seeking a job equals the number of jobs available so anyone wishing to work can do so. The decline in labor hours is a voluntary, optimal response by workers in the face of a reduced real wage (Lucas, 1978).

It is also important to highlight the interpretation of recessions in RBC. In many economic theories, downturns are inevitably characterized by harmful, involuntary unemployment. Of course, this cannot happen when markets adjust instantly in RBC theory. Rational expectations also destroys Friedman's AEH explanation for recessions and depressions, which are caused when falling prices leads firms to offer lower nominal wages that are rejected by workers whose adaptive expectations belief is that this offer is a decline in real wages. The gap between what firms are willing to pay and what workers are willing to accept creates unemployment and recessions. This explanation, based as it is on mistaken beliefs about wages and prices, is impossible under rational expectations. Workers would immediately know that although their nominal wages had fallen, the decrease in prices would leave their real wage unchanged, destroying the AEH explanation of unemployment. With the twin assumptions of rational expectations and price and wage flexibility, neither the Keynesian nor the AEH explanation can be correct. Rather, downturns are caused when workers withdraw their labor due to decreases in productivity and real wages.

The RBC logic of recessions caused by intertemporal changes to working hours in a context of equilibrium also has important implications for how recessions and depressions are interpreted. The standard post-war interpretation was that the reductions in income and increase in unwanted unemployment that accompany a downturn are societally harmful and should be avoided if at all possible. It is this logic that created the case for Keynesian counter-cyclical policy. However, the RBC explanation of fluctuation implies that recessions are, in fact, optimal responses to technology shocks. While the economy would have been better off without a negative shock, if and when a shock occurs, and Prescott's evidence suggests that it will, the optimal response by firms will be to reduce real wages. Given the decline in real wages, workers will want to work less. Given that each of these decisions is a desirable adjustment to falling productivity, the fluctuation is actually an appropriate response to the fall in technology. Prescott puts this quite explicitly: "the policy implication of this research is that costly efforts at stabilisation are likely to be counter-productive. Economic fluctuations are optimal responses to uncertainty in the rate of technological progress" (Prescott, 1986, p. 21). It is not quite true that RBC theorists argue that recessions are positive, since it would be a superior result if negative technology shocks could be avoided. However, RBC theory does suggest that if a negative shock occurs, the recession is a desirable consequence. Therefore, government policy that strives for something called "full employment" is misguided, because the economy is always in such a state (Snowdon & Vane, 2005, p. 331). For RBC authors, like Prescott, the term "business cycle" is undesirably misleading because it creates the impression that the economy goes through cycles of better and worse times, when, in fact, a better statement would be that there is no such thing as a business cycle in the sense that fluctuations are a normal, acceptable feature of economic growth (Prescott, 1986).

Government policy to correct for a recession is not only unnecessary, it is also ineffective. Or, if we are going to be a bit more careful with our language, if rational expectations are taken seriously, then anticipated changes to monetary policy will affect prices, but will have no impact on either output or employment (Sargent & Wallace, 1975, 1976).[3] Let's say a central bank were to reduce interest rates, encourage borrowing and, therefore, increase consumption and investment. This increase in demand in the economy would drive up prices. Since actors in the economy have rational expectations, workers will increase their wage demands to reflect the higher prices. Because the real wage then remains unchanged, the profit of firms would not change and neither would their output and employment (Sargent, 1999).

On the other hand, anti-inflationary policy is not only effective but also painless. In most Keynesian (and Friedman's AEH) theory, inflation could only be controlled at the expense of employment and output. Increasing interest rates would increase unemployment and slow down the economy, which would, in turn, put downward pressure on prices as demand fell. In the Sargent and Wallace economy, on the other hand, if the increase in the interest rate is credibly announced by the central bank, it will create the same chain of events outlined in the previous paragraph but in the opposite direction. When the interest rate increase is announced, people will rationally revise their price and wage expectations downward, resulting in a decreased price level without the sacrifice of declining output and employment. In the early 1980s context of rapidly rising prices, this theory had a certain utopian appeal, since it implied that inflation could be tamed without the nasty adjustment costs predicted by either the Keynesians' or Friedman's adaptive expectations (Gordon, 1978, p. 338; Snowdon & Vane, 2005, p. 248).

The RBC model turned the Keynesian theory of economic fluctuations on its head. Rather than being caused by insufficient demand, recessions and depressions are caused by supply-side productivity shocks. Rather than an undesirable stagnation to be corrected by counter-cyclical government policy, recessions represent optimal responses to shocks for which the government cannot, and should not, correct. For these RBC authors, barring any undesirable government policy, technology shock, or environmental disaster,

---

3   Kydland and Prescott's RBC theory would go a step further and argue that even unanticipated changes in monetary policy will have no effect, going as far as calling it a "monetary myth" (Kydland & Prescott, 1990).

whatever the state of the capitalist economy, it is the best of all possible worlds.

Rational Expectations and RBC: Problems and Criticisms

RBC theory and rational expectations have come under attack on a variety of fronts, from the ability of humans to actually behave as rational expectations hypothesizes, to the assumption of equilibrium and voluntary unemployment, to the implications for policy. Turning first to the idea of rational expectations, questions have been raised about people's ability to process and adopt "correct" information in forming their expectations. Indeed, even among those professional few who dedicate their working lives to analyzing the economy, uncertainty reigns and disagreements rage over the impact of changes to the macroeconomy. To argue that people can correctly anticipate the price increase that will stem from reduced interest rates appears to grant people predictive powers beyond even those of the central banks responsible for monetary policy (see, for example, Evans & Honkapohja, 1999).

Questions have also been raised about the dependence on technology as a driver of economic ups and downs. First, technological change is most likely not sufficiently large or sudden to cause the kind of swings in productivity required by RBC theory (Muellbauer, 1997). Second, Solow residual evidence for technology shocks may not prove what RBC scholars claim. Recall that the Solow residual measures the difference between the change in output and the change in the quantity of inputs. If output is increasing with the same number of inputs, then the RBC school claims that this is evidence of a technology shock, loosely defined since it doesn't actually have to be technology. However, the Solow residual could be capturing a whole host of changes that have nothing to do with the RBC supply-side productivity explanation. One possibility is that firms "hoard" labor in recessions. If there are some fixed costs to hiring and letting workers go, firms will keep workers during downturns despite a decline in their sales. These "underutilized" workers will be less productive in the sense that the same inputs now produce less output (Mankiw, 1989, p. 1984). This would show up as a negative productivity shock in the Solow residual, but what it would be really measuring was a reduction in demand. If the Solow residual represents something other than the productivity shocks that RBC authors claim, then the productivity explanation that is so crucial to RBC theory remains unproven.

RBC insistence that only supply-side productivity changes can cause economic fluctuations is a particularly extreme version of the more general tendency in much of mainstream economics to focus on shocks, external to the economic system, as the source of instability. This analysis ignores the possibility that the economic system is not stable. The position taken by what might be called "radical" economists is that the economic system generates internal contradictions that will cause repeated crises. As one example of how this might happen, in Chapter 2 we outlined the policy transformation in the US in response to the low profits of the 1970s. In Chapter 3, we discussed how the deregulation and income stagnation caused by that transformation laid the foundation for the economic crisis of 2008. The 2008 decline was not due to a shock external to an otherwise smooth system. Rather, the crisis came from an economic structure set up to restore profits starting in the 1980s. One interpretation of the 2008 crisis was that it was a specific example of a general type of crisis in which capital is "too strong," in the sense that the compensation that firms pay their employees is not sufficient to guarantee demand for their products. This is not the only theory of the cause of the 2008 crisis. Radical economists agree, in general, about the system's tendencies, conflicts and contradictions, but differ over the proximate cause. For example, economic historian Robert Brenner of UCLA claimed that overproduction (too many factories in too many countries producing the same products) has resulted in falling prices and profits (Brenner, 2006). A contrasting explanation was put forward by The New School's Anwar Shaikh, who argued that firms' tendency to increase their fixed capital costs in order to keep ahead of the competition and undermine the demands of labor for higher wages will also lead to long-term declines in the rate of profit (Shaikh, 2010). Despite the differences between scholars in this tradition, they all look *inside* the system to explain crises, rather than resorting to external shocks.

Beyond questions about the rational expectations hypothesis and relying on shocks to explain instability, the assertion of price flexibility and market equilibrium has also raised a few eyebrows. Recall that wage and price flexibility means that markets instantly clear. If prices and wages do not adjust as quickly as these equilibrium theories suggest, then prolonged periods of disequilibrium can occur where supply does not equal demand in markets. In fact, this disequilibrium is a fundamental component of many mainstream Keynesian theories to explain economic fluctuations. While arguments have been put forward supporting sticky prices, the more common objection to flexibility revolves around wages. Casual observation and empirical evidence suggests that wages do not fall rapidly, even in the face of large surpluses of labor (Mankiw, 1989). There have been many justifications for this. For example, many contracts, like those negotiated by unions in collective bargaining, lock workers and employers into multi-year wage deals. An even more permanent explanation is the "efficiency wage" hypothesis that states that it is profit maximizing for firms to pay higher than equilibrium wages in order to attract better-quality employees and induce more effort out of their workforce. In either event, wages will not fall even in the face of involuntary unemployment. Regardless of the specific justification for a prolonged situation in which those seeking work exceeds the number of jobs available, the RBC denial of the very possibility that this can happen appears to be contradicted by a casual glance at the labor market, especially during recessions or depressions.

A related concern is the interpretation of unemployment. RBC theory suggests that the reduction in hours that perpetuates a recession is caused by voluntary decisions by workers. Expansions are caused by workers choosing more hours following positive productivity shocks. For this to be true, workers must be quite responsive to changes in the real wage. Yet statistical studies find that workers do not greatly alter the amount they work when wages change (Altonji, 1986). This certainly makes intuitive sense. Few workers have the flexibility in either their work schedules or their budgets to cut back on the number of hours they work. A second problematic implication of the RBC version of voluntary unemployment is that the number of workers quitting their jobs should increase during a recession. Yet this is the opposite of what occurs. During recessions, the number of voluntary quits decreases while the number of job listings decreases. Recessions and depressions are times when the unemployed, desperate to find a job at virtually any wage, line up to apply for those few jobs that become available. This is precisely what is implied by an explanation of downturns that rests on involuntary unemployment, but it flies in the face of RBC theory.

Perhaps even more perniciously, RBC theory implies away the very real and very damaging effects of unemployment on the unemployed. In RBC theory, unemployment is not something forced on an unwilling worker, but something chosen and welfare improving. However, unemployment has been linked to increased mortality, worse mental health, and unhealthy behavioral changes like alcohol consumption and marriage breakdown. Both men and women who are unemployed report being in bad health more often than those who are employed. In terms of stressful life events, unemployment is ranked as equivalent to the death of a family member (McKee-Ryan et al., 2005; Bartley et al., 2006; Mustard et al., 2006). These facts do not lie comfortably alongside an assertion that choosing "more leisure" is a voluntary, welfare-improving choice by workers.

RBC theory's lack of understanding of the functioning of the labor market is underlined in their assumption about the connection between productivity and wages. For the authors in this chapter, the labor market is competitive and wages are flexible. As a result of competition between firms for workers, when productivity increases, the value of workers' production will rise, and wages will go up. Yet, as we have seen in Chapter 3, while prior to 1980 wages did increase with productivity, since 1980 wages have lagged well behind productivity growth. RBC theory would have difficulty explaining this trend because of its erroneous assumptions about a perfectly competitive labor market. We have argued that the labor market is not a place of perfect competition, where equally powerful employers and employees bargain a wage contract. Rather, the labor market is characterized by the power of the firm over the worker, which waxes and wanes with the changing structure of the labor market, from the level of unemployment to regulations that help workers like favorable unionization rules. The changing relative power of workers and firms in the labor market can explain the changing relationship between wages and productivity before and after 1980, a theory that assumes perfectly competitive labor markets cannot.

Finally, the RBC policy ineffectiveness conclusion appears to be falsified by economic evidence. It is ironic that RBC theory rose to prominence in the 1980s, the precise moment that the unemployment sacrifice, something that RBC claims does not exist, was so conclusively proven. RBC theory implies that with rational expectations and price and wage flexibility, there should be no decline in output or employment when contractionary monetary policy causes interest rates to rise. In the US during the late 1970s and early 1980s, the Federal Reserve under Paul Volcker followed a restrictive monetary policy that forced nominal interest rates up above 15 percent. A severe recession followed. Unemployment rose from 6 to 10 percent between 1979 and 1983. Inflation was also reduced, falling from 11 to 3 percent during the same period. The debate between non-RBC economists was not so much whether the high interest rates contributed to the recession as whether the benefits in terms of reduced inflation were worth the costs of higher unemployment.

The difference between Friedman's adaptive expectations monetarism from Chapter 3 and RBC theory can be highlighted in this context. Friedman argued that the inflationary tolerance of the Fed prior to 1979 meant that people did not believe that it was going to seriously combat inflation. As a result of people's continued expectation of inflation, the Fed had to raise interest rates sufficiently high to convince people that its anti-inflationary policy was credible, which created a greater recession than would have been necessary had the Fed's contractionary policy been believed (Friedman, 1984). However, the benefit of establishing the credibility of the Fed's low inflation target is that people would now expect inflation to be lower in the future. As William Poole more explicitly stated, "a recession may be necessary to provide the evidence that the central bank is serious" (Poole, 1988, p. 98). Even those in favor of the high interest-rate effort to control inflation recognized that there would be recessionary costs. RBC theorists insisted that this was not the case. For RBC theorists, the high interest-rate policy and subsequent recession must have been coincidental events, not causal ones.

Kydland and Prescott's RBC theory, however, creates the misleading impression that high interest rates are not associated with higher unemployment or reduced output. Nor will lower interest rates increase output and reduce employment. As Mankiw noted:

... to the extent that it trivializes the social cost of observed fluctuations, real business cycle theory is potentially dangerous. The danger is that those who advise policy-makers might attempt to use it to evaluate the effects of alternative macroeconomic policies or to conclude that macroeconomic policies are unnecessary. (Mankiw, 1989, p. 79)

Even Mankiw's telling critique does not explicitly acknowledge the distributional consequences of RBC policy. Stabilization policy aimed at promoting full employment, a policy that RBC theory views as ineffective and unnecessary, improves the bargaining position of workers in the labor market. Conversely, RBC theory dismisses anti-inflationary policy's very real negative impact on workers who find themselves unemployed or in a diminished bargaining position if they manage to hold onto their job.

In total, RBC theory is sufficiently at odds with actual economic events that it led one researcher to conclude that "anyone who believes that theories must be warranted by evidence has little reason to date to place much confidence in real business cycle models" (Hartley et al., 1997, p. 51). In a more dramatic vein, the rational expectations revolution was summarily dismissed by Robert Solow:

> Suppose someone sits down where you are sitting right now and announces to me that he is Napoleon Bonaparte. The last thing I want to do with him is to get involved in a technical discussion of cavalry tactics at the Battle of Austerlitz. If I do that, I'm getting tacitly drawn into the game that he is Napoleon Bonaparte. Now, Bob Lucas and Tom Sargent like nothing better than to get drawn into technical discussions, because then you have tacitly gone along with their fundamental assumptions; your attention is attracted away from the basic weakness of the whole story. Since I find that fundamental framework ludicrous, I respond by treating it as ludicrous—that is, by laughing at it—so as not to fall into the trap of taking it seriously and passing on to matters of technique. (Klamer, 1984, p. 146)

In some ways RBC's economic theory amounts to little more than assuming away the problematic impacts of economic downturns. Further, even an economist like Mankiw, who as we saw in Chapter 1, is fairly amenable to pro-business policy, was concerned that RBC policy recommendations are dangerously misguided.

Conclusion: RBC and Profits

The problems associated with RBC theory are, in fact, sufficiently grave that it could lead one to question why it was so influential. The answer might be that RBC was more useful than it was accurate. By useful, we mean that, given the economic conditions of the time, RBC theory justified the policies that played an important role in restoring profits.

First, it suggests that unemployment is not caused by monetary policy. Since recessions can only be caused by supply-side shocks and employees' choices about hours of work that follow, high interest-rate policy cannot cause unemployment in RBC theory. As a result, the high interest-rate policy is justified by RBC theory. In doing so, it not only disguises the attack on labor as an attack on inflation, as does Friedman, but also goes a step further in arguing that fighting inflation actually harms no one. In the context of the 1980s, this provided an intellectual justification for the turn away from using monetary policy to maintain higher levels of employment and focusing instead on fighting inflation—a policy change that, as we have seen, has been beneficial to the profitability of US firms, but has had problematic consequences for US workers.

Second, RBC downplays the negative impacts of unemployment on workers by suggesting that unemployment is a welfare-improving voluntary response to supply-side shocks and declining real wages. RBC theory suggests that policy should focus on alleviating productivity-decreasing shocks but not using either counter-cyclical policy (deficit spending and lower interest rates) or social insurance to alleviate the impacts of that unemployment. According to the RBC model it would appear, for example, that increasing payments to the unemployed would make it more likely for workers to substitute leisure for labor when real wages fall, exacerbating the duration of downturns. This is the opposite of the Keynesian implication that maintaining consumer demand in a recession can help maintain sales for business and shorten a recession. Of course, the debate around the merits of providing income to the unemployed is not only about the impact on unemployment, but also on the relative power of workers and employers in the labor market. The less government assistance is provided to those out of work, the more desperate workers become to either keep or find a job. The RBC insistence that unemployment is caused by workers freely choosing leisure very nicely dovetails with business desires to get labor costs down after the 1970s.

Third, as RBC theory moved from a more narrow technological explanation of productivity swings, to one that included government policy, the policies that RBC authors deemed harmful were revealing. Government policies that are harmful to productivity according to RBC include protective regulation, like environmental or worker safety, and corporate taxation. In this respect, RBC reinforced the claim that business was being dragged down by the cost of government, which we saw in both Friedman's work in Chapter 4 and public choice theory in Chapter 5. The obvious policy solution is to reduce these costs to create a more hospitable climate for productivity-enhancing investment by the private sector. However, this ignores any socially beneficial uses corporate taxes might be put to, and any benefits that flow from regulatory protection of workers and the environment.

It is, perhaps, no surprise that rational expectations and RBC came to prominence during the 1980s. The idea of rational expectations was first credited to a 1961 paper by Muth, but it took a decade for it to be applied by Lucas (Muth, 1961). Even Lucas's 1972 paper only really rose to prominence a decade later. Some analysts have explained this by arguing that prior to the 1970s, the Keynesian analysis was the "only game in town" (Snowdon & Vane, 2005, p. 230). But this begs the question of why an alternative was needed after this and why this particular alternative gained so much traction. According to corporate America, profits had fallen in the 1970s because American labor worked too little and was paid too much. A Business Roundtable report in the 1970s claimed that profits were being squeezed by accelerating unit labor costs as wages rose and productivity stagnated (Kotz, 2015, p. 77). The policy implications that flow from RBC theory, like abandoning the Keynesian commitment to full employment, limiting income support for the unemployed, and reducing corporate taxation, were precisely the policy changes for which business, and its organizations like the Business Roundtable, were lobbying to restore their profits after the 1970s.

7
Bursting Bubbles: Finance, Crisis and the Efficient Market Hypothesis

It is difficult to get a man to understand something, when his salary depends on his not understanding it. (Upton Sinclair, 1934, p. 109)

Introduction

The world of finance can seem a bit above the pay grade of most people. The realm of stock values and diversifying risk seems more commonly populated by Warren Buffet-style billionaires than people of more modest means. As we saw in Chapter 3, it is certainly true that the ownership of assets in the US is the privilege of a very select, fortunate few, but this does not mean that the world of finance has no bearing on the lives of those with much more limited investment portfolios. This was brought crashing home for most people by the 2007 financial crisis in the US that bankrupted several giants in the investment industry, cost many families their homes and put millions out of work when the subsequent economic collapse forced the unemployment rate up from 4 to 10 percent. Purportedly, the role of the financial sector is to channel money from those with savings to socially desirable investments. This includes a wide variety of functions, from banks taking deposits and issuing loans to the stock market distributing the ownership of firms. In an ideal world, the financial system would work to channel investments into those activities that society considered to be most desirable, and much of the debate in financial economics is the extent to which this is likely to be achieved without government oversight, and whether there are features of financial markets that make them prone to instability.

The authors featured in this chapter generally come down on the "no oversight" side of the debate. Eugene Fama started his under-graduate university career in the Romance languages, a considerable disciplinary distance from finance economics where he made his name. However, he quickly grew bored of Voltaire and turned his attention to finance and business economics, becoming yet another off the Chicago graduate school assembly line in 1964. He immediately took a job at Chicago where he remained for the rest of his career. He credits fellow Nobel-winning finance economist Merton Miller as his mentor (Fama, 2013). His work ethic has become the stuff of legend. In a 2007 interview with the Minneapolis Fed, he claimed that working every day, including holidays, is really nothing out of the ordinary (Clement, 2007). Fama's 2013 Nobel Prize, shared with fellow Chicagoan Lars Peter Hansen and Yale's Robert Shiller, was awarded for "their empirical analysis of asset prices." Awarding the Nobel simultaneously to Shiller and Fama raised a few eyebrows since, as we shall see, their theories appeared to contradict each other. While they both conducted, in the highly generic terms of the Nobel award, "empirical analysis of asset prices," Fama's work suggested that the market is efficient and that investors are rational, while Shiller's argued that investor irrationality can lead to asset bubbles.

Fama claims that his "extreme libertarian" views make him something of a political outsider. He admires both Friedrich Hayek's *Road to Serfdom* and Milton Friedman for arguing that "to the extent you let government take over economic activity you're basically giving up freedom" (Sommer, 2013). Despite his claims to being outside the normal political spectrum, Fama is an active participant in debates over economic policy. He is on the American Enterprise Institute's (AEI) Council of Economic Advisors and won its 2014 Irving Kristol Award for "exceptional intellectual and practical contributions to improve government policy, social welfare, or political understanding." Some indication of the type of contribution that wins the Kristol Award can be gleaned from past winners: Dick Cheney, Clarence Thomas, Ronald Reagan, Paul Ryan and Henry Kissinger (AEI, 2014). He has justified skyrocketing CEO compensation, arguing that, although their wages are undeniably very high, they could only be too high if the process is somehow "corrupted," a claim for which Fama says there is no evidence: "So my premise would be that you're just looking at market wages. They may be big numbers; that's not saying they're too high" (Clement, 2007). In general, he also argues that government intervention and regulation are harmful to the economy. Although Fama argues that "some regulation" is necessary in the financial system, he thinks that the fairly limited Dodd-Frank bill, which was designed to prevent a recurrence of the 2007 financial crisis, went "too far." The collapse of the housing market in 2007 was due to government policy, "not a failure of the market. The government decided that it wanted to expand home ownership. Fannie Mae and Freddie Mac were instructed to buy lower grade mortgages" (Cassidy, 2010a). For Fama, the worst lesson from the ensuing financial collapse was that government was willing to bail out companies that were "too big to fail," which created risky investment strategies by firms that knew they would not be allowed to go under (Fisher, 2012). However, in a seeming contradiction of both his libertarian leanings and Hayek's threat about encroaching socialism, Fama recommended nationalizing the banks that failed after the 2007 crisis rather than bailing them out (Sommer, 2013).

In some ways, Robert C. Merton's future career in financial economics was apparent from childhood. His father was a social scientist of considerable renown at Columbia. In fact, he coined the phrase "self-fulfilling prophesy" in which people's belief that something will happen makes it happen, for example, when people's belief that a share price will go up makes people buy that share causing its value to increase. Merton's childhood years were dedicated to baseball and cars, but even in these he showed a penchant for obsession to detail, memorizing batting averages and engine horsepower. He claims that he grew up fascinated with stocks and money. He even created his own fictitious bank, RCM Savings of Dollars and Cents Company (Merton, 1997). With an academic father and an interest in money, his career path should not be hugely surprising. Although Merton started off his university life in math and engineering, he opted to jump to economics and completed his PhD at MIT in 1970, where he subsequently took a faculty position alongside Fischer Black and Myron Scholes. In 1988, he moved to Harvard where he is currently a Professor Emeritus.

Despite dying his hair red after winning the Nobel, Merton has been described as a reserved academic (Lowenstein, 2011, p. 35). Unlike Fama, he doesn't belong to any think tanks and has made fewer public pronouncements on his economic ideology. However, he has weighed in with some carefully measured words on the role of government in the financial sector. Like Fama, although he acknowledges that there is some role for government, successful public policy involves "recognizing when government inaction is the best choice" (Merton & Bodie, 1995, p. 266). Following the financial crisis, Merton advocated a national financial oversight board, which would investigate financial failures in the same manner that the transportation safety board deals with air plane crashes: "a forensic team, highly trained, comes in and examines what happened" (Klein et al., 2013a, p. 459).

Scholes is portrayed as the more gregarious of the Merton-Scholes duo. He grew up in Ontario, Canada, the son of a dentist. Entrepreneurial from an early age, he started a string of businesses with his brother including selling satin sheets. His career path mirrored many of the others summarized in these pages. He completed his MBA and PhD at Chicago under Fama, who he described as his mentor. After graduation in 1968, he took a job teaching financial economics at MIT's Sloan School along with Merton and Black, with whom he did his most famous work. As was so often the case with its graduates, Scholes returned to Chicago in 1973. He moved again after a decade, taking a job at Stanford in 1983, where he currently enjoys the lengthy title, Frank E. Buck Professor of Finance, Emeritus.

Scholes is a little more forthcoming about his policy stances than Merton. Scholes was a Senior Research Fellow at the Hoover Institution. Like others profiled here, he signed a petition supporting Mitt Romney's "bold economic plan for America" during the 2012 presidential campaign (Hoover Institution, 2012). In a 2008 debate with Joseph Stiglitz, Scholes argued in favor of a light regulatory touch in the wake of the financial crisis. Market failures, he claimed, "do not lead to the conclusion that re-regulation will succeed in stemming future failures. Or that society will be better off with fewer freedoms." After all, he continued, those who favor regulation inevitably overlook "the vast increase in the wealth of the global economy that has resulted from the freedom to innovate" (Scholes, 2008). As we will see, Scholes's academic work facilitated the dramatic expansion of financial markets, opening him up to considerable criticism after the 2008 crash. Yet, he remains unrepentant about the growing financialization of the economy, claiming that despite the crash, "I haven't changed my ideas" (Solomon, 2009).

Merton and Scholes won the Nobel in 1997 for "a new method to determine the value of derivatives." The original work was laid out by

Scholes and Black (who died in 1995, or he would have undoubtedly shared the award), who developed a pioneering formula for valuing stock options, coined the Black-Scholes Formula. Merton expanded and generalized the formula. According to both Merton and the Nobel Committee, the work of these three facilitated more efficient risk management in society and "laid the foundation for the rapid growth of markets for derivatives in the last ten years" (The Royal Swedish Academy of Sciences, 1997). In more general terms, the decision to award the Nobel to economists who argued that prices in financial markets were accurate reflections of the real value of an asset was "a clear statement: markets work" (Henderson, 1997).

The world of financial economics is a little different than other fields in the discipline. In every field, academic work and the policy implications that stem from that work, have different costs and benefits for different groups in society. We have attempted to demonstrate in previous chapters that economic ideas that support the profitability of business became increasingly prominent after the 1970s. We have attempted to trace this influence, in part, to the ability of business to fund and promote the ideas of sympathetic scholars. In all of these cases, there is an alignment of interests. The ideas of particular academics dovetail nicely with the interests of business and are therefore promoted and disseminated. Where financial economics differs from other disciplines is that it has not, generally, been the case that academic economists routinely benefit directly from their intellectual work—at least not to the degree that exists for those actually working in finance. The relationship between financial economics and the corporate world is more intimate. Most financial economists—Fama, Merton and Scholes included—have very direct relationships with investment firms. As a result, their interest in the regulatory environment surrounding these firms is not that of an impartial academic observer, but rather someone with a vested interest. For example, an economist who receives income from a company that trades in derivatives would be financially harmed by a government decision to regulate derivatives trading. If, as is often the case, that economist were in a position to offer policy advice or to publish literature on the topic of derivatives regulation, that would commonly be thought of as a conflict of interest, and yet this is frequently what happens in the world of financial economics (Mirowski, 2013, p. 220).

The hidden financial connections of economists and their advocacy for the deregulation of the financial system were dramatically illustrated in the film, *The Inside Job*. In a more academic vein, economists Jessica Carrick-Hagenbarth and Gerald Epstein investigated the business affiliations of 19 financial economists who were involved in two groups proposing reforms to the financial system following the 2008 crisis, the Squam Lake Working Group on Financial Regulation, and the Financial Reform Task Force associated with the Pew Charitable Trusts Financial Reform Project. They found that between 2005 and 2009, 15 of the 19 economists in their sample had affiliations with private financial institutions. Further, 13 of the 15 did not disclose their affiliations in their academic or policy work. The consensus policy view of these economists was that any reform needs to be market based and involve relatively less government regulation (Carrick-Hagenbarth & Epstein, 2012, p. 59). While it is impossible to determine whether the material interests of these economists influenced their academic policy stances, the two align conveniently.

All three of the economists highlighted here have one foot in the academic world and one foot in business. Fama was on the board of Dimensional Fund Advisors (DFA), an investment firm founded by Fama protégé David Booth, who described Fama's Chicago course as a life-changing experience. As a mark of his appreciation, Booth donated $300 million to the University of Chicago and credited Fama for his success (Allen, 2013). Merton and Scholes are even more involved in the private sector. Scholes was the chairman of Platinum Grove Asset Management, on the board of the DFA, and is on the American Century Mutual Fund Board of Directors. He was also a managing director at Salomon Brothers (Scholes, 2016). Merton was a resident scientist at Dimensional Holdings, Inc., where he is the creator of Managed DC, "a global integrated retirement-funding solution system" (Merton, 2016).

Most famously, Merton and Scholes were partners in Long-Term Capital Management (LTC). Although Merton operated more in the background, the outgoing Scholes was a crucial element of the company's sales pitch. His academic credentials impressed potential clients and investors, who he bewildered with the math behind LTC's investment strategy, which he compared to "vacuuming up nickels others couldn't see" (Lowenstein, 2011, p. 34). Scholes was also valuable to LTC because of his intimate knowledge of tax rules and his ability to put his claim, that "no one actually pays taxes," into practice (Lowenstein, 2011, p. 35). When Merton and Scholes won their Nobel in 1997, things were on the up for LTC. Merton could legitimately boast that LTC had raised $1 billion from investors, had 180 employees, and had opened an office in Tokyo. One dollar invested in LTC in early 1994 would have been worth $4 in early 1998 (Lowenstein, 2011, p. i). According to Merton in 1997, LTC "characterizes the theme of the productive interaction of finance theory and finance practice" (Merton, 1997). Yet, by the end of the summer of 1998, LTC had lost everything in a remarkable five-week period after Russia declared a debt moratorium and refused to defend the value of the ruble. The refusal of any government or international actor to step in and prop up the Russian financial system, as the US had done for Mexico earlier in the decade, made investors leery of first, emerging markets, and then, of any risky investment. In one day, LTC lost 15 percent of its capital, over $500 million. Although LTC made its money gambling on firms that it felt were over- or under-valued, it was completely unprepared for a general downturn in the financial market (Lowenstein, 2011, p. 143).

Ironic may be a much-abused term, but surely the bankruptcy of an investment firm in which two of the partners won the Nobel Prize for their work in valuing assets fits the definition. In the context of this chapter, perhaps the more important lesson from LTC is that highlighted by Carrick-Hagenbarth and Epstein. These three scholars, especially Merton and Scholes, are not disinterested impartial observers of the world of finance. Rather they are practitioners with a material interest in the conditions of that market. Unlike many of the economists in this book, whose ideas accord with those that benefit business, the economists in this chapter are members of the business community.

Asset Pricing: The Theory

Merton and Scholes are most famous for their work inventing and refining the Black-Scholes formula for valuing options. An option,[1]

---

[1] To be precise, this is an example of a European option. An American option can be exercised on any date between the option sale and an end date.

as the name suggests, provides the purchaser with the right (not the obligation, which is why it is called an option) to buy (call option), or sell (put option), an asset at a certain price at a certain future date. When X buys an option from person Y, they pay Y for the right to purchase an asset at a later date. If the actual value of the asset at that later date is greater than the agreed on price, then X will take the option. If the difference between the agreed on price of the asset and the actual price is greater than the price paid by X for the option, X has gained on the transaction. The worst X can do from the transaction is the loss from the price paid to Y for the option (Shah, 1997).

The problem that Fischer, Black and Merton were able to solve was how to price the option. Prior to the Black-Scholes formula (coined by Merton – the name is extended to the Black–Merton–Scholes model by some), pricing an option was equal parts guesswork and gambling because of the uncertainty surrounding the risk premium. As a result of this uncertainty, at the time Fischer and Black were coming up with their formula, there was no institutionalized, organized market for options. Black, Merton and Scholes argued that the risk premium is already included in the price of the asset. Their equation related the price of the option to three things that can be readily measured: the amount of time until the option date, the price of the asset upon which the option is secured, and the interest that could be earned by an investment with zero risk, such as government bonds. The fourth element, which is not as obviously observable, is the volatility of the asset, but this is assumed to be constant for the lifetime of the option. The price of the option then depends on these variables. For example, if the price of the asset increases, then the price of the option, should also increase since there is a greater likelihood that the asset price will be greater than the agreed-on sale price when the agreement comes due.

One of the important discoveries of Black, Merton and Scholes is that hedging—making an offsetting investment—can be used to eliminate risk, using a mix of the option and the underlying asset. They then asserted that this riskless mix of investments should earn the same return as a riskless interest rate-bearing investment like a bond. The logic behind this is that if the return were any different between two equally risk-free assets, people would flee the lower return asset and flock to the one that earned a higher return equalizing the returns between the two (Schaefer, 1998). The Black Scholes formula is a partial differential equation that determines the rate of change of the option price in terms of the rates at which the other variables, like the price of the asset, are changing (Black & Scholes, 1972, 1973; Merton, 1973; for a popular account of the equation see Jarrow, 1999; Stewart, 2012a).

A fancy partial derivative may not sound like a particularly ground-breaking discovery. However, it opened up not only the market for options but a wide variety of other financial instruments, including derivatives. The techniques invented by Black, Merton and Scholes revolutionized not just academic economics or even economic policy, but provided a valuable tool for the practitioners of finance used by "literally thousands of individuals" (Schaefer, 1998, p. 425). When Scholes and Black wrote their article in the early 1970s, it was possible to speak of options as being a small market. By 2007, $1 quadrillion per year worth of derivatives were traded internationally, ten times the real value of all products manufactured in the world over the last century (Stewart, 2012b).

Fama was known more as an empiricist than a theorist. He is best known for his support for the Efficient Market Hypothesis (EMH). The claim that markets are "efficient" demands some definition of what is meant by efficiency. What Fama means by "efficient" might be thought of as "accurate" in the sense that he argues that efficiency means a fairly narrow definition of: "a market in which prices always 'fully reflect' available information" (Fama, 1970, p. 383). He claims that because of competition between rational investors, the value of assets, like stocks, incorporates all relevant information. This claim was formulated very early in Fama's career, appearing in his doctoral dissertation (Fama, 1965; Clement, 2007). Part of the problem in testing this idea is defining what "information" means. In his 1970 paper, Fama defines three types: information on historical prices (weak form), all publicly available information, such as annual corporate earnings announcements (semi-strong form), and investors having "monopolistic" information, by which he means that some have a special advantage over others in obtaining or processing data (strong form). He finds that "evidence in support of the efficient markets model is extensive and (somewhat uniquely in economics) contradictory evidence is sparse" (Fama, 1970, p. 416). Fama's definition is different than allocative efficiency, which would mean that the prices of assets would channel money into the most socially desirable investments, a fact that some of Fama's critics seem to miss (Mirowski, 2013, p. 266). Having said this, Fama does claim in his 1970 article, "Efficient Capital Markets: A Review of Theory and Empirical Work," that "the ideal is a market in which prices provide accurate signals for resource allocation," which would seem to imply something much broader and more normatively desirable than Fama's information definition, involving the capital market's ability to channel investment into those areas that society would find most valuable (Fama, 1970, p. 383).

Fama continued this work in various forms throughout his career. Fama's work with Dartmouth economist Ken French found that asset prices are "highly related to business conditions," and that "the variation in expected returns is rational" (Clement, 2007). He has also surveyed the existing work on "event studies," which are essentially tests of how asset prices respond to new information (events), such as mergers or unexpected earnings announcements. Fama argues that there is no systemic bias to how investors react to these kinds of events. Apparent under-reaction to events occurs as often as over-reaction and continuation of abnormal returns after the release of the information is as frequent as reversals of above-normal returns (Fama, 1998; Malkiel, 2003). The implication is not that prices are efficient in the sense that they are always correct. Because asset prices are based on future earnings, it would require perfect foresight for them to be completely accurate and no one has a magic crystal ball. Rather, it means that new information is quickly incorporated into asset prices and that investors do not make any predictable, systematic errors in using that information.

While it might not seem particularly ground-breaking to discover that stock prices are "related to business conditions," Fama's EMH has two important implications. The first is less controversial from a policy standpoint, but does suggest an investing strategy. If new information is quickly adopted by rational investors into the price of the asset, then future prices are essentially random because they will only reflect unpredictable upcoming events. Because there are no predictable future patterns to asset prices, it is impossible to "beat the street," even for the professional investor. According to Fama, "only the top 3%" of portfolios that are actively managed by professionals earn returns high enough to cover their additional costs (Harrison, 2012). The implication of this for investing strategies is that paying for managed funds in which analysts use supposedly innovative strategies to pick winners is a waste of money. Fama's research implies that a much more cost-effective strategy is to invest in an index of stocks, which contributed to the spread of low-cost passive investing through index funds (Campbell, 2014; Malkiel, 2003).

The second implication of the EMH is more controversial from a policy standpoint. If markets are efficient and prices accurately reflect available information, this would seem to dismiss the possibility of investor behavior that leads to systematically incorrect pricing of assets. This is important because it suggests that there should be no such thing as an asset bubble caused by investor over-confidence or exuberance. In a *New York Times* interview, Fama declared, "I don't even know what a bubble means ... These words have become popular. I don't think they have any meaning" (Appelbaum, 2013). Fama's claim that asset bubbles cannot exist seems to run up against some prominent recent examples. On Black Monday in 1987, the Dow Jones Industrial Average fell 22.6 percent in a single day, which seems to suggest either over-exuberance leading up to that date, or panic on the day itself. In the early 2000s, the decline in value of Internet-related business caused a rapid decline in the stock market. More recently, in 2007, the mortgage market in the US collapsed, taking the market for mortgage-based derivatives with it. Fama argues that these declines were not due to the collapse of inflated prices caused by overly optimistic investors, but, rather, were a rational adjustment to asset prices based on changing economic circumstances (Lowenstein, 2011, p. 74). For example, one theory about the collapse of the mortgage derivative market is that the derivatives made up of bundled mortgages were so complex that investors didn't know what they were buying and were easily misled by the artificially high credit rating on these assets assigned by rating agencies like Moody's, which suggests a certain degree of "inefficiency." Fama argued that this is a misreading of the information, saying that "I'm very skeptical of these stories" (Clement, 2007). According to Fama, it was not financial collapse that sparked off economic crisis but the other way around: "I think you can't reject the hypothesis that it was an economic disaster that caused the financial disaster" (Harrison, 2012). The logic behind this is that the financial collapse was a rational response by investors to a rapidly deteriorating economy that would produce lower profits in the near future.

The idea that asset markets are always rational and efficient is not merely an academic assertion. It has important policy implications. If asset bubbles and their subsequent collapse are not a realistic possibility, then governmental oversight of the financial system is not necessary. The financial industry was steadily deregulated after the 1980s. Much of intellectual justification for this move was provided by the belief that asset prices were accurate and that the financial instruments that were being developed, like options and derivatives, made the economy less risky, making damaging asset bubbles nigh on impossible.

Taken together, the three Nobel winners in this section laid the ground work for the dramatic expansion and deregulation of the financial sector. Merton and Scholes's work opened up new kinds of financial instruments such as options and derivatives. Fama's EMH suggested that the market for these new assets was as accurate a reflection as possible of their underlying value, negating the need for government oversight.

Asset Pricing: Criticisms

By now, readers should recognize a recurring theme in this book. Many of the theories being analyzed assume that humans want, and have the ability, to act as rational maximizers. As Real Business Cycle (RBC) theorists assumed that people would take new information on the macro economy, like a change in interest rates, into their decisions about the future, so too the financial economists in this chapter assume that investors can make rational use of public information in valuing assets. Merton viewed investors as little more than calculators, going so far as to always put the term "speculative" in quotes so as to dismiss it as a possible motive (Lowenstein, 2011, p. 74). Much of the criticism of their work, including that of Nobel co-winner Shiller, is based on the extent to which people behave in this manner. If the Nobel Committee were attempting to make the economics profession look slightly foolish, they couldn't have named a better combination of academics in 2013. Shiller's theory of finance is almost impossible to reconcile with Fama's. It was as though the best explorer of the year were given jointly to someone who proved the earth is round and someone else who claimed to have fallen off its edge. This controversy was not lost on Shiller, who described the EMH as "the most remarkable error in the history of economic theory" (Lowenstein, 2011, p. 74). In a slightly more measured tone, he also stated that the EMH

> ... makes little sense, except in fairly trivial ways. If the theory said nothing more than that it is unlikely that the average amateur investor can get rich quickly by trading in the markets based on publicly available information, the theory would be spot on ... But the theory is commonly thought, at least by enthusiasts, to imply much more. Notably, it has been argued that regular movements in the markets reflect a wisdom that transcends the best under-standing of even the top professionals, and that it is hopeless for an ordinary mortal, even with a lifetime of work and preparation, to question pricing. (Shiller, 2013)

For Shiller, investors are not the rational automatons of EMH. Rather, they are subject to psychological influences that result in them being overly optimistic or unduly pessimistic, depending on which way the prevailing winds are blowing. This can create a "bandwagon" effect, where confident investors flock to assets in the belief that values are on the up, or vice versa, creating more volatility in asset prices than would be the case than if investors were, strictly speaking, rational (Shiller, 2015). Shiller supports this with empirical evidence showing price volatility in the stock market is 5–13 times too high to be attributed to only new information about future real dividends (Shiller, 1981). According to Shiller, "I emphasize the enormous role played in markets by human error, as documented in a now-established literature called behavioral finance" (Shiller, 2013; see also Bernard & Thomas, 1990; DeBondt & Thaler, 1985; Kahneman & Rupe, 1998).

The idea that investors are prone to flights of fancy is not merely a matter of whether a few investors end up on the losing end of a gamble. If stock values are not correct, then the production and investment decisions based on those prices will also be incorrect. For example, in the early 2000s, this fancy new thing called the Internet was really taking off. Any company that could stick a "dot.com" after its name saw its value skyrocket. At the time, the optimistically high valuations of such unlikely successes as "pets.com" were justified by the dot.com world as a new way of doing business that was poorly understood by the old analytics. As the price of these stocks increased, the Internet and technology sectors benefitted from a rush of new investment. Although hindsight is always perfect, it is now apparent that investment money was being channeled into areas that were unlikely to succeed. The EMH implies that because asset prices are as well-valued as possible, investment will be channeled into profitable avenues. Or, at least, avenues that people's best rational judgment deems to be profitable. If Shiller is correct, investment money is often likely to be wasted on fads and trends. The debate between the supporters of the rationalist EMH and the behavioralist Shiller camp remains completely unresolved, despite an Everest-like mountain of research on the subject using increasingly advanced statistical techniques. Part of the reason for the ongoing uncertainty is that testing the EMH involves actually knowing what the "correct" prices of asset would be and what is causing their fluctuations, so any test of the EMH is simultaneously a test of other hypotheses, such as how to price an asset (Lo & MacKinlay, 2002). As a result of the difficulty of testing the EMH, additional research seems not to have brought any resolution of the debate. Rather, it has merely hardened the positions of both sides (although the debate around the EMH hardly stands alone in the economic landscape in this regard) (Mirowski, 2013, p. 265). Perhaps part of the reason for the dogmatism of each group is that they both understand the enormous implications of the contrasting theories. The gravity of the irrationality critique was not lost on Merton, who acknowledged, in his rebuttal of Shiller's empirical studies, that if Shiller is correct "then serious doubt is cast on the validity of this cornerstone of modern financial economic theory" (Marsh & Merton, 1986, p. 484).

If investors are, at times, irrational, it does not only lead to misplaced investment. In stark contrast to Fama's assertion that the financial system cannot create asset bubbles and the Merton-Scholes claim that options can reduce risk, heterodox economist Hyman Minsky of Washington University in St. Louis argued that the inherently unstable financial system can destabilize the broader economy. Like Shiller, Minsky believed that people have a bandwagon mentality. When the economy is booming, the growing confidence of both borrowers and lenders leads to increasingly speculative loans on the expectation of growing asset prices. At the beginning of a cycle, lenders will only provide credit in instances when both the interest and principle can be repaid. Minsky termed this "hedge finance." As the boom continues and investors gain confidence in the second phase, "speculative finance" emerges, when loans are extended to those whose revenues will only cover interest. Finally, during the over-confident height of the boom, the "Ponzi finance" phase is reached, when revenues do not even cover the interest, and repayment is dependent on capital gains of increasing asset values. This bubble will then collapse when asset values decline, creating a short-term boom-and-bust cycle. In addition to these short-term fluctuations, there is a longer-term, overarching cycle in which the institutions that regulate and protect society from the inherently risky financial sector are eroded by the demands of the financial industry for a more laissez-faire approach (more on this in the next chapter). As a result of a policy environment that permits progressively more risk over this overarching cycle, the financial sector can be thrown into full-blown crisis (Minsky, 1977, 1982; Minsky & Vaughan, 1990; Minsky, 1993).

The very idea that bubbles and speculation are not a recurring theme in the world of finance is belied by its history of manias, panics and crises. As early as 1636, the price of tulips in the Netherlands skyrocketed and then crashed amid stories of investors selling their houses in order to buy into the booming bulb business. While it is true that bubbles and their nasty, inevitable burst have a long history, they have increased in the deregulated and increasingly financialized world after 1980. In their history of financial crises, economic historians Charles Kindleberger and Robert Aliber note that the years since the late 1970s have been unprecedented in terms of the "frequency and severity" of financial shocks (Kindleberger & Aliber, 2005; see also Bilginsoy, 2015). Part of the reason for this must surely be the rapidly expanding range of financial instruments for the purposes of speculation. Prior to 1970, if an investor wanted to gamble on the future US mortgage values, there was no real market or financial instrument with which to do it. With the Black-Merton-Scholes formula and the expansion of asset trading that followed, speculation and the volatility that accompanied it increased dramatically (Lowenstein, 2011, p. 241). An International Monetary Fund (IMF) report counted a total of 147 banking crises worldwide between 1970 and 2011. The decade of the 1970s was comparatively peaceful, with no crises in the first part of the decade and only four in the second half. After 1980, the story is very different. Not a year went by between 1980 and 1998 without at least one banking crisis somewhere in the world, with 1995 marking a particularly turbulent year featuring 13 crises, mostly centered on the nations of Latin America. The early years of 2000s were calm relative to the turbulent 1990s but, of course, this came crashing to an end with the 2007 wave of crises that engulfed over twenty countries (Laeven & Valencia , 2012, p. 10; for an early World Bank report along the same lines, see Caprio , 2003). As a reminder of just how damaging the 2007 crash was to financial markets, the Dow Jones Industrial Average fell by 40 percent, from 14,000 to 8,000, between November 2007 and November 2008. Authors, like Fama, who question the existence of bubbles and argue that rational investors price assets as accurately as possible, are faced with the uphill task of explaining away the very existence of crises stemming from asset bubbles, let alone the coincidence that crises of unprecedented "frequency and severity" have accompanied an increasingly large, deregulated financial system.

A closer examination of the financial crisis reveals that the increased use of exotic financial instruments and deregulation were contributing factors. Although the Black-Merton-Scholes formula was purported to permit the calculation of the value of an asset, it actually provided a sense of false confidence in many of the outrageously complicated instruments that were being developed, such as mortgage-backed securities. In fact, no firm, let alone an individual investor, had the time or ability to accurately calculate the risk associated with them. As a result, buyers relied on ratings agencies, like Moody's, to provide a credit score to indicate the riskiness of the asset. There were two problems with this. First, it appears as though the credit agencies did not fully understand many of these complex assets. Second, there was little incentive for them to dig very deeply to find problems with the assets and, if they did, giving an investment a low credit rating was against the interests of rating agencies. The problem was that the profits of rating agencies were dependent on maintaining the business of the investment banks who sold these derivatives. If one credit agency gave an asset a low rating, the investment bank selling the asset would simply take its business to another agency to get a higher rating. Reassured by a naively secure impression of the risk of these assets, over-confident investors were snapping up mortgage-backed derivatives at prices that did not reflect their underlying value. House prices in the US fell by 7.2 percent in the year after the third quarter of 2007, the largest decline in the 39 years the Federal Home Loan Mortgage Corporation (Freddie Mac) has been keeping statistics. When housing prices began to collapse in 2007, the value of these securities plummeted, sparking the global financial crisis (Crotty, 2009). In his assessment of the extent to which the Black-Merton-Scholes formula was to blame for the crash, mathematician Ian Stewart gives a slightly equivocal "Yes and no. Black-Scholes may have contributed to the crash, but only because it was abused. In any case, the equation was just one ingredient in a rich stew of financial irresponsibility, political ineptitude, perverse incentives and lax regulation" (Stewart, 2012b).

This brings us to the deregulatory causes of the crash. As economist James Crotty has pointed out, the policy implications of Minsky's theory are dramatically different than those of Fama. While Minsky's theory insists on the importance of maintaining protective regulation to minimize the risky activity of the financial system, Fama's ideas imply that they are unnecessary. If Minsky's ideas were taken more seriously, it is extremely unlikely that the deregulation of the financial sector would have been so wide-ranging, the assets so complex, and the investments so risky as was the case in the run-up to the 2007 collapse. According to Shiller, Fama's EMH was harmful because it provided the intellectual justification for "authorities in the United States and elsewhere to be complacent about asset mispricing, about growing leverage in financial markets and about the instability of the global system" (Shiller, 2013). With the increasing complexity of exotic financial instruments like options and derivatives, the financial world was becoming more, not less, risky and unstable. Yet the EMH was a falsely comforting theory that dismissed the possibility of asset bubbles and, therefore, the need to regulate against their possibility. The fact that asset bubbles have a long history and have increasingly plagued the world economy were explained away by Fama's EMH as rational market adjustments to new information, rather than a financial world subject to swings of exuberance and panic.

Increasing financialization of the economy not only raises the specter of instability and crisis, it may also create longer-term problems for economic growth. While most economists agree that finance plays a crucial role in the economy by channeling savings into socially useful investment, the extent to which specific financial institutions actually play this role, and the appropriate size of the financial sector, is subject to much more debate, with some questioning the desirability of the recent expansion and direction of finance. There is no question that the profitability of finance has increased since 1980. Financial sector profits as a percent of GDP increased from around 1 percent in the early 1980s to 3 percent in 2004 (Crotty, 2008, p. 169). Between 1966 and 1984, financial sector profits hovered around 15–20 percent of total corporate profits in the US, but on the eve of the financial crisis in 2006 they accounted for over 40 percent of the total (Khatiwada, 2010, p. 2). Since 1980, employment in the US finance sector has increased from around five million to more than seven-and-a-half million (Cassidy, 2010b). In 1980, the financial sector contributed 4.9 percent of GDP. By 2006, that number had increased to 8.3 percent (Greenwood & Scharfstein, 2013, p. 3). Even firms traditionally outside of the financial sector were switching into the world of finance. In 1980, financial assets made up about 15 percent of total assets in the non-financial sector. By the early 2000s, that percentage had almost doubled, to 29 percent (Tomaskovic-Devey et al., 2015).

Some of the major financial institutions also do less of what would be considered traditional investment in favor of more exotic financial activities of the kind that exploded with the creation of the Black-Merton-Scholes formula. This trend continued even after the 2007 financial collapse, in which investment giants Morgan Stanley and Goldman Sachs would have failed without government bailouts. Just to provide a quick snapshot for a few large financial firms, the traditional investment business of raising money for companies contributed less than 15 percent of revenue for Morgan Stanley in the first nine months of 2010. Between July and September of 2010, 63 percent of Goldman Sachs's revenue came from simply trading assets such as derivatives, while corporate finance added a much more modest 13 percent. In Citi's investment-banking section about 80 percent of revenues came from buying and selling securities, compared to 14 percent from raising capital for companies (Cassidy, 2010b). The financial sectors that expanded most rapidly since 1980 were asset management and "credit intermediation," especially the rise of new forms of mortgage lending (Greenwood & Scharfstein, 2013), not the more traditional capital-raising activities of finance.

The concern is that high profits in the finance industry, particularly that which is speculative rather than real investment, channel money and people away from "real" parts of the economy that actually produce goods and services and into finance, which does not actually produce anything. This was succinctly expressed by Christina Romer, the chair of President Obama's Council of Economic Advisers, in 2009, when she claimed that the US economy was suffering under the weight of a bloated financial sector that attracted investment that could have gone into "real" sectors of the economy, and talent that could otherwise have become doctors and engineers. A smaller financial sector, she argued, would actually allow the US to "make things" (quoted in Henwood, 2010, p. 2; see also Baragar & Chernomas, 2012). The chair of Britain's Financial Services Authority, Lord Adair Turner, was blunter, arguing that while finance has an important role in society, much of what is done in the financial centers of New York and London is "socially useless activity." Rather than helping with production, many financial instruments "extract rents from the real economy" (cited in Cassidy, 2010b). There appears to be some empirical support for these claims. An IMF study examining the effects of "financial development" on economies (using an index of the size of the financial sector, access and cost as a measure) found that a growing financial sector can actually have a negative impact on economic growth if the nation is already at a high level of financial development, as is the case in the US. The authors argue that this is because high levels of financial development can impair "allocation of financial resources toward productive activities" and create misallocation of "human capital across sectors" (Sahay et al., 2015, pp. 15–16; for more support for the negative connection between financialization and economic growth, see Stockhammer, 2004; Krippner, 2005; Palley, 2007; Freeman, 2010; Khatiwada, 2010; Arcand et al., 2012, and Tomaskovic-Devey et al., 2015).

Conclusion: Finance and Profits

Crotty describes the EMH as a "fairy-tale theory," based on "crudely unrealistic" assumptions, yet, although it was controversial, it became widely accepted in both academic and policy circles. At least part of the answer to its popularity must turn on its benefits to the financial community (how this happened in policy circles will be covered in the next chapter) (Crotty, 2013; see also Roubini & Mihm, 2010).

The problems caused by selling complicated mortgage-backed derivatives in an increasingly deregulated environment may have contributed to the indebtedness of US households, but it increased the profitability of US firms. We have previously discussed the role of subprime mortgages in increasing the debt of US families and increasing the profitability of lenders. Of course, the problem with subprime loans is that the lender is extending loans to borrowers increasingly unlikely to be able to repay. This leads to the question of why banks would find these risky loans so attractive. Part of the answer is undoubtedly that they, along with most other observers, were overly optimistic about the US housing market. In addition, the innovation of mortgage-backed securities allowed them to access funds well beyond their own deposits. However, a crucial part of this story is the role of the incentive structure of mortgage-backed derivatives, which grew from $19 billion in 1995 to $508 billion in 2005 (Getter et al., 2007, p. 3), as opposed to the more traditional relationship between bank and household. Mortgage-backed derivatives severed the traditional risk of default that in the past had made banks cautious lenders. Traditionally, banks made money on loans by having the principal repaid along with a bit of interest. This made banks fairly conservative lenders, since they would not get repaid in full if the borrower defaulted. When banks (or any other lending institution, but we'll use banks as a shorthand) sell a bundled package of mortgages as a financial instrument, they earn income on the sale of the mortgage bundle, not on the repayment of the mortgage. The risk of repayment is transferred from the bank to the buyer of the mortgage-backed security, reducing the incentive for banks to loan only to households who are likely to repay. In fact, the incentive for the bank is to sign as many families up for mortgages as possible, since that creates more derivatives for it to sell. While it might seem that if banks were a little looser with their purse strings, this would have the beneficial effect of providing families with lower incomes access to the American dream of home ownership, the reality was that by preying on people's hopes, banks increased the number of families making larger debt payments. Family incomes were not only stretched as a result of stagnating incomes due to changes in the labor market discussed earlier, but also because that limited income now had to stretch to cover the additional costs of interest and principle on loans. It would be a gross overstatement to lay the blame for the collapsed housing market at the feet of the Black-Merton-Scholes formula. Every stage in the mortgage and finance industry created an incentive for borrowers to overextend. Real estate agents on a commission have an incentive to sell a more expensive house. Lenders have an incentive to maximize their interest income by approving high mortgage limits and higher interest rates. Yet it is also certainly true that providing the foundation for the market in derivatives created a new and risky form of lending in which the incentive for banks was to have a large quantity of loans but the quality of those loans was of secondary importance at best. The result of all the links in this chain is that lending institutions extended larger loans to more families, increasing the interest payments from families and increasing the profits of firms in the financial sector.

The Black-Merton-Scholes formula also contributed to profits in the financial industry, because their formula for option pricing opened up a largely undiscovered market in new financial instruments. As the expansion of both the finance industry as a share of the whole economy and the rise of specific financial instruments, like mortgage-backed securities demonstrates, firms rushed in to take advantage of these new opportunities. As financial firms created, bought and sold these increasingly complicated but highly lucrative instruments, their profits were protected from the unwanted constraints of regulatory oversight by Fama's EMH, which suggested that asset prices were generally priced accurately, removing the possibility of bubbles and their problematic popping. As we shall see in the next chapter, a number of concerns were raised about the deregulated financial market and regulations were proposed to rein it in. For example, limits on how much financial firms could borrow were proposed, as were restrictions on banks' ability to function as investment houses. Each of these pieces of legislation would have constrained firms and lowered their profits. The intellectual justification for rejecting these regulatory moves was that the financial market was efficient.

The finance sector has enjoyed unprecedented profits over the last three decades or so. Yet these profits contributed to increasing indebtedness of homeowners, economic instability and perhaps even reduced economic growth. Fama, Merton and Scholes were not directly responsible for the economic collapse or growing debt of the average American. Yet, as economist and former Greek Finance Minister Yanis Varoufakis remarked:

> I don't blame my fellow economists for pulling the trigger that created so much devastation in 2008 and before that and after that, but I blame them for providing the economic, the mathematical models, the sermons which steadied the hand of the financiers and allowed them to believe that what they were doing was perfectly okay, consistent with science, provable mathematically that it was riskless, and therefore allowed them the mental and emotional strength to do a lot more damage than they would have done otherwise. (Varoufakis, 2016)

8
Economists Go to Washington: Ideas in Action

Introduction

In the 1939 movie *Mr. Smith Goes to Washington*, James Stewart plays a naïve but wholesome leader of the "Boy Rangers," who is somewhat randomly plucked from the comfort of his small-town Midwestern life and thrust into the world of high politics when he is chosen to replace a recently deceased senator. The new senator falls afoul of the Machiavellian dirty dealing inside the Washington Beltway and is on the brink of being falsely charged for another's corruption, when he saves himself with a filibuster so honest and impassioned that he sways the actual guilty party into confessing. It's a movie that highlights the dishonesty and corruption of the political world while reaffirming the potential of US democracy when morally upstanding individuals take charge. This romantic version of politics, which places the faults in the system squarely on the shoulders of bad individuals, is considerably different than the interpretation offered in this book. In Chapters 2 and 3, we emphasized an interpretation of policy based on the powerful actors who can influence political results in their favor. These actors were not corrupt politicians or greedy bureaucrats but the business community, who were doing nothing more than acting in the political system in the same manner that they act in the rest of their operations—to maximize their profits. Most of the rest of the book has aimed to demonstrate that economists provided what might be called the ideological justification for the transformation of economic policy that has so favored the business community. In most of these examples, the economists played an arms'-length role. With the exception of the financial economists in the previous chapter, they did not have a direct material interest in the policies that they were advocating and they did not have their hands directly on the levers of power. They were not corrupted in the Mr. Smith manner. Rather, the theories that they developed had distributional consequences that favored business, which promoted these ideas to the public and within the halls of political power. In this chapter, we will examine two economists who were known not for their intellectual achievements in the economics profession, but who did have their hands on the levers of power. These individuals enacted the kind of pro-business policies that the other economists in this book advocated. There will be no Nobel Prize winners here. Rather a look at two economists in particularly high-ranking bureaucratic positions will illustrate the specific types of policies that led to the transformation of the US economy after 1980. Unfortunately, the story of Alan Greenspan and Lawrence Summers doesn't have the same kind of feel-good ending as the tale of Mr. Smith.

For about twenty years, Alan Greenspan had a realistic claim to be the most famous, powerful economist alive. His position of influence did not come from clever economic theory, but from his long-standing position as chair of the Fed, the US central bank. It was a classic rise from humble beginnings to riches and power for a boy who was raised in his grandparents' tiny apartment in New York, where his mother moved after splitting with Greenspan's father. The most commonly bandied-about "revelation" about the young Greenspan by his various biographers was that he attended the Julliard School of Music, which he left to tour in a dance band. This is a pleasantly colorful bit of history for a man whose dour speaking style could only generously be described as deadly dull.

Greenspan traded music for economics. However, he was less academically driven than others whom we have discussed here, finishing his PhD in between his pursuits outside the ivory tower. While earning his bachelor's and master's degrees from New York University, Greenspan worked on Wall Street for one of the largest private banks in the United States, Brown Brothers Harriman, until opening his own consulting firm, Townsend-Greenspan & Co, where he worked from 1955 to 1987 (Biography, n.d.). An old music friend, Leonard Garment, started Greenspan's life in the public sector when he convinced Greenspan to help out on the 1968 presidential campaign of Richard Nixon, who was Garment's law partner (Martin, 2000).

He briefly interrupted his private-sector career to serve on President Gerald Ford's Council of Economic Advisers from 1974 to 1977. His 1977 PhD from New York University was not based on a traditional dissertation but rather on a collection of other writings, including the annual report of the president, which Greenspan prepared for Ford in his role on the Council of Economic Advisers. In fact, Greenspan never completed his planned dissertation. When Ronald Reagan was voted in, Greenspan served on his Economic Policy Advisory Board from 1981 to 1983. Of course, his biggest government role was chair of the Fed, where he became the most important setter of monetary policy and financial market regulator in the world (Crotty, 2009, p. 9).

Like the economists highlighted in Chapter 7 on finance, Greenspan was intimately connected to the private sector. He not only ran his own consulting firm but also served as a director for some of the biggest corporate names in America, including ALCOA, JP Morgan, General Foods and Mobil. According to former financial regulator Bill Black, Greenspan worked as a "de-facto" lobbyist for Charles Keating, whose Lincoln Savings and Loan fraud was a critical part of the Savings and Loan (S&L) collapse in the late 1980s. Greenspan enlisted the "Keating Five" senators who pressured regulators to forgo enforcement action against Keating's S&L. Greenspan, himself, also sent a memo encouraging regulators to be more lenient, arguing that Lincoln "posed no foreseeable risk of loss" (Black, 2013; see also Fingleton, 2013). For his casual and very misleading look at the Lincoln books, Greenspan reportedly received $30,000–40,000 (Madrick, 2011, p. 224).

Greenspan describes himself as a "lifelong libertarian Republican" (Ip & Steel, 2007); he has been described by others as an Ayn Rand acolyte. Rand is famous for her books, *Atlas Shrugged* and *The Fountainhead*, in which she espouses the ethics of self-interest through the fiction of heroic capitalists struggling against the drag of intrusive governments. Greenspan co-edited a book, *Capitalism: the Unknown Ideal*, with Rand and contributed an essay, "The Assault on Integrity," to the volume, in which he argued that "the 'greed' of the businessman or, more appropriately, his profit-seeking ... is the unexcelled protector of the consumer." He claimed that this was true for banks as well as other firms since they needed to be able to maintain the trust of the customers to survive. Overall, he described free market, unregulated capitalism as a "superlatively moral system" (Greenspan, 1967). Greenspan's own interpretation of his relationship with Rand is that it was a youthful fling that waned as he matured, but his policy pronouncements throughout his career remained consistent with the broad thrust of Rand's philosophy (Greenspan, 2008; Monbiot, 2012; Weiss, 2012). One example of Greenspan's ideology comes from Bob Woodward's fawning biography, called *Maestro* (2000). In 1994, Democratic President Bill Clinton appointed Alan Blinder as vice chair of the Fed under Greenspan. The outgoing vice chair, David Mullins, whom Greenspan had asked to check into Blinder's bona fides, reported back, "it's not like he's a Communist or anything. It's just in his early publications he's noticeably soft on inflation." Greenspan responded, "I would have preferred he were a Communist." After less than two years as vice chair, Blinder resigned, frustrated by the cold relationship between the two, in which Blinder's desire to allow a little more inflationary wiggle room in an effort to bring down unemployment was repeatedly foiled by Greenspan (Woodward, 2000; see also Tuccille, 2002). Later in his tenure as the Fed chair, Greenspan endorsed Bush's tax cuts, a foray into the political realm that had previously been taboo for supposedly impartial Fed chairs. His support of the cuts, despite the fact that the benefits went almost entirely to the richest income group and that they would increase the deficit, was based on his fear that a government surplus might be used to purchase private-sector stocks and bonds, a public intervention in the private sphere that he found unpalatable (Madrick, 2011, p. 243).

Lawrence Summers is more of an academic intellectual and had less policy clout than Greenspan, although admittedly that sets the academic bar low and the clout bar high. Unlike Greenspan, Summers was born to the academic world. His parents, Robert and Anita Summers, were both academic economists, first at Yale and then at the University of Pennsylvania. His uncles, Paul Samuelson and Ken Arrow, are two of most famous post-war economists. Summers is generally held to be remarkably intelligent. At age 10, he appeared on a local sports-radio quiz show and answered everything so quickly that the show ran out of questions (Bradley, 2005).

After earning his doctorate at Harvard in 1982, Summers flitted between the academic life and the public sector. After a very brief stint teaching at MIT, Summers went to work with the Reagan presidency's

Council of Economic Advisers, but that lasted only until 1983 when he returned to Harvard and stayed there until 1991. In 1988, he signed on as an economic adviser with the presidential campaign of Massachusetts Governor Michael Dukakis, where he met future bosses Bill Clinton and Robert Rubin (Bradley, 2005). It was after his departure from Harvard that Summer's star really rose as a public figure. In 1991, he went to work as the chief economist at the World Bank. In 1993, he joined the US Treasury, where he rose from undersecretary to deputy to secretary of the Treasury under Clinton. It is this portion of Summer's career that will be the primary focus of this chapter. After leaving government, Summers returned to academia, but not to the drudgery of lectures and seminars with the professoriate. Instead, he became Harvard's president until he was forced out in 2006. In 2008, he rejoined the federal government as Obama's assistant to the president for economic policy and director of the National Economic Council until 2010, where he was tasked with organizing the federal response to the economic crisis. In 2011, he returned to Harvard as the Charles W. Eliot University Professor.

One of the common criticisms of Summers is that he projects an abrasive combination of superiority and crassness. Two high-profile instances are often cited to illustrate Summers' tendency to court controversy. First, as chief economist at the World Bank he released a memo (written by Lant Pritchett, but signed by Summers) arguing that because wages were lower in the developing world than in richer countries, lives shortened by pollution were less costly. The inevitable conclusion, the memo claimed, was that "just between you and me, shouldn't the World Bank be encouraging more migration of the dirty industries to the LDCs?" After all, lives shortened by pollution in poor nations did not represent a great loss compared to the economic benefits of more industry (Bradley, 2005). Needless to say, when this memo was leaked, it was not greeted with enthusiastic support. Summers' defense was that it was sarcastic, designed to be controversial in order to start a conversation on the limits of using narrow cost-benefit analysis. However, there is nothing in the memo that suggests this context (for a critique of the logic behind this memo, see Hausman & McPherson, 1996, pp. 9–16).

His diplomatic skills again failed him as president of Harvard. At a 2005 lecture at a conference on "Diversifying the Science and

Engineering Workforce: Women, Underrepresented Minorities, and their S. & E. Careers," in which Summers was asked to be provocative, he certainly complied (Goldenberg, 2005). He started out by pointing out that women are not the only group to be underrepresented in desirable professions. For example, "white men are very substantially underrepresented in the National Basketball Association." He then went on to dismiss discrimination as a likely culprit for the lack of women in science and math, using an economic framework developed by Chapter 5's Gary Becker:

> If it was really the case that everybody was discriminating, there would be very substantial opportunities for a limited number of people who were not prepared to discriminate to assemble remarkable departments of high quality people at relatively limited cost simply by the act of their not discriminating. (Quoted in Jaschik, 2005)

In addition to women's unwillingness to work long hours, Summers put forward the possibility that women's underrepresentation in science and math careers might be down to "issues of intrinsic aptitude," citing as evidence the fact that fewer women than men score at the very top end of high school math scores (quoted in Jaschik, 2005). His comments created a firestorm of negative publicity that played a significant role in his subsequent resignation after a no-confidence vote by the Harvard faculty.

Fellow economist Blinder once claimed that "everybody knows, Larry is very smart, and he likes to show it" (quoted in Hirsch, 2013). At Treasury, one aide described his management style in the following manner: "If you're in a meeting, whatever you say, he will make you feel like you're an idiot" (Bradley, 2005). This confidence in his own intellectual ability literally cost Harvard hundreds of millions. As President, Summers invested billions of dollars of Harvard's cash in risky derivatives and stocks of the kind discussed in the previous chapter. When these markets collapsed in 2007 and 2008, Harvard lost $1.8 billion (Healy, 2009).

Unlike Greenspan, Summers did not join the public service from the private sector. However, according to Charles Ferguson, director of *The Inside Job*, Summer's career does reflect an increasingly common "convergence of academic economics, Wall Street, and political power" (Ferguson, 2010). Between 2001, when he left the Treasury, and 2008 when he returned to the federal government with Obama, Summers made a tidy personal fortune of $20 million from consulting and speaking engagements with financial firms. He earned $5 million a year for working one day a week at finance company D.E. Shaw and made some tidy speaking fees from big finance companies such as Goldman Sachs ($135,000), JP Morgan ($67,000) and Lehman Brothers ($67,500) (Mirowski, 2013, p. 206). His 2009 federal financial disclosure form listed his net worth as somewhere between $17–39 million (Ferguson, 2010). Long-time Summers critic, economist Joseph Stiglitz, argued that Summers was "seen to be, and probably is, captured" by the finance industry (Hirsh, 2013).

Unlike Greenspan, Summers is not an acolyte of Rand-style freedom for firms. In his writing and public pronouncements, he would much more accurately be described as a liberal new Keynesian. In a 2001 speech, he claimed that he went into economics to research "the most important problems in the world: poverty, unemployment, helping poor people. But I knew that I didn't want to just shout and rant about them" (Bradley, 2005). His subjects of interest reflect noble goals, and his desire to move beyond "ranting" mirrors many economists' justifications of the rigor of the discipline. Summers is a great admirer of Friedman, declaring that "we are all now Friedmanites" and that he had "great respect for his ideas" (quoted in Mirowski, 2013, p. 207). Yet, Summers made his name, and won a John Bates Clark Award for the best US economist under 40, for applying economics to the real world, frequently in a manner that justified government intervention. One example of this kind of research is his attack on Real Business Cycles's anti-government macroeconomic policy described in Chapter 5. He has also produced research advocating raising government revenue by taxing financial transactions, based on the argument that financial markets may no longer be playing their one-time role of "efficiently guiding the allocation of capital" (Summers & Summers, 1989, p. 262). Further, discouraging financial activity may actually be desirable since so little finance "has to do with the financing of real investment in any very direct way" (Summers & Summers, 1989, p. 173). A final example came in 1997 when the US was engaged in a debate over the merits of cutting the tax on inheritances. Summers again took the pro-taxation side, arguing that "when it comes to the estate tax, there is no case other than selfishness" (quoted in Bradley, 2005). These comments by Summers are particularly interesting, because, as we shall see, they are difficult to reconcile with his actions while at the Treasury. While Greenspan is remarkably consistent across his writing, his public opinions and his policy actions, Summers appears to don one hat as a writer or academic and another while in office. Greenspan and Summers were not only the two most ungainly tennis partners at the St. Alban's Tennis Club (Bradley, 2005), but also were surprisingly in sync when it came to overseeing the rapidly growing financial industry.

Economics in Action: Monetary Policy and Deregulation in Finance

In their prominent roles in the Treasury and the Fed, Summers and Greenspan operationalized many of the ideas that had been championed by economists in the previous chapters. As chair of the Fed, Greenspan was the driving force behind the monetary policy responsible for the increased debt of US households. He also combined with Summers to support the financial deregulation that helped create the speculative frenzy that contributed to the financial collapse in the US.

Monetary Policy

Greenspan's monetary policy choices can be divided into two distinct periods. The first period, which lasted until the late 1990s, continued his predecessor Paul Volcker's policy of aggressively attempting to subdue what they thought were dangerously high rates of inflation. In 1989, Greenspan testified that he viewed an acceptable level of inflation as one in which "the expected rate of change of the general level of prices ceases to be a factor in individual and business decision-making" (Greenspan, 1990, p. 6). In fact, he immediately increased interest rates on taking office in 1987 to signal his inflation-fighting credentials and combat what he thought were entrenched inflationary expectations. The concern about inflationary expectations, for someone like Greenspan, is that they are a bit of a self-fulfilling prophecy. If people believe that inflation will exist in the future, they build this into their economic actions such as contract negotiations. If people want a 2 percent increase in their spending power and inflation is going to be 7 percent, they need to ask for a 9 percent raise. This becomes self-fulfilling because now the 9 percent wage increase is built into the costs that firms pass on to customers. So, inflationary expectations create inflation. His goal in office was to drive inflation down and keep it there so that people's expectations about inflation would fall. For the first part of Greenspan's tenure, interest rates were occasionally reduced, as was the case between 1991 and 1994, but in general he was willing to sacrifice employment and growth to reduce inflation. For example, from the beginning of 1988 to the end of the year, interest rates increased from 6.5 to 8 percent. As the economy slowed, Greenspan informed the Fed's Open Market Committee that "those who think that we are in a recession … are reasonably certain to be wrong" (quoted in Madrick, 2011, p. 234), and he refused to cut rates until 1991 and 1992, despite growing unemployment and slow economic growth. George H.W. Bush blamed his election defeat on the sluggish economy brought on by Greenspan's monetary policy (Madrick, 2011, p. 234). After lowering interest rates during the worst of the recession of the early 1990s, Greenspan increased rates by a remarkable three-quarters of a point, a very large rise, worried about the inflationary consequences of unemployment falling below 5.5 percent. By 1995, he had increased interest rates from 3 to 6 percent in just over a year (Madrick, 2011, p. 236).

An approving review of monetary policy in the 1990s by Mankiw noted that interest rates were more "responsive" to inflation than in previous periods and that the Fed may have been involved in "covert inflation targeting" of about 3 percent (Mankiw, 2001). Greenspan's successor as Fed chair, Ben Bernanke, described the Greenspan policy as "de facto very similar to inflation targeting" (Bernanke & Mishkin, 1997, p. 113). Monetary policy expert Marvin Goodfriend agreed, claiming that while Greenspan was in charge, the Fed acted to keep "core inflation" at around 2 percent (Goodfriend, 2007, p. 54). These three approving reviews of Greenspan's inflation targeting reflect our claims from Chapter 2, that one of the dramatic changes in economic conventional wisdom in the post-1980 period was the abandonment of Keynesian stabilization. Much of the momentum for this change was provided by Friedman, and even more forcefully, the Real Business Cycle (RBC) scholars. In monetary policy, this reflected a change from focusing on the twin goals of low inflation and high employment to fighting inflation alone. Goodfriend, for example, argues that inflationary targeting was a remarkable success despite the fact that it came "at some cost in unemployment" (Goodfriend, 2007, p. 54).

William Grieder of *The Nation* disagreed with the notion that Greenspan had followed a wise monetary policy. Grieder argued that Greenspan "deliberately restrained economic growth for many years, effectively suppressing employment and wages. The economy, he [Greenspan] argued, cannot grow faster than 2–2.5 percent without igniting price inflation, so the Fed was duty bound to prevent it" (Grieder, 2005). As we highlighted in Chapter 3, high interest policy is commonly justified on the grounds of combating the horrors, as elusive as those may be, of inflation, but the unstated concern about high employment is that it causes wage increases that might cut into profits. According to Greider, prior to 1997, Greenspan used monetary policy to keep the unemployment rate above 6 percent because he feared creating more jobs would lead to inflationary pressures (Greider, 2001).

The second period was Greenspan's low interest-rate, high employment monetary-policy regime that lasted a little less than a decade, from the late 1990s to the mid-2000s. According to Greider, the ability of the US economy to withstand low rates of unemployment without creating excessive inflation surprised even Greenspan. It was only in early 1997, under the threat of a potential worldwide financial meltdown (and collapse of LTC), that Greenspan relaxed monetary policy sufficiently to let US unemployment fall below the feared 6 percent rate and accidentally discovered that his ceiling was artificially high. Even when unemployment fell to 4 percent, while wages increased slightly, it did not lead to what Greenspan considered to be "wage inflation" (Greider, 2001). The reason that Greenspan could lower interest rates to levels unprecedented in recent history, and so against his natural proclivity, was, as we have said in Chapter 3, that US workers were traumatized by a number of forces from previous high unemployment to international trade to labor market policy changes, which meant that they would not seek, or could not get, wage increases despite high levels of employment. Once Greenspan realized that he could relax interest rates, much more than he previously believed, he used low interest rates in his attempt to keep the US economy bobbing along (although the inflation fighting Greenspan did briefly re-emerge when he increased rates from 4.75 to 6.5 percent between 1997 and May 2000: Madrick, 2011, p. 242). Inflation and unemployment were low and growth was high. In 1998, Greenspan told Clinton, "This is the best economy I have ever seen in fifty years of studying it every day" (Madrick, 2011, p. 241). Of course, low interest rates had the advantageous effect of maintaining consumer demand despite stagnant labor incomes. Unemployment dropped to very low rates during this period, and wages even increased a little. However, the downside of low rates and modest incomes was the steadily increasing household debt of the US population as detailed in Chapter 3. At the start of the 1980s, personal saving as a percent of personal disposable income was 11.5 percent. By 2005, it was 2.6 percent (US Bureau of Economic Analysis, 2016).

In the context of debt-driven consumption, it is important to recognize the importance of the prolonged period of low interest rates starting in the late 1990s and early 2000s. The low interest rates played a dual role in maintaining consumer spending. Most obviously, it kept debt payments manageable for increasingly indebted households. Secondly, by keeping borrowing costs low, it helped inflate the value of the US housing market that was a cornerstone of the growing wealth against which households were borrowing. During this period, Greenspan dismissed concerns that the housing market might collapse, arguing that housing prices had never suffered a broad nationwide decline (Andrews, 2008).

Despite Greenspan's confidence about the solidity of the housing market, it did collapse in 2007, after Greenspan raised rates by more than 4 percentage points between 2004 and 2006. Households with precariously high debt loads, many with dangerous subprime and variable-rate mortgages, could not manage the increasing payments brought on by increased interest rates. According to the Mortgage Bankers Association, the share of loans that "were seriously delinquent or beginning the foreclosure process" were more than two times their previous record highs by the mid-2008 (US Department of Housing and Urban Development, 2010, pp. 4–6). Predictably, defaults were especially pronounced in the subprime market, but spread to mortgages with adjustable rates. As defaults increased, housing prices collapsed in the US, declining by 8 percent in the year between November of 2007 and 2008 (Avery et al., 2010). This was precisely the decline that Greenspan claimed was unlikely to occur. As housing prices fell and families defaulted on their mortgages, the bottom fell out of the mortgage derivative market, causing the failure of financial giants like Lehman Brothers and insurance firm AIG.

Greenspan continued his predecessor Volcker's tight monetary policy in his early years as Fed chair. However, limiting inflation meant creating unemployment, which holds down the income of workers. Only when he realized that low unemployment would not result in escalating wage pressure did Greenspan lower rates. Those lower rates played a crucial role in maintaining demand in an economic environment of low wages that Greenspan himself had helped create. The problem with this method of maintaining demand is that it is very precarious. A high-debt economy is inherently unstable, but it is especially vulnerable if interest rates rise, as they did in 2006 and 2007.

Financial Deregulation

The other piece of the policy puzzle that contributed to the 2008 crisis was the deregulation of the financial sector. This policy was consistent with the ideas of Friedman, the public choice school and the Efficient Market Hypothesis (EMH), which argue against state oversight of private-sector activity. Both Greenspan and Summers played important roles in first deregulating and then resisting restoration of regulations in financial markets. Before delving into the history of the deregulatory 1990s, it might be instructive to provide a quick look at the post-Depression regulatory regime that was dismantled.

The Great Depression was, in part, caused by a massive wave of bank failures across the country, creating a consensus that regulation was needed to create an industry less prone to risky behavior. Part of the reason for the banks' failure was that they were doing two things: the traditional banking role of taking deposits and making loans, as well as acting as an investment house. This created two sources of risk. First, it created a potential conflict of interest because banks could make loans to, underwrite securities for, and hold stock in the same company (Wigmore, 1985). Second, in the bull market of the late

1920s, banks were as eager as anyone else to cash in by purchasing stocks. Unfortunately, when the market crashed in 1929, banks were left holding rapidly declining stocks, contributing to their financial woes. The Glass-Steagall Act (or Banking Act) of 1933 separated the deposit collecting and loaning activities of commercial banks from other investment activities by prohibiting banks from dealing with financial securities (Kroszner & Rajan, 1994). This legislation was designed to create a firewall to prevent the conflict of interest and reduce the risk that existed when commercial banks could both loan money and deal in securities.

The banking industry was never happy with the legislated separation of commercial banking and investment. In the 25 years between 1975 and 1999, the banking industry unsuccessfully attempted to get Glass-Steagall overturned twelve times. Despite these political failures, Glass-Steagall had been whittled down, starting in the late 1980s. The language of the Act allowed for a certain degree of inter-pretation of how strict the separation of commercial and investment banking needed to be. The Fed started to allow banks to own securities companies as long as they were a very small percent (initially 5 percent) of revenue. This limit was raised to 25 percent by 1997 (Barth et al., 2000).

Glass-Steagall was finally repealed and replaced after more than sixty years with the Gramm-Leach-Bilely Act (GLBA) in 1999. The general thrust of the GLBA was to allow banks to engage in a wider range of activities, including the previously forbidden roles of selling securities and insurance. It also eliminated many federal and state restrictions on affiliations between banks and investment and insurance firms (National Commission on the Causes of the Financial and Economic Crisis in the United States, 2011). The new regulations were enacted in spite of a prescient warning in the rationale for preserving Glass-Steagall, written by the Congressional Research Service in 1987: "Securities activities can be risky, leading to enormous losses. Such losses could threaten the integrity of deposits. In turn, the Government insures deposits and could be required to pay large sums if depository institutions were to collapse as the result of securities losses" (Jackson, 1984, p. 3).

The elimination of Glass-Steagall did not come from a groundswell of popular anger against unjust and archaic legislation. The pressure for regulatory change came directly from the banking and finance industry. Citigroup was especially keen on advancing this agenda. In 1998, it had merged with Travelers Insurance into exactly the kind of corporation Glass-Steagall was designed to prevent, so it needed deregulation to keep the new corporation intact. What is perhaps most remarkable about this merger is that Citigroup was so confident that it could obtain the required deregulation that it pursued the merger with Travelers, despite knowing that the resulting corporate structure contravened the existing Act. More generally, banks were concerned that corporations were bypassing the traditional avenues of bank lending to raise money directly in the financial markets (Kroszner & Rajan, 1994). Getting traditional loans from commercial banks is only one avenue that firms can choose to pursue when they need to raise capital. Banks were eager to participate in these alternative measures, but were prohibited from doing so due to the restrictions of Glass-Steagall. They further argued that the ancient Glass-Steagall restrictions disadvantaged US banks and investment firms compared to their foreign competitors who were not fettered by the same regulatory requirements. Finally, they argued that the legislation was completely unnecessary, since competition in the industry would ensure that firms would be careful with their clients' money.

In the push for banking deregulation, the financial sector had a number of cards to play. Economic common sense and the general policy environment in the 1990s were certainly in favor of deregulation. In other industries, from telecommunications to energy, the role of the state had been pared back. The banks could also rely on the intellectual justification provided by ideas like the EMH. Not leaving favorable legislative change to the winds of chance, the financial sector also engaged in more direct political activity. Unsurprisingly, Citigroup was especially active on this front, spending $9 million on lobbying in 1998 (Center for Responsive Politics, 2016a), and $2.8 million on political donations in the 1998 election cycle (Center for Responsive Politics, 2016b). Citigroup could also count on some very well-placed support in the government. In the days before the merger with Citigroup, Travellers head Sandy Weill made phone calls to Summers' boss, Robert Rubin about the deal. (Rubin went on to a very lucrative job at Citigroup when he left the Treasury.) Weill also met with Greenspan who gave the merger his personal approval (PBS, 2003).

Both Greenspan and Summers supported the replacement of Glass-Steagall with the GLBA. Greenspan personally used his influence to advocate for the repeal of Glass-Steagall, arguing that financial institutions had strong incentives to protect their shareholders and would therefore regulate themselves, and that removing barriers imposed by regulation would result in increased efficiency and better services for the public (National Commission on the Causes of the Financial and Economic Crisis in the United States, 2011, pp. 64, 84). Speaking when GLBA was passed in 1999, Summers claimed, "This historic legislation will better enable American companies to compete in the new economy" (Labaton, 1999). The following year, while speaking to what was surely a sympathetic audience of the Securities Industry Association, Summers first played up the importance of "the unparalleled strength and dynamism of our financial markets" as an engine of US economic success and then lauded the 1999 deregulation as providing "the appropriate balance between high-quality regulation and the absence of excessive state interference" (Summers, 2000). It was precisely the elimination of the Glass-Steagall restrictions that permitted banks to speculate in the mortgage-backed investments that were such a crucial feature of the financial crisis.

The finance industry could also count on Greenspan and Summers to fight against any regulation that would limit its use of increasingly complex investment instruments, including the mortgage-backed derivatives that helped spark the crisis. Summers' opinions on financial regulation were nicely illustrated at a 2005 conference of central bankers. IMF economist Raghuram Rajan presented a paper that warned that the structure of financial-sector compensation combined with newly developed complex financial products, created an incentive for bankers to take substantial investment risks. Rajan warned that this could create a "full-blown financial crisis." After he had finished his presentation, Summers called Rajan a "Luddite," dismissing his concerns, and cautioning that regulation would harm the financial sector (Ferguson, 2010; Hirsch, 2013).

In the late 1990s, the Commodities Futures Trading Commission (CFTC), a federal agency that regulates options and futures trading, grew concerned about the increasingly complex and opaque nature of many of the financial instruments being traded. This unease stemmed in part from a 1994 General Accounting Office report on the growing use of exotic financial instruments in the US that concluded that there were "significant gaps and oversights" in regulation of derivatives (GAO, 1994). The head of the CFTC, Brooksley Born, recommended legislation calling for more transparent reporting of trades and higher reserves. She was opposed vehemently in these proposals by the banking industry, which feared that increased regulation would cause investors to flee the US for less heavily policed shores. According to the *New York Times*, she was also pilloried by deregulatory enthusiasts Greenspan, Rubin and Summers, who argued that the mere passage of this regulation could destabilize financial markets that they thought were functioning smoothly. Summers testified that regulation was unnecessary in the derivatives market as those participating were "largely sophisticated financial institutions that would appear to be eminently capable of protecting themselves" (Summers, 1998). Taking a more direct tack, Summers phoned Born to, in the words of a *Newsweek* article, "dress her down, loudly and rudely," according to Born's deputy Michael Greenberger, who walked in on the call. Born was astonished that Summers could claim that "you shouldn't even ask questions about a market that was many, many trillions of dollars in notional value—and that none of us knew anything about" (Hirsch, 2009). Greenspan, Rubin and Summers successfully convinced Congress to freeze the regulatory authority of the CFTC for six months. Born quit soon after.

In the years prior to the financial crisis, both Summers and Greenspan repeatedly argued that the expanding derivatives market did not need regulation. In 2004, Greenspan claimed that as a result of this wonderful innovation in finance, "Not only have individual financial institutions become less vulnerable to shocks from underlying risk factors, but also the financial system as a whole has become more resilient" (Greenspan, 2004). He also claimed prior to 2006 that the possibility of financial failure was extremely remote, if not impossible: "I believe that the general growth in large institutions has occurred in the context of an underlying structure of markets in which many of the larger risks are dramatically—I should say, fully—hedged" (quoted in Goodman, 2008). Blinder offered this opinion of Greenspan following the crash: "I think of him as consistently cheerleading on derivatives" (quoted in Goodman, 2008). As late as 2007, Summers maintained his confidence in the state of the US financial sector, claiming that finance does not "just oil the wheels of economic growth—they are the wheels" (quoted in Murray, 2007).

In 1999, after Born's resignation, Greenspan and Summers were members on the President's Working Group on Financial Markets, which issued a report urging Congress to further deregulate derivatives (Goodman, 2008). This led to the passage of the Commodities Futures Modernization Act (CFMA) of 2000, which was Summers' big legislative accomplishment as Treasury secretary (Ferguson, 2010; Hirsch, 2013). The CFMA effectively deregulated the market in derivatives. According to former Born deputy Greenberger, "The CFMA did not just stop the CFTC from regulating. It stopped every federal regulatory entity from regulating swaps, and even state law was also almost completely pre-empted" (Hirsch, 2013). The benefit to financial corporations was immediate, as the value of over-the-counter derivatives grew from $95.2 trillion in 2000 to $672.6 trillion globally by 2008 (National Commission on the Causes of the Financial and Economic Crisis in the United States, 2011, p. 77). The Financial Crisis Inquiry Commission of Congress in 2009 placed the failure to regulate the derivatives market at "the center of the storm" (National Commission on the Causes of the Financial and Economic Crisis in the United States, 2011, p. 77).

After the crisis, Greenspan and Summers took different approaches to the criticisms that inevitably came their way. Greenspan, although certainly not admitting to the role that monetary policy played in creating the conditions of the crisis, did make a *mea culpa* of sorts about his distrust of regulation: "I made a mistake in presuming that the self-interests of organizations, specifically banks and others, were such that they were best capable of protecting their own shareholders and the equity and the firms" (quoted in Clark & Treanor, 2008). Summers, on the other hand, was characteristically unrepentant, claiming that he was not "a great deregulator," but that he opposed the specifics of the regulations being proposed. According to Summers, he "expressed the strong view of Secretary Rubin, chairman Greenspan and SEC chief Levitt that the way the CFTC was proposing to go about it was likely to be ineffective and itself imposed major risks into the market" (Hirsch, 2009).

Conclusion: Policy and Profits

Surely no recent economist, and possibly no other public figure in the US, has fallen as far, from as high, as Greenspan in his Icarus-like plummet. At the time of his retirement in 2006, he was feted as the greatest Fed chair of all time—a monetary manager without peer, who had ushered in a new era of low inflation and unemployment. Mankiw's evaluation of monetary policy during the 1990s claimed that the "macroeconomic performance of the 1990s was exceptional, especially if judged by the volatility of growth, unemployment, and inflation" (Mankiw, 2001, p. 52). A review of two fawning Greenspan tributes, including Woodward's *Maestro*, concluded: "He doth bestride the Fed like a colossus, and if these books are correct, we should hope he goes on bestriding" (Kuttner, 2000). In 2007, Republican presidential candidate John McCain wanted a recently retired 81-year-old Greenspan to oversee an overhaul of the country's tax code. Such was the strength of the Greenspan legacy that McCain joked, whether, "he's alive or dead it doesn't matter. If he's dead, just prop him up and put some dark glasses on him like, like 'Weekend at Bernie's'" (CBS News, 2007).

Following the crisis, Greenspan's legacy took a beating in both academic circles and the popular press. Greenspan was criticized for both his overly expansionary monetary policy and his deregulatory enthusiasm, both of which stemmed, in part, from his belief, reminiscent of the EMH, that the housing market could not produce a bubble. According to the *New York Times*'s "reassessment of the Greenspan legacy": "If Mr. Greenspan had acted differently during his tenure as Federal Reserve chairman from 1987 to 2006, many economists say, the current crisis might have been averted or muted" (Goodman, 2008). Writing for *Forbes*, Eamonn Fingleton is less reserved, claiming that "It is fair to say that Greenspan emerges as probably the biggest—and most dangerous—fool in American financial history," which given the history of skullduggery in American finance is a high bar indeed (Fingleton, 2013). More academically, EMH critic Robert Shiller argued that Greenspan was derelict in his duty as a financial watchdog: "A public official who fails to alert investors to such risks is no better than a doctor who, having diagnosed high blood pressure in a patient, says nothing because he thinks the patient might be lucky and show no ill effects" (quoted in Grieder, 2005).

Because he was seen as more of a supporting member of the economic policy cast, rather than its genuine star, Summers was not the subject of the same sort of glowing tributes as Greenspan. However, along with Greenspan and Rubin, Summers took his fair share of blame for the crisis. In fact, it probably cost him the coveted position as successor to Bernanke as Fed chair in 2013. Although he was reportedly Obama's first choice, his nomination drew the scorn of several liberal Democrats who threatened to oppose his candidacy based on his deregulatory zeal during the Clinton years and his close relationship with Wall Street (Graham, 2013). A summary of Summers' record in public service in *The Atlantic* concluded, "As a government official, he helped author a series of ultimately disastrous or wrongheaded policies" (Hirsch, 2013).

The post-crisis upbraiding of Summers and Greenspan was accurate as far as it went. Monetary policy and deregulation did foster an increase in consumer debt, the mortgage housing bubble and the financial collapse. However, what is less remarked on is that even in the supposed good times, when Greenspan especially was being applauded for his careful economic stewardship, things were not going particularly well for the average American. Greenspan's continuation of the Volcker war against inflation had important redistributive consequences. The increased level of unemployment caused by high interest rates put downward pressure on wages and improved profits during the early 1990s. Greenspan's explicit concerns about rising wages were instructive about where he thought that economic danger might come from. Greenspan only opted for a low interest-rate and high employment monetary-policy regime when it did not foster wage growth. In fact, the low interest rates were necessary to maintain profits through debt-fueled consumption precisely due to the limited growth of wages during the Greenspan period. His fear of rising wages makes an interesting contrast to his exuberance at the growth in asset prices. As Greenspan critic Grieder put it: "If working-class wages rose smartly, that was a sign of inflation threatening prosperity. If stock prices rose explosively, that was evidence of good times ahead" (Grieder, 2005).

Deregulation of the financial sector was also a part of a broader transformation of the policy environment that favored firms during the 1980s and 1990s. We have seen that the economic theories of the EMH, in finance, and public choice, more generally, support the idea that government intervention is both unnecessary and harmful. In Chapter 3, we showed that the growing debt of American households was caused, in part, by stagnant incomes, but, as we demonstrated in Chapter 7, the deregulation of the financial sector, especially the mortgage and banking sectors, also played an important role. The increasing debt payments of American families translated into profits for firms extending credit. While most of the criticisms of the Summers-Greenspan legacy focus on the instability associated with their policies, what this overlooks is that the supposed boom times of the 1990s and early 2000s were not only unstable, they were also grossly unequal.

9
Conclusion: Dissenters and Victors

Faced with the choice between changing one's mind and proving that there is no need to do so, almost everyone gets busy on the proof. (John Kenneth Galbraith, 1971, p. 50)

Capital will always go where it's welcome and stay where it's well treated. Capital is not just money. It's also talent and ideas. They, too, will go where they're welcome and stay where they are well treated. (Walter Wriston, Citibank CEO, quoted in Karlgaard, 2006)

Economics is not a discipline without debate or controversy. There are very real, even vitriolic, disputes about theory and policy. As we have seen, the ideas of economists of the neoliberal age have not been universally embraced or undisputed. In fact, critics of neoliberal ideas such as Franco Modigliani and Robert Shiller can claim their own Nobel prizes and are, arguably, every bit as respected in the discipline as those we have discussed in this book. Perhaps two of the most famous dissenters are Joseph Stiglitz and Paul Krugman.

In 2002, Joseph Stiglitz's *Globalization and its Discontents* was released and became a bestseller. The book was especially critical of the International Monetary Fund (IMF), which advised (or forced, depending on your view of the IMF's relationship as lender of last resort to desperately indebted nations) developing countries to follow policies along the neoliberal lines described in Chapter 2. Stiglitz did not mince words when it came to the IMF and its policies, once famously describing its economists as "third-rank" (quoted in *The Economist*, 2006b). Among the IMF's many rebuttals of Stiglitz's work was a remarkably vitriolic "open letter" from the IMF's Economic Counsellor and Director of Research Kenneth Rogoff.[1] Rogoff's

---

1   Ironically, Rogoff himself was found to be peddling snake oil when three University of Massachusetts, Amherst researchers found that the conclusion of a famous paper co-authored by Rogoff, which argued that

rejoinder included the following choice quotes about Stiglitz: "Your ideas are at best highly controversial, at worst, snake oil." "Do you ever lose a night's sleep thinking that just maybe, Alan Greenspan, Larry Summers, (and) Bob Rubin ... had it right?" "I don't have time here to do justice to some of your other offbeat policy prescriptions." "Do you ever think that just maybe, Joe Stiglitz might have screwed up? That, just maybe, you were part of the problem and not part of the solution?" (Rogoff, 2002)

Stiglitz is a professor at Columbia University. Along with George Akerlof and Michael Spence, he was the co-winner of the 2001 Nobel Prize for "their analyses of markets with asymmetric information." Basically, what Stiglitz argued was that imperfect information is pervasive in economies and when it exists, markets do not work well and government interventions can improve welfare (Stiglitz, 1975, 1979; Grossman & Stiglitz, 1980, 1986). Like Summers, Stiglitz held some very prominent positions at powerful institutions. Between 1997 and 2000, he was the senior vice president and chief economist at the World Bank. In this position, he was already a vocal critic of what he viewed as the IMF's neoliberal policies around the world. There have been allegations that his tenure at the World Bank was shortened due to pressure from the IMF and the US Treasury, particularly Summers (Wade, 2001). Prior to that, from 1993 to 1997, he served on President Clinton's Council of Economic Advisers, first as a member and then as the chair. He has also belonged to a wide variety of research institutions, from the centrist Brookings Institution to the more conservative Hoover Institute at Stanford University.

Krugman is a professor at the City University of New York, where he moved after his tenure at Princeton from 2000 to 2015. He won the Nobel Prize in 2008 for "his analysis of trade patterns and location of economic activity," which is an overly brief description of his work that uses the idea of economies of scale to predict patterns of trade. While the theory of comparative advantage argues that countries will trade different goods between each other, Krugman developed a theory that

---

higher levels of government debt are associated with lower growth, was premised upon some fundamental errors. Rogoff's paper "omitted relevant data, weighted their calculations in an unusual manner, and made an elementary coding blunder," and when these errors were corrected, its conclusions no longer held (Herndon et al., 2013).

uses the idea of product differentiation to explain why most trade is between countries that make different models of the same product. He also used economies of scale to show that regions that already have large amounts of profitable production will be more likely to attract more investment. The implication is that rather than spreading out around the globe, production will concentrate in a few regions (Krugman, 1979, 1980, 1981, 1991). Interestingly, for someone who viewed himself as a staunch defender of the welfare state, Krugman worked for Reagan's Council of Economic Advisers in the 1980s, an experience that did not last very long and which he described as "first thrilling, then disillusioning" (Krugman, n.d.). Although Krugman is well respected as an economist, has had positions at the most prestigious universities, has written over twenty books and published numerous articles, he is probably most famous for his columns in the *New York Times* starting in 1999.

Both Krugman and Stiglitz have been very critical of most neoliberal policies and the economic theory that justified them. Stiglitz has consistently criticized contractionary macroeconomic policy, deregulation and growing income inequality. Despite serving in Clinton's Council of Economic Advisers, he distanced himself from most of the policies implemented during the 1990s, and is especially critical of Greenspan and Rubin, who he sees as the chief economic architects of the time. In contrast to Milton Friedman and the Real Business Cycle (RBC) school, Stiglitz argues that monetary and fiscal policy should be used to achieve high levels of employment. As we have done, Stiglitz lamented that although the Federal Reserve is supposed to have twin goals of maximizing employment and limiting inflation, Greenspan, like Paul Volcker before him, was exclusively concerned with the latter, often at the expense of the former. Stiglitz also makes the important point that while achieving balanced budgets hurt the poor in the 1990s, deficits in the 2000s benefited the rich. Stiglitz argues that in the 1990s Clinton was elected, and wanted to deliver, on his promise of "for people, for a change," but was dissuaded by Greenspan (despite the fact that as chair of the Fed he was not directly responsible for fiscal policy) and Rubin, who were obsessed with eliminating the deficit. The result was that social programs that were much needed were not implemented and even existing ones were cut back in real terms. In the 2000s, the budget was plunged into deficit when George W. Bush implemented massive tax cuts that almost exclusively benefitted the rich. Stiglitz makes two important points. The first is that Greenspan made a revealing about-face on deficit reduction. When budget deficits would have resulted from Clinton's promises to provide assistance to the poor, Greenspan favored balanced budgets. Yet Greenspan favored deficits when they resulted from Bush's tax cuts for the rich. Second, the impacts of fiscal policy are about more than just deficits and surpluses, although these are obviously important in terms of their overall impact on employment and output. The manner in which those deficits or surpluses are achieved also have crucial distributive consequences (Stiglitz, 2003).

Stiglitz's concern about the manner in which budget deficits are usually tamed has now extended to the austerity policies being implemented across Europe. If anything, the spending cuts in Europe are even more ill-advised than those in the US during the 1990s, because Europe is suffering through an economic crisis. As Stiglitz notes, deficit cutting during recessions has a long and troubled history:

> Austerity had failed repeatedly, from its early use under President Herbert Hoover, which turned the stock-market crash into the Great Depression, to the IMF programs imposed on Eastern Asia and Latin America [and also Africa] in recent decades. And yet when Greece got into trouble, it was tried again. (Stiglitz, 2015)

Eliminating deficits by cutting public services during a downturn is twice damned, according to Stiglitz. It is the incorrect counter-cyclical stabilization policy, and it cuts programs to those who need them the most during the recession.

Stiglitz also opposes Friedman's claim that the market delivers a fair distribution of income. In both a much-discussed article in *Vanity Fair* (Stiglitz, 2011) and his book *The Price of Inequality* (Stiglitz, 2013), he lamented the rising inequality in the US and argued that there is little connection between income and merit:

> Those who have contributed great positive innovations to our society, from the pioneers of genetic understanding to the pioneers of the Information Age, have received a pittance compared with

those responsible for the financial innovations that brought our global economy to the brink of ruin. (Stiglitz, 2011)

Growing inequality has been fostered by deliberate policy decisions that favor the wealthy at the expense of the majority of the population, from lowering tax rates on capital gains, to lax enforcement of anti-trust laws to manipulation of the financial system. According to Stiglitz, the will of the rich is translated into policy through influence in the political system:

> Virtually all U.S. senators, and most of the representatives in the House, are members of the top 1 percent when they arrive, are kept in office by money from the top 1 percent, and know that if they serve the top 1 percent well they will be rewarded by the top 1 percent when they leave office. (Stiglitz, 2011)

Unlike Greenspan, the RBC economists and Friedman, Stiglitz argues in favor of higher taxes, both in order to raise revenue and to decrease after-tax income inequality. In a recent paper, Stiglitz proposed dramatic changes to the US tax code. In addition to the obvious increase in the top marginal income tax rate, he also recommended raising tax rates on corporations while reducing their ability to avoid taxation, implementing environmental taxes, a financial transaction tax, a tax on the bonuses of financial-sector executives, and an inheritance tax (Stiglitz, 2014). These policy prescriptions are consistent with Stiglitz's objections to growing inequality and insistence that the market distribution of income is not necessarily a reward for merit, but they also represent a stark contrast to the recommendations of the economists profiled in this book and economic policy trends after 1980.

Stiglitz has also consistently opposed the deregulatory moves, especially in the financial sector, justified by Friedman and public choice scholars, which were implemented by Greenspan and Summers. Coming at these matters from the perspective of theory, he argued that his own work on "imperfect and asymmetric information in markets had undermined every one of the 'efficient market' doctrines" (Stiglitz, 2010a). For example, the Efficient Market Hypothesis (EMH) and much RBC macroeconomic theory require that people acquire and correctly use information, but Stiglitz claims that his work with Sanford Grossman demonstrated that people won't actually do this (Grossman & Stiglitz, 1980). However, despite its intellectual shortcomings, the EMH comforted deregulators, like Greenspan and Summers, who stripped away regulatory constraints on financial markets. Further, those in positions to implement economic policy were not in those roles by chance. They were in those positions precisely because they were favored by those who benefitted from deregulation in the financial sector. Interestingly, considering that he was part of it, Stiglitz was very critical of the Clinton administration's economic agenda, claiming that it was set and implemented by Wall Street insiders like Greenspan and Rubin (Stiglitz, 2003). In general, "banks had invested well, not in the housing or the real sector, but in politics ... they had bought deregulation" (Stiglitz, 2010c, p. 326). The result, according to Stiglitz, was that the regulatory environment in the financial sector created incentives for firms to peddle their inefficient and dangerous mortgage products that increased instability and household debt (Stiglitz, 2010b).

Krugman shares many of the opinions held by Stiglitz, making them something of a dissenters' one-two punch when it comes to opposing neoliberal economic policy. Perhaps the main difference between the two is that Krugman is a more recent convert to the opposition. Prior to the mid-2000s, Krugman was an avid supporter of the welfare state, but also advocated some important neoliberal policies. For example, unlike Stiglitz, who was very critical of the Clinton 1990s, Krugman was overwhelmingly positive. His book, *The Great Unraveling*, stated that "by decade's end 'Rubinomics' was triumphant," and that "at the beginning of the new millennium, then, it seemed that the United States was blessed with mature, skillful economic leaders" (Krugman, 2003a, pp. xxxi–xxxii). In a triumphal article in 1999, he chose to cheerlead for two particularly ill-fated firms, claiming that they were on the cutting edge of a new way of doing business that was dramatically improving the competitiveness of the economy:

The retreat of business bureaucracy in the face of the market was brought home to me recently when I joined the advisory board at Enron ... It's sort of like the difference between your father's bank, which took money from its regular depositors and lent it out to its regular customers, and Goldman Sachs. (Krugman, 1999c)

With hindsight, it is difficult to imagine two firms less worthy of this praise, but for Krugman the new economy and financial speculation were not the only positive attributes of the 1990s. So, too, was Greenspan's use of monetary policy to control the wage demands of the working population: "Even liberal economists like myself grudgingly accept the conclusion that a responsible Fed must sometimes raise interest rates in order to limit the number of jobs and maintain a suitably high rate of unemployment." Greenspan's error, according to Krugman, was not that he engineered sufficient unemployment to ensure that wages did not increase faster than labor productivity, but rather that he described that policy "so explicitly and so honestly" (Krugman, 1999a).

In the late 1990s and early 2000s, Krugman made unfavorable comparisons between what he argued was the sluggish European and the dynamic US economies. The rise of the Anglo economies was due to the rise of smart economists, like Greenspan and Summers, to positions of power and the "ideological groundswell in the English-speaking world in favor of markets" represented by Thatcher in England (Krugman, 1999b). In contrast, in France, policies protecting workers, like "generous health and unemployment benefits, long mandatory paid vacations, maybe even a limit on individual working hours," created unemployment and sluggish growth, despite their seeming appeal: "I'd say that given the alternatives, the American system, though not beautiful, still takes the prize" (Krugman, 2000a). At this point, Krugman was still arguing that the 1990s were not particularly hard on the US worker. In an exchange with economist James Galbraith, Krugman claimed that the statement, "workers are hurting because labor has failed to share in national productivity gains," was demonstrably false (Krugman, 1996a).

In the early 2000s, when the world was embroiled in a debate over the merits of free trade (or more specifically, free trade as operationalized by institutions like the World Trade Organization (WTO)), and protestors were out in the streets of Seattle in running battles with security forces, Krugman sided firmly with the WTO. His argument had two components. First, free trade had transformed the economies of many nations in the developing world and lifted hundreds of millions out of poverty. For example, it was Thailand's "export-led success stories that are the best advertisement for the WTO and its free-trade agenda" (Krugman, 2000b). In fact, "globalization, driven not by human goodness but by the profit motive, has done far more good for far more people than all the foreign aid and soft loans ever provided by well-intentioned governments and international agencies" (Krugman, 2000c). Krugman not only credited free trade with improving the economic position of the world's poor, but it also improved their political lives: "When a nation opens to the world, its businesses become less dependent on government favor, its citizens become more aware of how politics is conducted in advanced countries. The result, repeatedly, has been a peaceful transition to true democracy" (Krugman, 2000d). It follows that any opposition to free trade was opposition to improving the lot of the poorest in the world. Krugman argued that the "anti-globalization movement already has a remarkable track record of hurting the very people and causes it claims to champion," because their dogmatic and simplistic understanding of the world failed to appreciate that "unless they [developing nations] are allowed to sell goods produced under conditions that Westerners find appalling, by workers who receive very low wages," those countries will not attract investment and will remain poor (Krugman, 2001).

The second component of Krugman's pro-trade argument was that, to the extent that US workers were being left behind in the decades following the 1980s, it was the result of deliberate policy choices rather than the detrimental effects of international trade. While international trade may put some pressure on American workers' wages and cause some corporate downsizing, "it is hardly the most important cause of the phenomenon." It also couldn't explain the race to the bottom for worker protection rules like minimum wages and a social safety net: "None of the important constraints on American economic and social policy come from abroad ... if policies have become increasingly mean spirited, that is a political choice" (Krugman, 1997).

During this period, Krugman was careful to distance himself from what he considered to be overly radical commentary and commentators. For example, he characterized consumer advocate and presidential candidate Ralph Nader as having a "general hostility toward corporations," that so clouded his judgment that he was willing to "prevent patients from getting drugs that might give them a decent life and prevent a moderate who gets along with business from becoming president" (Krugman, 2000e). He made similar disparaging comments about think tanks that opposed free trade, like the Economic Policy Institute, which he described as "hacks," in contrast to the reasonable opinions held by the honest scholars at "Harvard or the University of Chicago" (Krugman, 2000f).

However, as the 2000s wore on, Krugman became a more consistent opponent of the neoliberal economic status quo. Like Stiglitz, he was very critical of growing income inequality and stagnant incomes for many in the US. Interestingly, this involved a reconsideration of his support of the 1990s Clinton era, when he correctly pointed out that although corporate profits have boomed, "the stagnation of real wages—wages adjusted for inflation—actually goes back more than 30 years" (Krugman, 2006a; see also Krugman, 2005a, 2008a). He described the current US income distribution as the outcome of an "oligarchy" in which income and wealth was being concentrated in an increasingly narrow and protected privileged elite (Krugman, 2011a). The US also failed to live up to its famous slogan about being the land of opportunity. Citing research from economist Alan Krueger, Krugman argued that compared to other nations, the US had a "more static distribution of income across generations with fewer opportunities for advancement" (Krugman, 2002a).

For the later Krugman, rising inequality was a result of precisely the kinds of neoliberal transformations to the labor market that we highlighted in Chapters 2 and 3. Krugman argued that obvious policies "like tax rates for the rich and the level of the minimum wage" were creating inequality, but so, too, were less obvious but important changes, "like the shift in Labor Department policy from protection of worker rights to tacit support for union-busting" (Krugman, 2006b; see also Krugman, 2005b). His concern about the conditions of the average US worker also appears to have led to a reconsideration of the attractiveness of European-style labor policies. Krugman noted in 2005 that although GDP per hour worked, a measure of productivity, was actually a bit higher in France than the US, French GDP per person was lower than the US primarily because French workers put in fewer hours on the job and more with their families. Further, it was government regulations that "actually allow people to make a desirable tradeoff. And whatever else you may say about French economic policies, they seem extremely supportive of the family as an institution" (Krugman, 2005c). All of the policies that Krugman has supported are precisely the kinds of policies that Friedman opposed because they decrease competition in the labor market and increase the non-accelerating inflation rate of unemployment (NAIRU).

Finally, the dire condition of the US worker also caused Krugman to take a slightly less dismissive line on the impacts of free trade on wages. Although he maintained his support for free trade on the basis of its benefits for poorer nations, he conceded that, "fears that low-wage competition is driving down U.S. wages have a real basis in both theory and fact ... And no, cheap consumer goods at Wal-Mart aren't adequate compensation" (Krugman, 2007a). In contrast to his earlier claim that those who opposed trade were following their hearts but ignoring their heads, by 2007 he also conceded that "those who are worried about trade have a point, and deserve some respect" (Krugman, 2007b).

Krugman also favors regulation and government intervention, in contrast to Friedman and the public choice authors. Unlike capture and rent-seeking theories, Krugman argues that strong industry regulation in areas as diverse as food and finance are beneficial for both consumers and firms. Krugman follows the logic of information asymmetry to argue that when it is difficult for consumers to know how their food is prepared and how healthy it is, firms that cut corners will have a price advantage over those who do not. Quoting the president of the United Fresh Produce Association, Krugman argued that the safety issues facing the food industry "can't be solved without strong mandatory federal regulations" As a result, both the food industry and consumer groups are eager for stronger regulations (Krugman, 2007c; see also Krugman, 2008b). Krugman takes a similar line in his strong pro-regulatory stance in the financial industry, a position he clearly felt was vindicated by the financial collapse of 2007. He warned of the dangers of replacing the Glass-Steagall Act with the Gramm-Leach-Bliley Act (GLBA), and the underfunding of regulatory agencies like the Securities and Exchange Commission (SEC) ("the whole point is to prevent the agency from doing its job": Krugman, 2002b), an analysis of the financial crisis very much along the lines described in this book, and in opposition to the EMH authors and regulators in the previous chapter (Krugman, 2008b, 2009a).

In addition to regulatory oversight, Krugman has also come out in favor of outright government ownership and control of many industries. In the wake of the financial crisis, he advocated nationalizing the banks (Krugman, 2009b). One of his most controversial recommendations is to create a universal public health care system in the US. Krugman correctly pointed out that the health of US citizens fares poorly compared to people in nations with public health insurance like the UK and Canada:

> ... the richest third of Americans is in worse health than the poorest third of the English. It's possible that Britain's National Health Service, in spite of its limited budget, actually provides better all-around medical care than our system because it takes a broader, longer-term view than private insurance companies. (Krugman, 2006c)

He argues that part of the reason that the US system is so expensive and delivers such poor results compared to a public system is that "in the United States administrative expenses eat up about 15 percent of the money paid in premiums to private health insurance companies, but only 4 percent of the budgets of public insurance programs" (Krugman, 2005d). The inevitable conclusion, according to Krugman? "Does this mean that the American way is wrong, and that we should switch to a Canadian-style single-payer system? Well, yes" (Krugman, 2004a). The flip side of Krugman's policy stance on nationalization is that he opposed privatization of services that were being effectively provided by the government. Perhaps most vocally, he is a long-term opponent of privatizing social security (Krugman, 2002c). As we have done in Chapter 2, Krugman attributed the privatization drive to the well-funded political activities of companies and the lobby groups to which they donate, including the American Legislative Exchange Council (ALEC), which he particularly criticized for drafting legislation that would turn "the provision of public services, from schools to prisons, over to for-profit corporations" (Krugman, 2012a).

Much like Stiglitz, Krugman favors expansionary fiscal and monetary policy during downturns. In the aftermath of the 2008 economic crisis, when unemployment surged to 10 percent, there was considerable debate in the US about whether President Obama was correct in running large deficits in an effort to stimulate the economy. Krugman was not only on the side of deficit spending, but argued that Obama's stimulus package was both too small and poorly targeted. His message to Obama was unequivocal: "you need to get both your economic team and your political people working on additional stimulus, now" (Krugman, 2009c). He also lamented deficit cutting at the state level, which he argued was undercutting the limited federal attempts at resurrecting the economy: "The nation will be reeling from the actions of 50 Herbert Hoovers—state governors who are slashing spending in a time of recession" (Krugman, 2008c).

While Krugman supported deficits during the crisis, he was not as enamored about where the money was going. Much of the stimulus package went to bail out the insolvent banks that had created the financial crisis in the first place, under the assumption that they were "too big to fail." Krugman argued that this amounted to nothing more than "lemon socialism: taxpayers bear the cost if things go wrong, but stockholders and executives get the benefits if things go right" (Krugman, 2009d). The fact that government bailouts were going to executive bonuses in failed financial firms may have been undesirable, but it was also predictable, given Wall Street's influence over the National Economic Council (NEC), the agency responsible for organizing the response to the crisis. The NEC was populated with "Wall Street insiders and establishmentarians" like Mike Froman, from Citigroup, and Summers (Krugman & Wells, 2012).

Also like Stiglitz, Krugman supported a range of tax increases, especially on the rich, to help fund government programs. He has repeatedly pointed out the fiscal constraints imposed by tax cuts. During the debate about the Bush administration's tax cuts, he noted that "once the new round of cuts takes effect, federal taxes will be lower than their average during the Eisenhower administration" (Krugman, 2003b). He not only opposed the Bush presidency's tax cuts that favored the rich, but has also been more generally critical of the numerous tax evasion and avoidance schemes that allowed the rich to pay very little tax, especially the corporate shell game of setting up in low tax jurisdictions like the Cayman Islands (Krugman, 2002d, 2004b). His dismay at the hollowing-out of fiscal capacity during the 2000s prompted an apology of sorts, when he admitted that Nader "wasn't all wrong" in lumping the Democrats and Republicans together in their subservience to corporations and the wealthy when even the supposedly more left-leaning party waffled over whether managers of hedge funds should be taxed at the same rate as other income earners (Krugman, 2007d). Like Stiglitz, Krugman has been careful to point out that taxes and spending impact different groups in the population and has been critical of those who advocate balancing budgets on the backs of spending cuts. He favorably contrasted France's budget balancing through tax increases to the rest of Europe's choice of cutting social programs, claiming that "France has committed the unforgivable sin of being fiscally responsible without inflicting pain on the poor and unlucky" (Krugman, 2013).

Stiglitz and Krugman have both been steadfast opponents of the neoliberal policies that we have detailed in Chapters 2 and 3. They have also been critical of the economics discipline that justified these policies. Krugman described the state of macroeconomics in the three decades prior to the 2008 crisis as "spectacularly useless at best, positively harmful at worst" (quoted in Mirowski, 2013, p. 292). After 1970, financial economics consisted largely of researchers imitating "Voltaire's Dr. Pangloss, who insisted that we live in the best of all possible worlds" (Krugman, 2009e). For his part, Stiglitz argued that what he described as the neoclassical paradigm that emphasizes the efficiency of markets and market equilibrium, to which most of the economists listed in this book subscribe, does not have a great deal of theoretical or empirical support. Its continued popularity within the economics profession may be, in part, due to its ability to provide "insights into many economic phenomena," but the possibility that "belief in that paradigm, and the policy prescriptions, has served certain interests" must also be considered (Stiglitz, 2001).

Yet the dissent of even these two critics, whose analysis, in many respects, accord with that presented in this book, has some important limits. Krugman and Stiglitz are simultaneously very critical of much of the work in economics and supportive of the quest for scientific rigor that we have identified in Chapter 2 as a hallmark of the post-1970s discipline. Stiglitz has claimed that his work stemmed from a belief that "the most effective way of attacking the paradigm was to keep within the standard frameworks as much as possible" (Stiglitz, 2001, p. 519). He argued that it was not the traditional tools of economics that were to blame for the direction of economics after 1980, but the uses to which these tools were put. In fact, used correctly, the traditional tools of maximized modeling actually explain the crisis fairly well: "The disaster that grew from these flawed financial incentives can be, to us economists, somewhat comforting: our models predicted that there would be excessive risk taking and shortsighted behavior... economic theory was vindicated" (Stiglitz, 2010b, pp. 150, 153). Perhaps not coincidentally, the traditional models that Stiglitz argued explain the economic crisis were his own models of asymmetric information, in which one party in a transaction has more knowledge about the product being sold than the other (Stiglitz, 2003). This interpretation of the crisis focuses on the fact that people were purchasing complicated financial investments that they did not fully understand and could not properly value.

Krugman has declared himself "basically a maximization-and-equilibrium kind of guy. Indeed, I am quite fanatical about defending the relevance of standard economic models in many situations." For Krugman, an economist like John Kenneth Galbraith, who did not use these techniques, "looks to most serious economists like an intellectual dilettante who lacks the patience for hard thinking" (Krugman, 1996b). Krugman's academic work is in the tradition of Samuelson's Keynesianism, which he admits is "intellectually unstable," because it combines the assumptions of "rational individuals and rapidly clearing markets" in its microeconomics and "frictions and ad hoc behavioral assumptions" in macro (Krugman, 2010). Krugman argues that despite the inconsistency that this version of Keynesianism requires of its adherents, it is the correct theoretical framework for analyzing macro phenomena, including the 2008 economic crisis: "Basic sensible macro—what we learned from Keynes and Hicks—has actually held up very well in the crisis." A fundamental rethinking of how the discipline is practiced is not necessary. Rather, the problem with economics has been that too many economists rejected the sensible approach (Krugman, 2012b). Although both Stiglitz and Krugman think that there is a great deal wrong with modern economics, it is not the fault of the mainstream theory itself, rather the direction that the technique has been taken:

Why, then, do people like Stiglitz or myself so often seem to be in the position of defending economic orthodoxy? Because when you enter the real world of policy debates, you find out that the great majority of those who attack standard economic prescriptions may imagine that they have transcended textbook economics, but, in fact, have simply failed to understand it. (Krugman, 1996a)

History of economic thought scholar Philip Mirowski character-izes the Stiglitz-Krugman position on the state of the discipline as: economics has made some unfortunate mistakes, but we've sobered up and we are working hard to rectify them. However, Mirowski argues that this is an overestimation of the extent to which mainstream theory of the Stiglitz-Krugman variety can explain the crisis. To illustrate this, we can draw on one example each from Stiglitz and Krugman.

Stiglitz argued that the financial crisis can be explained by one of his papers (Grossman & Stiglitz, 1980), which analyzes how the problem of information acquisition can cause markets to fail. According to Mirowski, Stiglitz's model frames the problem as people being unwilling to pay for information when there is risk. Yet the financial crisis was characterized by people who were willing to pay receiving falsely optimistic information because of the profit-maximizing activities of the credit agencies (Mirowski, 2013, p. 273). Stiglitz's analysis, which rests on people's lack of information about asset values, is an inadequate explanation of the financial crisis and an even more incomplete explanation of the ensuing economic crisis.

Mirowski also argues that Stiglitz conflates welfare loss with system breakdown and crisis. Stiglitz's work highlights the fact that individual markets can function poorly or even break down in situations where information asymmetry exists. Even if information problems were a complete explanation of the financial crisis, although we have just suggested this is not the case, there is still a considerable jump from a failure of one market, even the financial market, to a full-blown economic crisis (Mirowski, 2013, p. 274). After all, the S&L and dot. com financial busts failed to spark entire system failure of the kind experienced in 2008. What Stiglitz's information theory leaves out is that workers were not in a position to demand higher wages. This permitted the low interest-rate policies that reduced unemployment and increased indebtedness. In his review of Stiglitz's *The Roaring Nineties*, Robert Pollin connects the dots, arguing that when people's wealth increases, as it did when stock markets and housing values hit record highs, people will increase their consumption. Pollin estimated that between 1995 and 1999, the increases of wealth resulted in consumption increases "injecting between $275–$460 billion, or roughly 2–4 percent more spending into the economy" (Pollin, 2004). An economy built on debt-fueled consumption was both possible and necessary because of the limited income gains of workers after 1980, but this more complete explanation is hidden, if one focuses on models of information asymmetry.

The limits of Krugman's analysis can be highlighted by recalling our discussion of Hyman Minsky, who argued that finance will create an inevitable source of instability in an economy. Although Krugman has some sympathy for Minsky's work, he criticized Minsky for rejecting the micro theory that Krugman argues is part of good, although inconsistent, macroeconomics. Krugman especially objects to Minsky's rejection of the marginal productivity theory of distribution (Krugman, 2009f, 2014), which states that "factors of production," like workers, get paid the value of what they produce in a competitive market. Even fellow dissenter Stiglitz argued that it is an ideologically useful but theoretically and empirically bankrupt means to explain income distribution in capitalist society (Stiglitz, 2011). This theory implies that as the productivity of workers increases, their wages should increase at the same rate. However, as we pointed out in Chapter 3, although this did happen in the decades prior to 1980, wage gains have lagged behind productivity in the post-1980 years. The problem with marginal productivity theory is that workers' income does not only rely on their productivity, but also on their ability to capture the gains from that productivity, which depends on their power in the labor market. Marginal productivity theory does not, in fact, explain worker incomes in the post-1980 economy, due to labor market policies that have turned against workers, a fact that Krugman acknowledges in some of his *New York Times* articles. Yet he still cannot reject marginal productivity theory, since it forms such a common linchpin of his standard economic theory (Mirowski, 2013, p. 292). This is important because it is precisely those labor market policies, and the fact that labor income lagged behind productivity, which crucially contributed to the large inequality that characterizes the US economy and was an important factor in the build-up of debt.

Despite these misgivings, Krugman attempted to incorporate some Minsky, at least in name (a Fisher-Minsky-Koo approach), into the usual Keynesian model. Krugman's "Minsky moment" occurs when there is reconsideration in society about how much debt is safe, forcing indebted households to pay off their debts. In order to pay off debts, households will cut back their spending, creating a recession that even a very expansionary zero-interest-rate monetary policy may not solve. Expansionary, deficit-inducing, fiscal policy, on the other hand, is effective in ending the recession by compensating for the temporary decrease in spending (Eggertsson & Krugman, 2012). According to Mirowski, despite the title, Krugman's model fails to incorporate the most important of Minsky's insights. Minsky's primary focus was to show how finance creates a systematic source of instability (Mirowski, 2013, p. 294). Krugman's analysis does not do this. There is no source of inherent instability built into the working of Krugman's economic system. Rather, it comes from a sudden change in how much debt is acceptable. How that debt came to be also remains an unexplored issue for Krugman.

The reason that the academic work of both Krugman and Stiglitz ignores crucial components of both the economic crisis, in particular, and the problematic economic trends in the post-1980 economy, in general, is that the structural features of a capitalist economy are absent from their analysis. Specifically, the power wielded by firms due to the importance of a policy environment that maintains their profitability is not included. For Stiglitz, information asymmetry is inherent in certain industries. It is either present or not. But as we saw in the credit market, who has the most influence over information is rooted in the same power relations that have determined the policy outcomes characteristic of neoliberal capitalism. Naturalizing asymmetric information makes it possible to ignore the capitalist character of the crisis. Similarly, Krugman's insistence on relevance of the marginal productivity theory removes the issue of power relationships in the labor market. In addition, his sanitized version of a "Minsky moment" cleanses the term of its implications for capitalism's dynamics, which suggest that crisis is an inherent part of the workings of the economic system. In Chapter 2, we discussed the controversy about the extent to which scientific pretension, the use of mathematical modeling and statistical empiricism, aided the rise of neoliberal economics. Stiglitz and Krugman are both economists committed to this type of analytical rigor and their academic work leads to conclusions about market failure necessitating government intervention, so there is nothing inevitable connecting scientific pretension and neoliberal ideas. Yet their theories are also limited because of their failure to tether those models to structural features of a capitalist economy.

The point here is not to argue that Krugman and Stiglitz's economic policy prescriptions are incorrect. The vast majority of them are actually very reasonable. Rather, the point is that Krugman and Stiglitz suffer from the weakness of which Krugman accused Friedman. Recall that Krugman argued that there were two Friedmans, the careful economist of adaptive expectations and the irresponsible free market policy advocate. We have argued that this dichotomy is, in fact, a mirage, and that Friedman's academic work contains the same pro-business biases as his policy stances. Krugman and Stiglitz, however, do suffer from this dichotomy. Their progressive policy stances cannot be justified by their academic work.

Even if the policy advice of inside-the-mainstream dissenters like Krugman and Stiglitz does present some possible answers, their preferred policies have not been enacted during this period. This is a bit more of an issue for Stiglitz because, as part of Clinton's economic advisory team, he was in a position to actually influence events. It may be true, as Stiglitz suggests, that he was simply overruled by the Greenspan-Rubin-Summers trio. However, Pollin points out that the 1996 Economic Report of the President, written under Stiglitz's supervision, generally approved of lowering regulatory standards, including the electric power industry that created the Enron scandal that devastated California in 2002 (Pollin, 2004). While one could debate the extent to which they are dissenters from the economic mainstream, what is absolutely true is that the kinds of policies that Stiglitz and Krugman publically advocated were largely ignored, leaving them increasingly frustrated with the direction of economic policy.

Conclusion

Rather than the more egalitarian, regulatory, high-employment Krugman-Stiglitz prescriptions, the post-1980s US economy has been characterized by policy that has created inequality, deregulation and higher unemployment in the service of combating inflation. These policies, not coincidentally, tilted the economic policy landscape toward the profits of firms and away from the rest of the population. In contrast to Krugman and Stiglitz, who looked on the economic policy landscape with increasing anger and dismay, the other economists featured in these pages must have experienced a sense of triumph at the growing influence of their ideas.

For much of Friedman's young career, he must have felt like a voice crying out in the wilderness. In an era wedded to Keynesian macro policy and an acceptance of government intervention, Friedman was calling for a withdrawal of the state. By the time of his death in 2006, he could look on the transformation of economic policy with no small satisfaction. In the world of macroeconomics, his theories of adaptive expectations, NAIRU and monetary rule unraveled the Keynesian consensus that governments and central banks should follow full-employment macro-stabilization policy. Further, his macro theory suggested that the economy would perform at its low-inflation, high-employment best when labor markets were at their most price flexible, by which he meant that unions were weak, unemployment benefits were low and workers' wage gains were modest. His micro-economic policy work was less original but no less influential. His insistence that competition in the free market would deliver the best products for the consumer and the best conditions for the worker, while government intervention would result in higher prices, fewer goods and more unemployment, became established wisdom and actual policy. While evidence for Friedman's contention that more government leads to a worse economy is falsified by history, the distributional consequences of his policies are clear-cut. Reducing the power of workers in the labor market, privatization and deregulation all improve the profitability of business.

The rational choice approach to politics, a cornerstone of public choice, ran with Friedman's ideas about the harm done by government. The innovation of public choice was to apply to politics the standard economic tools that were applied to markets. Its most famous pioneers argued that following this method permits a more rigorous, scientific examination of outcomes of the state. However, public choice has been accused of containing an anti-government bias. Certainly, the scholars investigated in this book (Buchanan, Stigler, Peltzman, Becker and

Tullock) view government intervention in the economy as damaging. Unsurprisingly, their positive approaches yield results that all but uniformly find evidence of government failure. If government failure creates rent seeking and capture, the policy solution is straightforward: less government.

The ideas of capture and rent seeking may actually describe a small subsection of government activity, in which firms use legislation to create an advantage over their competitors, but the concepts are more problematic when addressing the vast majority of regulations. Public choice predicts that firms should favor regulation, while consumers should be opposed. Yet, in reality, companies have spent considerable sums lobbying for either outright deregulation or gutting regulatory institutions' ability to fulfill their mandate, mostly against the wishes of the public. While public choice authors portray consumer support of regulation as the rational ignorance of voters misled by information bias created by interest groups that benefit from regulation, it is possible that the public actually understands the costs and benefits. People are often better protected with regulation than without, while the activity of firms is often constrained. Although some of the pioneers of public choice explicitly claim that it is a superior explanation for government activity than more radical, class-based explanations, in fact a class-based explanation offers a better account. It is the structural power of business in a capitalist economy rather than the different costs and benefits of interest groups that can best explain government outcomes like the deregulatory trend since the 1970s. As was the case with Friedman's deregulatory ideas, rational choice in politics may not be accurate but it is attractive, at least to a business community desperate to reduce what it considered to be the burden of an encroaching state in the 1970s. It is surely no coincidence that much of the funding for the centers of public choice comes from the corporate world.

Real Business Cycle theory did for Friedman's macroeconomic ideas what public choice did in micro. Although, in contrast to public choice, RBC theory took Friedman's ideas to such an extreme that they ended up actually dismissing his idea of adaptive expectations. The hallmarks of RBC theory are that prices and wages adjust quickly, information is quickly incorporated into decisions, and markets are in equilibrium. With these starting assumptions, RBC authors assert that economic fluctuations are caused by random productivity shocks to which employees optimally respond by altering the amount that they will work. This theory has some very important and controversial implications for macroeconomic policy. It implies that unemployment is not caused by tight monetary policy, which helps justify using high interest rates to control inflation. It also has a curious interpretation of unemployment, which is not seen as a case of firms shedding their labor force during economic downturns, but rather as voluntary quits in response to declining real wages caused by adverse productivity shocks. RBC theory suggests that, while avoiding negative productivity shocks, if possible, is desirable government policy, counter-cyclical policy like low interest rates and social insurance to ease the income shock of unemployment are to be avoided. Finally, as RBC theory moved away from narrow definitions of productivity shocks, which were not empirically justifiable, and turned to a broader definition, its list of productivity-damaging policies included protective regulation, like environmental or worker safety, and corporate taxation.

RBC theorists make a number of highly counter-intuitive claims (for example, that workers quit more frequently during recessions) which fail to hold up to even casual observation, but its policy conclusions definitely favor the interests of business. Corporate America was very concerned that US labor was overpaid and underproductive in the 1970s. An economic theory that claimed full employment policy was ineffective, that high interest-rate policies would not create unemployment, and that unemployment was in some ways optimal, was ideologically very useful for business. It created an intellectual justification for high interest-rate policy that did, despite RBC claims, create unemployment which dramatically reduced workers' power in the labor market during the 1980s and 1990s. It also implied that policies like social insurance for the unemployed, regulations on worker safety and corporate taxation either create or lengthen productivity shocks. As was the case with public choice, it is no coincidence that RBC-style theory rose to prominence in the 1980s when macroeconomic policy turned away from a focus on full employment, and labor market policy reduced its protection for unemployed workers. Both of these policies were crucial in creating a labor force that worked harder for stagnant wages.

The authors who rose to prominence in financial economics did so by inventing a formula that created large profits for firms in the finance industry and then shielded those profits from regulatory oversight. The Black-Merton-Scholes formula for option pricing opened up a largely undiscovered market in new financial instruments. As the market for options and derivatives expanded exponentially, the share of total profits in the US going to the financial industry increased. However, it also changed the incentive structure in the housing mortgage market. When banks earn money on the sale price of the bundle of mortgages in a derivative rather than by the homeowners paying back the mortgage, the incentive for the bank is to sign as many families up for mortgages as possible since that creates more derivatives for it to sell. The predictable result of this incentive structure is that increasingly large loans were given to increasingly marginal lenders. The murky complexity of the derivative market created growing concern among some in policy circles, like Brooksley Born, that asset bubbles were forming and regulation was needed. However, in the battle to get out from the regulatory restrictions of the Glass-Steagall Act and avoid any alternative oversight, the financial industry and its anti-intervention defenders could lean on the intellectual justification of Eugene Fama's EMH, which suggested that asset prices were generally priced accurately, and bubbles were therefore unlikely. The post-1980 economic policy environment was very lucrative for the financial industry. Yet these profits contributed to increasing indebtedness of homeowners and the 2008 economic crisis. The finance economists examined in the pages of this book were not directly responsible for the growth of the mortgage derivatives market that increased the debt of Americans, nor were they responsible for the deregulatory zeal that permitted the financial industry a free hand with its speculative adventuring. However, the authors did provide the intellectual ammunition for the expansion of the derivatives market and the academic shield from regulation.

Greenspan and Summers were among those high-placed economists who were directly responsible for the deregulatory zeal. After the 2008 crisis, both Summers and Greenspan were on the receiving end of a justifiable upbraiding for their contribution to the monetary policy and deregulation that fostered an increase in consumer debt, the mortgage housing bubble and the financial collapse. However, even had there not been a crisis, the economy fostered by Greenspan and Summers created a hostile environment for most Americans while being generous to firms. Greenspan's continuation of Paul Volcker's war against inflation increased unemployment, putting downward pressure on wages and improving profits during the early 1990s. His policy shift to a lower interest-rate environment only occurred once Greenspan was confident that workers were so traumatized that low unemployment would not create wage gains. The low interest-rate policy was important because growing household debt helped firms maintain their sales despite limited wage gains. Summers and Greenspan's deregulatory policy advocacy was part of a broader move to remove government obstacles to profitability in the post-1980 economic transformation. In the financial sector, this not only created instability but also increasing household debt, that transferred income from families to creditor firms. The supposed good times of the 1990s and early 2000s created by Greenspan and Summers were not only unstable, they were also a boom for only a very small minority of the population.

Some were anticipating that the 2008 crisis would do to neoliberal economics what the 1970s did to Keynesianism. Surely, this line of thought went, a crisis largely put down to lax regulation in subservience of corporate profits leading to widespread malfeasance and economic collapse would cause a profound rethinking of the economics discipline. While it is still not completely out of the realm of possibility, this outcome now seems extremely unlikely. If we return to the three factors that we identified in the rise of neoliberal economics after the 1970s (scientific pretension, economic conditions, and institutional support), it is only the change in economic conditions that might provide any cause for optimism among those looking for a transformation in economics. But even here, we have argued that it is not only the march of major economic events that helps to determine which theories rise to prominence and which are discarded. Who benefits from those economic events is also crucially important. The collapse of the Keynesian consensus and the rise of neoliberal policy did not occur only because Keynesian analysis could not explain the inflation unemployment trade-off. It happened because Keynesian analysis favored government intervention, that was seen as harming the profitability of business. The solutions offered by neoliberal economists were not only opposed to the Keynesian post-war doctrine; their particular form of opposition involved policies that were beneficial to the corporate world. The 2008 crisis did not lead to a comparable crisis for the business community, which weathered the storm remarkably well. As a result, although the march of events may yet create problems for neoliberal economics, the entrenched interests that benefit from those policy ideas remain the same. There are plenty of economic theories being put forward that run counter to the neoliberal ideas in this book, from the more moderate opinions of Krugman and Stiglitz to the more radical theories of prominent scholars such as Brenner, Duménil and Levy, Minsky, Pollin and Shaikh, yet they will only ever see the light of day as economic policy if the structural political influence currently wielded by the business class can be countered.

Bibliography

Abelson, D., 2009. *Do Think Tanks Matter? 2nd edn.* Montreal: McGill-Queens University Press.

AEI (American Enterprise Institute), 2014. *Eugene F. Fama to receive 2014 Irving Kristol Award.* [Online] Available at: https://www.aei.org/press/american-enterprise-institutes-irving-kristol-award-presented-to-nobel-winner-eugene-f-fama/ [Accessed 25 May 2016].

Akerlof, G. & Shiller, R., 2015. *Phishing for Phools.* Princeton, NJ: Princeton University Press.

Allegretto, S., 2011. *The State of Working America's Wealth 2011.* Washington, DC: EPI Briefing Paper #292.

Allen, S., 2013. *Nobel Awarded to Fama and Hansen.* [Online] Available at: http://www.uchicago.edu/features/nobel_awarded_to_fama_and_hansen/ [Accessed 24 May 2016].

Altonji, J., 1986. Intertemporal substitution in labor supply: evidence from micro data. *Journal of Political Economy*, 94, pp. S176–S215.

Andrews, E., 2008. Greenspan concedes error on regulation. *New York Times*, 23 October, p. B1.

Appelbaum, B., 2013. Economists clash on theory, but will still share the Nobel. *New York Times*, 15 October, p. A1.

Appelbaum, B., 2014. A Fed policy maker, changing his mind, urges more stimulus. *New York Times*, 27 January, p. B1.

Arcand, J.-L., Berkes, E. & Panizza, U., 2012. *Too Much Finance?*, s.l.: International Monetary Fund.

Arjona, R., Ladaique, M. & Pearson, M., 2002. *Social Protection and Growth, OECD Economic Studies, No. 35.*, s.l.: OECD.

Aron-Dine, A. & Shapiro, I., 2007. *Share of National Income Going To Wages and Salaries at Record Low in 2006,* Washington, DC: Center on Budget and Policy Priorities.

Atkinson, G., 1983. Political economy: public choice or collective action? *Journal of Economic Issues*, 17(4), pp. 1057–65.

Avery, R. et al., 2010. *The 2008 HMDA Data: The Mortgage Market during a Turbulent Year,* s.l.: Federal Reserve Bulletin.

Backhouse, R., 2005. The rise of free market economics: economists and the role of the state since 1970. *History of Political Economy*, 37(1), pp. 355–92.

Baragar, F. & Chernomas, R., 2012. Profits from production and profits from exchange: financialization, household debt and profitability in 21st century capitalism. *Science & Society*, 76.

Barry, N., 1984. Unanimity, agreement, and liberalism: a critique of James Buchanan's social philosophy. *Political Theory*, 12(4), pp. 579–96.

Barth, J., Brumbaugh, R. & Wilcox., J., 2000. Policy watch: the repeal of Glass-Steagall and the advent of broad banking. *Journal of Economic Perspectives*, 14(2), pp. 191–204.

Bartley, M., Ferrie, J. & Montgomery, S., 2006. Health and labour market disadvantage: unemployment, non-employment, and job insecurity. In: M. Marmot & R. Wilkinson, eds. *Social Determinants of Health*. Oxford: Oxford University Press.

Basen, I., 2011. Economics has met the enemy, and it is economics. *Globe and Mail*, 15 October.

Becker, G., 1958. Competition and democracy. *Journal of Law and Economics*, 1, pp. 105–9.

Becker, G., 1968. Crime and punishment: an economic approach. *Journal of Political Economy*, 76, pp. 169–217.

Becker, G., 1983. A theory of competition among pressure groups for political influence. *Quarterly Journal of Economics*, 98(3), pp. 371–99.

Becker, G., 1985. Public policies, pressure groups, and dead weight costs. *Journal of Public Economics*, 28, pp. 329–47.

Becker, G., 1992. *Gary S. Becker – Biographical*. [Online] Available at: http://www.nobelprize.org/nobel_prizes/economic-sciences/laureates/1992/becker-bio.html [Accessed 16 November 16 2015].

Becker, G., 1994. To root out corruption, boot out big government. *Businessweek*, 31 January, p. 18.

Becker, G., 2004. A 19-year dialogue on the power of incentives. *Business Week*, 12 July.

Becker, G., 2009. Interview by Karen Ilse Horn. In: I. Horne, ed. *Roads to Wisdom: Conversations with Ten Nobel Laureates in Economics*. Cheltenham, UK: Edward Elgar, pp. 132–52.

Berk, G., 1991. Corporate liberalism reconsidered: a review essay. *Journal of Policy History*, 3, pp. 70–84.

Bernanke, B. & Mishkin, F., 1997. Targeting: a new framework for monetary policy? *Journal of Economic Perspectives*, 11(2), pp. 97–116.

Bernard, V. & Thomas, J., 1990. Evidence that stock prices do not fully reflect the implications of current earnings for future earnings. *Journal of Accounting and Economics*, 13, pp. 305–40.

Bernstein, M., 2001. *A Perilous Progress: Economists and Public Purpose in Twentieth-Century America*. Princeton, NJ: Princeton University Press.

Bilginsoy, C., 2015. *A History of Financial Crises: Dreams and Follies of Expectations*. New York: Routledge.

Bilgrami, A., 2008. *Free Inquiry and the Evolution of the Research University*. New York, s.n.

Biography, n.d. *Alan Greenspan Biography*, s.l.: A&E Television Networks.

Black, B., 2013. *How Elite Economic Hucksters Drive America's Biggest Fraud Epidemics*. [Online] Available at: http://www.nakedcapitalism.

com/2013/06/bill-black-how-elite-economic-hucksters-drive-americas-biggest-fraud-epidemics.html [Accessed 18 July 2016].

Black, F. & Scholes, M., 1972. The valuation of option contracts and a test of market efficiency. *The Journal of Finance*, 27(2), pp. 399–417.

Black, F. & Scholes, M., 1973. The pricing of options and corporate liabilities. *Journal of Political Economy*, 81(3), pp. 637–54.

Blaug, M., 1997. *Economic Theory in Retrospect*, 5th edn. Cambridge: Cambridge University Press.

Blinder, A. & Krueger, A., 2004. What does the public know about economic policy and how does it know it? *Brookings Papers on Economic Activity*, 1, pp. 327–97.

Blyth, M., 2002. *Great Transformations: Economic Ideas and Institutional Change in the Twentieth Century*. Cambridge, UK: Cambridge University Press.

Bohme, S., Zorabedian, J. & Egilman, D., 2005. Maximizing profit and endangering health: Corporate strategies to avoid litigation and regulation. *International Journal of Occupational and Environmental Health*, 11(4).

Bowles, S., David, G. & Weisskopf, T., 1986. Power and profits: the social structure of accumulation and the profitability of the postwar U.S. economy. *Review of Radical Political Economy*, 18(1&2), pp. 132–67.

Bradley, R., 2005. Lawrence of Absurdia. *Boston Magazine*, March.

Brennan, G. & Hamlin, A., 1998. Expressive voting and electoral equilibrium. *Public Choice*, 95(1), pp. 149–75.

Brennan, G. & Lomasky, L., 1994. *Democracy and Decision: The Pure Theory of Electoral Preferences*. Cambridge: Cambridge University Press.

Brenner, R., 2006. *The Economics of Global Turbulence : The Advanced Capitalist Economies from Long Boom to Long Downturn, 1945–2005*. New York: Verso.

Buchanan, J., 1978. From private preferences to public philosophy: the development of public choice. In: Institute of Economic Affairs, ed. *The Economics of Politics*. West Sussex: Institute of Economic Affairs, pp. 1–20.

Buchanan, J., 1980. Rent seeking and profit seeking. In: J. Buchanan, R. Tollison & G. Tullock, eds. *Toward a Theory of the Rent Seeking Society*. College Station: Texas A & M University Press, pp. 3–15.

Buchanan, J., 1992. From the inside looking out. In: M. Szenberg, ed. *Eminent Economists: Their Life Philosophies*. Cambridge, UK: Cambridge University Press, p. 98–106.

Buchanan, J., 1999a. Better than plowing. In: G. Brennan, H. Kliemt & R. Tollison, eds. *The Logical Foundations of Constitutional Liberty* (The Collected Works of James M. Buchanan, Volume I). Indianapolis, IN: Liberty Fund.

Buchanan, J., 1999b. Politics without romance: A sketch of positive public choice theory and its normative implications. In: *The Logical Foundations of Constitutional Liberty* (The Collected Works of James Buchanan, Volume 1). Indianapolis, IN: Liberty Fund, pp. 45–59.

Buchanan, J., 1999c. Democracy in deficit: The political legacy of Lord Keynes [1977]. In: *The Collected Works of James M. Buchanan*. Indianapolis, IN: Liberty Fund.

Buchanan, J., 2001. *A Conversation with James Buchanan*. [Online] Available at: http://archive.fcpp.org/posts/a-conversation-with-james-buchanan [Accessed 14 March 2016].

Buchanan, J. & Tullock, G., 1999 [1962]. *The Calculus of Consent: Logical Foundations of Constitutional Democracy*. Indianapolis, IN: Liberty Fund.

Buiter, W., 2009. *The Unfortunate Uselessness of Most "State of the Art" Academic Monetary Economics*, http://blogs.ft.com/maverecon/2009/03/the-unfortunate-uselessness-of-most-state-of-the-art-academic-monetary-economics/#axzz1yBJ97Cll: Willem Buiter's Maverecon Blog.

Bureau of Economic Analysis, 2012. *National Income and Product Accounts Tables: Percent Change From Preceding Period in Real Gross Domestic Product*. [Online] Available at: http://www.bea.gov/national/index.htm [Accessed 11 July 2012].

Campbell, J., 2014. Empirical asset pricing: Eugene Fama, Lars Peter Hansen, and Robert Shiller. *Scandanavian Journal of Economics*, 3(116), pp. 593–634.

Caprio , G., 2003. *Episodes of Systemic and Borderline Financial Crises*, s.l.: World Bank.

Carpenter, D. & Moss, D., 2014. Introduction. In: D. Carpenter & D. Moss, eds. *Preventing Regulatory Capture*. New York: Cambridge University Press, pp. 1–22.

Carrick-Hagenbarth, J. & Epstein, G., 2012. Dangerous interconnectedness: economists' conflicts of interest, ideology and financial crisis. *Cambridge Journal of Economics*, 36(1), pp. 43–63.

Cassidy, J., 2010a. Interview with Eugene Fama. *The New Yorker*, 13 January.

Cassidy, J., 2010b. What good is Wall Street. *The New Yorker*, 29 November.

Cassidy, J., 2010c. Interview with Richard Posner. *The New Yorker*, 13 January.

Cato Institute, 2009. *With all due respect Mr. President, that is not true*. [Online] Available at: http://object.cato.org/sites/cato.org/files/pubs/pdf/cato_stimulus.pdf [Accessed 2009 May 12 2016].

Cato Institute, 2016. *Edward C. Prescott*. [Online] Available at: http://www.cato.org/people/prescott.html [Accessed 12 May 2016].

CBS News, 2007. *McCain Wants Greenspan, Dead Or Alive*. [Online] Available at: http://www.cbsnews.com/news/mccain-wants-greenspan-dead-or-alive/ [Accessed 30 July 2016].

CCC (Copenhagen Consensus Center), 2016. *Finn Kydland*. [Online] Available at: http://www.copenhagenconsensus.com/expert/finn-kydland [Accessed 12 May 2016].

Center for Responsive Politics, 2016a. *Annual Lobbying by Citigroup Inc 1998-2016*. [Online] Available at: http://www.opensecrets.org/orgs/lobby.php?id=D000000071 [Accessed 27 July 2016].

Center for Responsive Politics, 2016b. *Citigroup Inc: Total Contributions by Party of Recipient.* [Online] Available at: http://www.opensecrets.org/orgs/totals.php?id=D000000071&cycle=2012 [Accessed 27 July 2016].

Center for Study of Public Choice, 2014. *Contributors.* [Online] Available at: https://www.gmu.edu/centers/publicchoice/contributors2.html [Accessed 28 February 2016].

Chandra, S., 2009. Paul Samuelson, Nobel-winning economist, dies at 94. *Bloomberg Newsweek*, 13 December.

Clark, A. & Treanor, J., 2008. Greenspan – I was wrong about the economy. Sort of. *Guardian*, 12 October.

Clement, D., 2007. *Interview with Eugene Fama.* [Online] Available at: https://www.minneapolisfed.org/publications/the-region/interview-with-eugene-fama [Accessed 23 May 2016].

Cohen, N., 2003. *Gambling with Our Future.* [Online] Available at: http://www.newstatesman.com/200301130012 [Accessed 15 March 2007].

Cohen, P., 2009. Ivory tower unswayed by crashing economy. *New York Times*, 5 March, p. C1.

Concerned Students of Economics, 2011. An open letter To Greg Mankiw, *Harvard Political Review*, 2 November. [Online] Available at: http://hpronline.org/harvard/an-open-letter-to-greg-mankiw/.

Congressional Budget Office, 2011. *Long Term Analysis of a Budget Proposal By Chairman Ryan.* Washington, DC: US Government Printing Office.

Consumer Reports, 2002. Deregulated. *Consumer Reports*, July, pp. 30–35.

Conway, E., 2009. *Barack Obama accused of making "Depression" mistakes.* [Online] Available at: http://www.telegraph.co.uk/finance/economics/6147211/Barack-Obama-accused-of-making-Depression-mistakes.html [Accessed 18 March 2016].

Copeland, C. & Laband, D., 2002. Expressiveness and voting. *Public Choice*, 110: 351–63.

Cowen, T., 2011. *Cowen, Tyler. 2011. Thomas Sargent, Nobel Laureate. Marginal Revolution,.* [Online] Available at: http://marginalrevolution.com/marginalrevolution/2011/10/thomas-sargent-nobel-laureate.html [Accessed 11 May 2016].

Crotty, J., 2008. If financial market competition is intense, why are financial firm profits so high? Reflections on the current "golden age" of finance. *Competition & Change*, 12(2), pp. 167–83.

Crotty, J., 2009. Structural causes of the global financial crisis: a critical assessment of the "new financial architecture." *Cambridge Journal of Economics*, 33(4), pp. 563–80.

Crotty, J., 2013. The realism of assumptions does matter: why Keynes-Minsky theory must replace efficient market theory as the guide to financial regulation policy. In: G. Epstein & M. Wolfson, eds. *The Oxford Handbook of the Political Economy of Financial Crises.* New York: Oxford University Press, pp. 133–58.

Davis, B., 2004. In Washington, tiny think tank wields big stick on regulation. *Wall Street Journal*, 16 July.

Davis, D., 2007. *The Secret History of the War on Cancer.* New York: Basic Books.

De Vroey, M., 2001. Friedman and Lucas on the Phillips Curve: from disequilibrium to an equilibrium approach. *Eastern Economic Journal*, 27(2), pp. 127–48.

DeBondt, W. & Thaler, R., 1985. Does the stock market overreact? *Journal of Finance*, 40, pp. 793–807.

DeGregori, T., 1974. Caveat emptor: a critique of the emerging paradigm of public choice. *Administration and Society*, 6.

DeNavas-Walt, C., Proctor, B. & Smith, J., 2008. *U.S. Census Bureau Current Population Reports, P60-235, Income, Poverty, and Health Insurance Coverage in the United States: 2007*, Washington, DC: US Government Printing Office.

Devereaux, P. et al., 2002. Comparison of mortality between private for-profit and private not-for-profit hemodialysis centers: a systematic review and meta-analysis. *Journal of the American Medical Association*, 288(19).

Dubois, L., 2006. Food, nutrition and population health: from scarcity to social inequalities. In: J. Heymann, J. Hertzman, M. Barer & R. Evans, eds. *Healthier Societies: From Analysis to Action.* Oxford: Oxford University Press.

Dukes, G., Braithwaite, J. & Moloney, J., 2014. *Pharmaceuticals Corporate Crime and Pubich Health.* Cheltenham, UK: Edward Elgar.

Duménil, G. & Lévy, D., 2004. *Capital Resurgent.* Cambridge, MA: Harvard University Press.

G. Duménil & D. Lévy (2005), Costs and benefits of neoliberalism: a class analysis. In: G. Epstein, ed., *Financialization and the World Economy.* Aldershot, UK: Edward Elgar.

Duménil, G. & Lévy, D., 2011. *The Crisis of Neoliberalism.* Cambridge, MA: Harvard University Press.

Duménil, G. & Lévy, D., 2012. The crisis of the early 21st century. In: *The Great Recession and the Contradictions of Contemporary Capitalism.* Aldershot, UK: Edward Elgar.

Eilperin, J., 2009. Danish think tank calls to focus on geoengineering solutions to global warming. *Washington Post*, 4 September.

Eggertsson, G. & Krugman, P., 2012. Debt, deleveraging, and the liquidity trap: A Fisher-Minsky-Koo approach. *The Quarterly Journal of Economics*, 127(3), pp. 1469–513.

Etzioni, A., 1993. The U.S. Sentencing Commission on Corporate Crime: A critique. *Annals of the American Academy of Political and Social Science*, 525, pp. 147–56.

Evans, G. & Honkapohja, S., 1999. Learning dynamics. In: J. Taylor & M. Woodford, eds. *Handbook of Macroeconomics.* Amsterdam: New Holland, pp. 449–542.

Faber, D. & Krieg, E., 2002. Unequal exposure to ecological hazards: environmental injustices in the Commonwealth of Massachusetts. *Environmental Health Perspectives*, 110(2).

Fama, E., 1965. Random walks in stock market prices. *Financial Analysts Journal*, 21, pp. 55–9.

Fama, E., 1970. Efficient capital markets: a review of theory and empirical work. *Journal of Finance*, 25, pp. 383–417.

Fama, E., 1998. Market efficiency, long-term returns, and behavioral finance. *Journal of Financial Economics*, 49(3), pp. 283–306.

Fama, E., 2013. *Eugene F. Fama – biographical.* [Online] Available at: http://www.nobelprize.org/nobel_prizes/economic-sciences/laureates/2013/fama-bio.html [Accessed 23 May 2016].

Feiwel, G., 1975. Kalecki and Keynes. *De Economist*, 123(2), pp. 164–97.

Ferguson, C., 2010. Larry Summers and the subversion of economics. *Chronicle of Higher Education*, 3 October.

Fingleton, E., 2013. Alan Greenspan's epic incompetence: another shoe drops. *Forbes*, 6 June.

Fischer, S., 1996. Robert Lucas's Nobel Memorial Prize. *Scandanavian Journal of Economics*, 98, pp. 11–31.

Fisher, D., 2012. *Eugene Fama on inflation, the crisis, and why you can't beat the market after fees.* [Online] Available at: http://www.forbes.com/sites/danielfisher/2012/12/02/eugene-fama-on-inflation-the-crisis-and-why-you-cant-beat-the-market-after-fees/#3508714715d4 [Accessed 5 June 2016].

Formaini, R., 2002. Milton Friedman—economist as public intellectual. *Economic Insights, Federal Reserve Bank of Dallas*, 7(2).

Fourcade, M., Ollion, E. & Algan, Y., 2015. The superiority of economics. *Journal of Economic Perspectives*, 29(1), p. 89–114.

Freeman, J., 2009. *A Modest Proposal: Bribe the Insurance Companies.* [Online] Available at: http://medicinesocialjustice.blogspot.com/2009/08/modest-proposal-bribe-insurance.html [Accessed 26 April 2013].

Freeman, R., 1999. It's better being an economist (but don't tell anyone). *Journal of Economic Perspectives*, 13(3), pp. 139–45.

Freeman, R., 2010. It's financialization! *International Labour Review*, 149(2), pp. 163–83.

Friedman, M., 1962. *Capitalism and Freedom.* Chicago, IL: University of Chicago Press.

Friedman, M., 1968. The role of monetary policy. *American Economic Review*, 58, pp. 1–17.

Friedman, M., 1976. Inflation and unemployment. *Nobel Memorial Lecture*, 13 December.

Friedman, M., 1984. Lessons from the 1979–82 Monetary Policy Experiment. *American Economic Review*, 74(2), pp. 397–400.

Friedman, M. & Friedman, R., 1990. *Free to Choose.* New York: Harcourt Brace Jovanovich.

Friedman, M. & Heller, W., 1969. *Monetary vs Fiscal Policy: A Dialogue*. New York: W.W. Norton & Company.

Friedman, M. & Schwartz, A., 1963. *A Monetary History of the United States: 1867–1960*. Princeton, NJ: Princeton University Press.

Fullbrook, E., 2005. Post-autistic economics. [Online] Available at: http://www.paecon.net/PAEarticles/Fullbrook1.htm [Accessed 22 September 2016].

Galbraith, J., 1971. *Economics, Peace and Laughter*. New York: New American Library.

Galbraith, J., 2001. *The Essential Galbraith*. New York: Houghton Mifflin Company.

GAO (General Accounting Office), 1994. *Financial Derivatives: Actions Needed to Protect the Financial System*. Washington, DC: United States General Accounting Office.

Garg, P. et al., 1999. Effect of the ownership of dialysis facilities on patients' survival and referral for transplantation. *New England Journal of Medicine*, 341(22).

Garrett, B., 2014. *Too Big to Jail: How Prosecutors Compromise with Corporations*. Cambridge, MA: Harvard University Press.

Getter, D., Jickling, M., Labonte, M. & Murphy, E., 2007. *Financial Crisis? The Liquidity Crunch of August 2007*, Washington DC: Congressional Research Service.

Ginsburg, T., 2002. Ways of criticizing public choice: the uses of empiricism and theory in legal scholarship. *University of Illinois Law Review*, pp. 1139–66.

Goldenberg, S., 2005. Why women are poor at science, by Harvard president. *Guardian*, 18 January.

Goodfriend, M., 2007. How the world achieved consensus on monetary policy. *Journal of Economic Perspectives*, 21(4), pp. 47–68.

Goodman, P., 2008. Taking a hard new look at the Greenspan legacy. *The New York Times*, 9 October, p. A1.

Gordon, D., 1971. Class and the economics of crime. *Review of Radical Political Economics*, 3(3), pp. 51–75.

Gordon, R., 1978. What can stabilisation policy achieve? *American Economic Review*, 68(2), pp. 335–41.

Gordon, R., 1979 [1976]. Recent developments in the theory of inflation and unemployment. In: P. Korliras & R. Thorn, eds. *Modern Macroeconomics: Major Contributions to Contemporary Thought*. New York: Harper & Row, pp. 259–84.

Gordon, R., 1997. The time varying NAIRU and its implications for economic policy. *Journal of Economic Perspectives*, 11(1), pp. 11–32.

Graham, D., 2013. How a small team of Democrats defeated Larry Summers—and Obama. *The Atlantic*, 15 September.

Green, D. & Shapiro, I., 1996. *Pathologies of Rational Choice Theory: A Critique of Applications in Political Science*. New Haven, CT: Yale University Press.

Greenspan, A., 1967. The assault on integrity. In: A. Rand, N. Branden, A. Greenspan & R. Hessen, eds. *Capitalism: The Unknown Ideal*. New York: Signet, pp. 118–21.

Greenspan, A., 1990. *Statement before the U.S. Congress, House of Representatives, Sub-committee on Domestic Monetary Policy of the Committee on Banking, Finance, and Urban Affairs. Hearing, 101 Congress 1st Session*, Washington, DC: US Government Printing Office.

Greenspan, A., 1997. *Testimony Before the Committee on the Budget, United States Senate*. [Online] Available at: www.federalreserve.gov/BOARDDOCS/Testimony/1997/19970121.htm [Accessed 12 March 2007].

Greenspan, A., 2004. *Remarks by Chairman Alan Greenspan at the American Bankers Annual Convention*, New York: Federal Reserve Board.

Greenspan, A., 2008. *The Age of Turbulence: Adventures in a New World*. New York: Penguin Books.

Greenstone, M. & Looney, A., 2011. The Great Recession may be over, but American families are working harding than ever. *Brookings Up Front*, 8 July.

Greenwald, B. & Stiglitz, J., 1986. Externalities in economies with imperfect information and incomplete markets. *Quarterly Journal of Economics*, 101(2), pp. 229–64.

Greenwood, R. & Scharfstein, D., 2013. The growth of finance. *Journal of Economic Perspectives*, 27(2), pp. 3–28.

Greider, W., 2001. Father Greenspan loves us all. *The Nation*, 1 January.

Grieder, W., 2005. The one-eyed chairman. *The Nation*, 1 September.

Grossman, S. & Stiglitz, J., 1980. On the impossibility of informationally efficient markets. *American Economic Review*, 70(3), pp. 393–408.

Hall, R., 1996. Robert Lucas, recipient of the 1995 Nobel Memorial Prize in Economics. *Scandanavian Journal of Economics*, 98, pp. 33–48.

Harrison, M., 2012. *Unapologetic After All These Tears: Eugene Fama Defends Investor Rationality and Market Efficiency*. [Online] Available at: https://annual.cfainstitute.org/2012/05/14/eugene-fama-defends-investor-rationality-and-market-efficiency/ [Accessed 10 June 2016].

Hartley, J., Hoover, K. & Salyer, K., 1997. The limits of business cycle research: assessing the real business cycle model. *Oxford Review of Economic Policy*, 13(3), pp. 34–54.

Harvey, J., 2012. *How Economists Contributed to the Financial Crisis*. [Online] Available at: http://www.forbes.com/sites/johntharvey/2012/02/06/economics-crisis/ [Accessed 10 January 2013].

Hausman, D. & McPherson, M., 1996. *Economic Analysis and Moral Philosophy*. Cambridge: Cambridge University Press.

Healy, B., 2009. Harvard ignored warnings about investments. *Boston Globe*, 28 November.

Hedges, S., 2002. *Iraq Hawks have Bush's Ear*. [Online] Available at: http://articles.chicagotribune.com/2002-08-18/news/0208180309_1_

defense-policy-board-saddam-hussein-saudi-arabia [Accessed 18 March 2016].

Heilbroner, R., 1999. *The Worldly Philosophers*. New York: Simon & Schuster.

Heilbroner, R. & Milberg, W., 1995. *The Crisis of Vision in Modern Economic Thought*. Cambridge: Cambridge University Press.

Henderson, D., 1997. Message from Stockholm: markets work. *Wall Street Journal*, 15 October.

Henwood, D., 2010. How to learn nothing from crisis. *Left Business Observer*, 25 February.

Hirsch, M., 2009. The Reeducation of Larry Summers. *Newsweek*, 20 February.

Hirsch, M., 2013. The comprehensive case against Larry Summers. *The Atlantic*, 13 September.

Hodgson, G., 2004. On the problem of formalism in economics. *Post Autistic Economics Review, 28*.

Honderich, K., 1996. Producers and parasites: the uses of rent seeking. *Review of Radical Political Economics*, 28(2), pp. 54–76.

Hoover Institution, 2012. *Which Economists Are Throwing Their Support Behind Mitt Romney?*. [Online] Available at: http://www.hoover.org/research/which-economists-are-throwing-their-support-behind-mitt-romney [Accessed 5 June 2016].

Hoover Institution, 2016. *Thomas J. Sargent*. [Online] Available at: http://www.hoover.org/profiles/thomas-j-sargent [Accessed 11 May 2016].

Hudson, I., 2002. Sabotage versus public choice: Sports as a case study for interest group theory. *Journal of Economic Issues*, 36(4), pp. 1079–96.

Hudson, I., 2009. From deregulation to crisis. In: W. Anthony and J. Guard, eds. *Bankruptcies and Bailouts*. Winnipeg, MB: Fernwood.

Huff, J., 2007. Industry influence on occupational and environmental public health. *International Journal of Occupational and Environmental Health*, 13(1).

Ip, G. & Steel, E., 2007. Greenspan book criticizes Bush and Republicans. *Wall Street Journal*, 15 September, p. A1.

Isaacson, E., 1993. Prescription for change. *San Francisco Bay Guardian*, 14 April.

Jackson, W., 1984. *Glass-Steagall Act: Investment Banking*, Washington, DC: Economics Division Congressional Research Service.

Jarrow, R., 1999. In honor of the Nobel laureates Robert C. Merton and Myron S. Scholes: a partial differential equation that changed the world. *Journal of Economic Perspectives*, 13(4), pp. 229–48.

Jaschik, S., 2005. What Larry Summers said. *Inside Higher Ed*, 18 February.

Jenkins, H., 2011. Chicago economics on trial. *Wall Street Journal*, 24 September.

Jenkins, J. & Eckert, C., 1989. The corporate elite, the new conservative policy network, and Reaganomics. *Critical Sociology*, 16, pp. 121–44.

Jenkins, J. & Eckert, C., 2000. The right turn in economic policy: business elites and the new conservative economics. *Sociological Forum*, 15(2), pp. 307–38.

Kahneman, D. & Rupe, M., 1998. Aspects of investor psychology. *Journal of Portfolio Management*, 24, pp. 52–65.

Kalecki, M., 1991. *Collected Works of Michal Kalecki.* Oxford: Clarendon Press.

Kalt, J. & Zupan, M., 1984. Capture and ideology in the economic theory of politics. *American Economic Review*, 74(3), pp. 279–300.

Kapur, A., Macleod, N. & Singh N., 2005. *Plutonomy: Buying Luxury, Explaining Global Imbalances.* New York: Citigroup.

Karlgaard, R., 2006. Predicting the future: Part II. *Forbes*, 13 February.

Katz, R., 2012. Environmental pollution: corporate crime and cancer mortality. *Contemporary Justice Review: Issues in Criminal, Social, and Restorative Justice*, 15(1).

Keynes, J., 1936. *The General Theory of Employment, Interest and Money.* London: Macmillan.

Khatiwada, S., 2010. *Did the Financial Sector Profit at the Expense of the Rest of the Economy? Evidence from the United States.* Geneva: International Labour Organization.

Kindleberger, C. & Aliber, R., 2005. *Manias, Panics, and Crashes A History of Financial Crises.* 5th edn. Hoboken, NJ: John Wiley and Sons.

Klamer, A., 1984. *Conversations with Economists: New Classical Economists and Their Opponents Speak Out on the Current Controversy in Macroeconomics.* Totowa, NJ: Rowman & Allanheld.

Klamer, A. & Colander, D., 1990. *The Making of an Economist.* Boulder, CO: Westview.

Klein, D. & Daza, R., 2013. Robert E. Lucas Jr. *Econ Journal Watch*, 10(3), pp. 434–40.

Klein, D., Daza, R. & Mead, H., 2013a. Robert C. Merton. *Econ Journal Watch*, 10(3), pp. 457–60.

Klein, D., Daza, R. & Mead, H., 2013b. Edward C. Prescott. *Econ Journal Watch*, 10(3), pp. 556–9.

Klein, D., Daza, R. & Mead, H., 2013c. Finn E. Kydland. *Econ Journal Watch*, 10(3), p. 3.

Klein, N., 2008. *The Shock Doctrine.* Toronto: Random House.

Kolko, G., 1963. *The Triumph of Conservatism: A Reinterpretation of American History 1900–1916.* Chicago, IL: Quadrangle Books.

Kotz, D., 2009. The financial and economic crisis of 2008, *Review of Radical Political Economics*, 41(3), pp. 305–17.

Kotz, D., 2015. *The Rise and Fall of Neoliberal Capitalism.* Cambridge, MA: Harvard University Press.

Krippner, G., 2005. The financialization of the American economy. *Socio-Economic Review*, 3(2), pp. 173–208.

Kroszner, R. & Rajan, R., 1994. Is the Glass Steagall Act justified? *American Economic Review*, 84(4), p. 810–32.

Krueger, A. O., 1974. The political economy of the rent-seeking society. *American Economic Review*, 64, pp. 291–303.

Krugman, P., 1979. Increasing returns, monopolistic competition, and international trade. *Journal of International Economics*, 9(4), pp. 469–79.

Krugman, P., 1980. Scale economies, product differentiation and the pattern of trade. *American Economic Review*, 70(5), pp. 950–59.

Krugman, P., 1981. Intraindustry specialization and the gains from trade. *Journal of Political Economy*, 89(5), pp. 959–73.

Krugman, P., 1991. Increasing returns and economic geography. *Journal of Political Economy*, 99(3), pp. 483–99.

Krugman, P., 1996a. *James Galbraith vs Paul Krugman*. [Online] Available at: http://www.pkarchive.org/theory/dialogue.html [Accessed 16 August 2016].

Krugman, P., 1996b. *What Economists can Learn from Evolutionary Theorists*. [Online] Available at: http://www.mit.edu/~krugman/evolute.html [Accessed 3 August 2016].

Krugman, P., 1997. We are not the world. *New York Times*, 13 February.

Krugman, P., 1999a. Labor pains. *New York Times*, 23 May, p. 24.

Krugman, P., 1999b. Want growth? Speak English: That certain je ne sais quoi of les anglophones. *Fortune*, 26 April.

Krugman, P., 1999c. The ascent of e-man: RIP the man in the grey flannel suit. *Fortune*, 24 May.

Krugman, P., 2000a. Reckonings; pursuing happiness. *New York Times*, 29 March.

Krugman, P., 2000b. Reckonings; an American pie. *New York Times*, 16 February.

Krugman, P., 2000c. Reckonings; the magic mountain. *New York Times*, 23 January.

Krugman, P., 2000d. Reckonings; Mexico's new deal. *New York Times*, 5 July.

Krugman, P., 2000e. Reckonings; saints and profits. *New York Times*, 23 July.

Krugman, P., 2000f. Reckonings; how to be a hack. *New York Times*, 23 April.

Krugman, P., 2001. Hearts and heads. *New York Times*, 22 April.

Krugman, P., 2002a. The sons also rise. *New York Times*, 22 November, p. A27.

Krugman, P., 2002b. Business as usual. *New York Times*, 22 October, p. A31.

Krugman, P., 2002c. Fear of all sums. *New York Times*, 21 June, p. A21.

Krugman, P., 2002d. The great evasion. *New York Times*, 14 May.

Krugman, P., 2003a. *The Great Unraveling*. New York: W.W. Norton & Co.

Krugman, P., 2003b. Stating the obvious. *New York Times*, 27 May, p. A25.

Krugman, P., 2004a. America's failing health. *New York Times*, 27 August, p. A21.

Krugman, P., 2004b. Red ink realities. *New York Times*, 27 January, p. A23.

Krugman, P., 2005a. The joyless economy. *New York Times*, 5 December, p. A23.

Krugman, P., 2005b. Losing our country. *New York Times*, 10 June, p. A21.

Krugman, P., 2005c. French family values. *New York Times*, 29 July, p. A23.

Krugman, P., 2005d. Passing the buck. *New York Times*, 22 April.

Krugman, P., 2006a. The big disconnect. *New York Times*, 1 September, p. A15.

Krugman, P., 2006b. Wages, wealth and politics. *New York Times*, 18 August, p. A17.

Krugman, P., 2006c. Our sick society. *New York Times*, 5 May, p. A23.

Krugman, P., 2007a. Divided over trade. *New York Times*, 14 May, p. A19.

Krugman, P., 2007b. Trouble with trade. *New York Times*, 28 December, p. A23.

Krugman, P., 2007c. Fear of eating. *New York Times*, 21 May, p. A19.

Krugman, P., 2007d. An unjustified privilege. *New York Times*, 13 July, p. A19.

Krugman, P., 2007e. Who was Milton Friedman? *New York Review of Books*, 15 February.

Krugman, P., 2008a. The real plumbers of Ohio. *New York Times*, 20 October, p. A29.

Krugman, P., 2008b. Bad cow disease. *New York Times*, 13 June, p. A29.

Krugman, P., 2008c. Fifty Herbert Hoovers. *New York Times*, 29 December, p. A25.

Krugman, P., 2009a. Money for nothing. *New York Times*, 27 April, p. A23.

Krugman, P., 2009b. Banking on the brink. *New York Times*, 22 February, p. A27.

Krugman, P., 2009c. That 30s show. *New York Times*, 2 July, p. A27.

Krugman, P., 2009d. Bailouts for bunglers. *New York Times*, 1 February, p. A21.

Krugman, P., 2009e. How did economists get it so wrong? *New York Times Magazine*, 2 September, p. MM36.

Krugman, P., 2009f. *The Return of Depression Economics Part 3: The Night They Reread Minsky.* [Online] Available at: http://www.lse.ac.uk/newsAndMedia/videoAndAudio/channels/publicLecturesAndEvents/player.aspx?id=366 [Accessed 27 August 2016].

Krugman, P., 2010. The instability of moderation. *New York Times*, 26 November.

Krugman, P., 2011a. Graduates vs oligarchs. *New York Times*, 1 November.

Krugman, P., 2012a. Lobbyists, guns and money. *New York Times*, 25 March, p. A27.

Krugman, P., 2012b. Gadgets versus fundamentals (wonkish). *New York Times*, 13 July.

Krugman, P., 2013. The plot against France. *New York Times*, 10 November, p. A25.

Krugman, P., 2014. On Gattopardo economics. *New York Times*, 24 April.

Krugman, P., n.d. *Incidents From My Career.* [Online] Available at: http://web.mit.edu/krugman/www/incidents.html [Accessed 10 August 2016].

Krugman, P. & Wells, R., 2012. Getting away with it. *The New York Review of Books*, 12 July.

Kuhn, T. 1962. *The Structure of Scientific Revolutions.* Chicago, IL: University of Chicago Press.

Kuttner, R., 2000. Alan Greenspan and the Temple of Boom. *New York Times*, 17 December.

Kydland, F. & Prescott, E., 1982. Time to build and aggregate fluctuations. *Econometrica*, 50(6), pp. 345–70.

Kydland, F. & Prescott, E., 1991. Hours and employment variation in business cycle theory. *Economic Theory*, 1(1), pp. 63–81.

Laband, D. et al., 2009. Patriotism, pigskins, and politics: An empirical examination of expressive behavior and voting. *Public Choice*, 138, pp. 97–108.

Labaton, S., 1999. Congress passes wide-ranging bill easing bank laws. *New York Times*, 5 November.

Laeven, L. & Valencia, F., 2012. *Systemic Banking Crises Database: An Update*, s.l.: International Monetary Fund.

Landon, B. et al., 2001. Health plan characteristics and consumers' assessments of quality. *Health Affairs*, 20(2).

Lapham, L., 2004. Tentacles of rage: the Republican propaganda mill, a brief history. *Harpers Magazine*, September.

Lavoie, M., Rochon, L.P. and Seccareccia, M., 2010. *Money and Macroeconomic Issues: Alfred Eichner and Post-Keynesian Economics*. Armonk, NY: M.E. Sharpe.

Leonnig, C., 2008. U.S. rushes to change workplace toxin rules. *Washington Post*, 23 July, p. A01.

Lo, A. & MacKinlay, C., 2002. *A Non-Random Walk Down Wall Street*. Princeton, NJ: Princeton University Press.

Lopez-Carlos, A., 2005. *Video Interviews*. [Online] Available at: http://www.weforum.org/site/homepublic.nsf/Content/Global+Competitiveness+Report+2005-2006:+Interview [Accessed 12 August 2006].

Lowenstein, R., 2011. *When Genius Failed*. New York: Random House.

Lucas, R., 1972. Expectations and the neutrality of money. *Journal of Economic Theory*, 4, pp. 103–24.

Lucas, R., 1973. Some international evidence on output-inflation tradeoffs. *American Economic Review*, 63(3), pp. 326–34.

Lucas, R., 1976. Econometric policy evaluation: a critique. In: K. Brunner & A. Meltzer, eds. *The Phillips Curve and the Labor Market*. Amsterdam: North-Holland, pp. 19–46.

Lucas, R., 1978. Unemployment policy. *American Economic Review*, 68(2), pp. 353–7.

Lucas, R., 1996. Autobiography. In: T. Frängsmyr, ed. *The Nobel Prizes 1995*. Stockholm: Nobel Foundation.

Lucas, R. & Rapping, L., 1969. Real wages, employment and inflation. *Journal of Political Economy*, 77, pp. 721–54.

Lucas, R. & Sargent, T., 1981. *Rational Expectations and Econometric Practice*. Minneapolis: University of Minnesota Press.

Madrick, J., 2011. *Age of Greed: The Age of Finance and the Decline of America, 1970 To Present*. New York: Alfred A. Knopf.

Malkiel, B., 2003. The efficient market hypothesis and its critics. *Journal of Economic Perspectives*, 17(1), pp. 59–82.

Mankiw, G., 1989. Real business cycles: a new Keynesian perspective. *Journal of Economic Perspectives*, 3(3), pp. 79–90.

Mankiw, G., 2001. *U.S. Monetary Policy During the 1990s*, s.l.: NBER Working Paper No. 8471.

Mankiw, G., 2006. Defending pharma. *Greg Mankiw's Blog*, 23 July. Available at: http://gregmankiw.blogspot.ca/2006/07/defending-pharma.html.

Mankiw, G., 2009. That freshman course won't be quite the same. *New York Times*, 24 May, p. BU5.

Mansbridge, J., 1990. *Beyond Self Interest*. Chicago, IL: University of Chicago Press.

Marsh, T. & Merton, R., 1986. Dividend variability and variance bounds tests for the rationality of stock market prices. *American Economic Review*, 76(3), pp. 483–98.

Martin, J., 2000. *The Man Behind the Money*. Cambridge, MA: Perseus Publishing.

Martin, R., 2011. *Fixing the Game: Bubbles, Crashes, and What Capitalism Can Learn from the NFL*. Cambridge, MA: Harvard Business Review Press.

Marx, K., 1873. Afterward. In: *Capital, Second German Edition*. s.l.:s.n.

Marx, K., 1889. *Capital*, Volume 1. New York: Appleton & Co..

Mayer, J., 2010. Covert operations: The billionaire brothers who are waging a war against Obama. *The New Yorker*, 30 August.

Mazzucato, M., 2013. *The Entrepreneurial State: Debunking Public vs. Private Sector Myths*. London: Anthem Press.

McDonough, T, Reich, M. and Kotz, D., 2010. *Contemporary Capitalism and Its Crises: Social Structure of Accumulation theory for the 21st Century*. Cambridge: Cambridge University Press.

McGratten, E. & Prescott, E., 2012. The great recession and delayed economic recovery: a labor productivity puzzle. In: J. Ohanian & J. Taylor, eds. *Government Policies and the Delayed Economic Recovery*. Stanford, CA: Hoover Institution Press, pp. 115–54.

McKee-Ryan, F. et al., 2005. Psychological and physical well-being during unemployment: a meta-analytic study. *Journal of Applied Psychology*, 90(1).

McNally, D., 2010. *Global Slump: The Economics and Politics of Crisis and Resistance*. Winnipeg: Fernwood.

McQuiston, T., Ronda, Z. & Loomis, D., 1998. The case for stronger OSHA enforcement: evidence from evaluation research. *American Journal of Public Health*, 88(7).

Media Matters, n.d. s.l.: http://mediamattersaction.org/transparency/.

Mercatus Center, 2016. *About*. [Online] Available at: http://mercatus.org/content/about [Accessed 1 March 2016].

Merton, R., 1973. Theory of rational option pricing. *Bell Journal of Economics and Management Science*, 4, pp. 141–83.

Merton, R., 1997. *Robert C. Merton – Biographical*. [Online] Available at: http://www.nobelprize.org/nobel_prizes/economic-sciences/laureates/1997/merton-bio.html [Accessed 6 June 2016].

Merton, R., 2016. *Robert C. Merton*. [Online] Available at: http://www.hbs.
edu/faculty/Pages/profile.aspx?facId=6511 [Accessed 6 June 2016].

Merton, R. & Bodie, Z., 1995. Financial infrastructure and public policy: a
functional perspective. In: D. Crane et al., eds. *The Global Financial System:
A Functional Perspective*. Boston, MA: Harvard Business School Press.

Michaels, D., 2008. *Doubt is Their Product: How Industry's Assault on Science
Threatens Your Health*. Oxford: Oxford University Press.

Minsky, H., 1977. A theory of systemic fragility. In: E. Altman & A. Sametz,
eds. *Financial Crises: Institutions and Markets in a Fragile Environment*.
New York: John Wiley and Sons, pp. 138–52.

Minsky, H., 1982. *Can "It" Happen Again? Essays on Instability and Finance*.
Armonk, NY: M.E. Sharpe.

Minsky, H., 1986. *Stabilizing an Unstable Economy*. New Haven, CT:
McGraw-Hill.

Minsky, H., 1993. The financial instability hypothesis. In: P. Arestis & M.
Sawyer, eds. *Handbook of Radical Political Economy*. Cheltenham, UK:
Edward Elgar.

Minsky, H. & Vaughan, M., 1990. Debt and business cycles. *Business Economics*,
25(3), pp. 23–8.

Mirowski, P., 2009. Postface: defining neoliberalism. In: P. Mirowski, ed. *The
Road from Mont Pelerin: The Making of a Neoliberal Thought Collective*.
Cambridge, MA: Harvard University Press, pp. 417–56.

Mirowski, P., 2010. The Great Mortification: Economists' Responses to the
Crisis of 2007. *The Hedgehog Review*, 12(3).

Mirowski, P., 2013. *Never Let a Serious Crisis Go to Waste: How Neoliberalism
Survived the Financial Meltdown*. London: Verso.

Mishel, L., 2012. *CEO Pay 231 Times Greater Than the Average Worker*.
[Online] Available at: http://www.epi.org/publication/ceo-pay-231-times-
greater-average-worker/ [Accessed 25 June 2012].

Mitchell, W. & Munger, M., 1991. Economic models of interest groups: an
introductory survey. *American Journal of Political Science*, 35(2), pp. 512–46.

Modigliani, F., 1977. The monetarist controversy or, should we forsake
stabilization policies? *American Economic Review*, 67(2), pp. 1–17.

Monbiot, G., 2012. How Ayn Rand became the new right's version of Marx.
Guardian, 5 March.

Mortgage Bankers Association, 2007. *National Delinquency Survey, 4th quarter,
2007*, s.l.: Mortgage Bankers Association.

Muellbauer, J., 1997. The assessment: business cycles. *Oxford Review of
Economic Policy*, 13(3), pp. 1–22.

Murray, A., 2007. New economic models are failing while America Inc. keeps
rolling. *Wall Street Journal*, 8 December.

Mustard, C., Lavis, J. & Ostry, A., 2006. Work and health: new evidence
and enhanced understandings. In: J. Heymann, C. Hertzman, M. Barer &
R. Evans, eds. *Healthier Societies: From Analysis to Action*. Oxford: Oxford
University Press.

Muth, J., 1961. Rational expectations and the theory of price movements. *Econometrica*, 29(3), 315–35.

National Commission on the Causes of the Financial and Economic Crisis in the United States, 2011. *The Financial Crisis Inquiry Report: Final Report of the National Commission on the Causes of the Financial and Economic Crisis in the United States.* Washington, DC: Financial Crisis Inquiry Commission.

Nichols, J., 2011. ALEC exposed. *The Nation*, 1–8 August.

Nickerson, G., 1983. Analytical problems in explaining criminal behavior: neoclassical and radical economic theories and an alternative formulation. *Review of Radical Political Economics*, 15(4), pp. 1–23.

Nobelprize.org, 1976. *The Sveriges Riksbank Prize in Economic Sciences in Memory of Alfred Nobel 1976.* [Online] Available at: http://www.nobelprize.org/nobel_prizes/economics/laureates/1976/ [Accessed 9 July 2012].

Novak, W., 2014. A revisionist history of regulatory capture. In: D. Carpenter & D. Moss, eds. *Preventing Regulatory Capture.* New York: Cambridge, pp. 25–48.

OECD, 2010. *Economic Policy Reforms: Going for Growth.* s.l.: Organization for Economic Cooperation and Development.

OECD, 2011. *Social Justice in the OECD: How Do the Member States Compare?,* s.l.: Organization for Economic Cooperation and Development.

OECD, 2016. *OECD Health Data 2015.* [Online] Available at: http://stats.oecd.org/index.aspx?DataSetCode=HEALTH_STAT [Accessed 22 July 2016].

Office of Science and Technology Policy, 2000. *Fact Sheet on how Federal R&D Investments Drive the US Economy,* Washington, DC: Executive Office of the President.

Orren, G., 1988. Beyond self interest. In: R. Reich, ed. *The Power of Public Ideas.* Cambridge, MA: Harvard University Press, pp. 13–30.

Palley, T., 2006. *Milton Friedman: The Great Conservative Partisan.* [Online] Available at: http://www.thomaspalley.com/?p=59 [Accessed 6 August 2012].

Palley, T., 2007. *Financialization: What it is and why it Matters,* Düsseldorf: IMK Working Paper. No. 04/2008.

Passell, P., 1991. *George Joseph Stigler Dies at 80; Nobel Prize Winner in Economics.* [Online] Available at: http://www.nytimes.com/1991/12/03/us/george-joseph-stigler-dies-at-80-nobel-prize-winner-in-economics.html [Accessed 16 November 2015].

PBS, 2003. *The Long Decline of Glass-Steagall.* [Online] Available at: http://www.pbs.org/wgbh/pages/frontline/shows/wallstreet/weill/demise.htm [Accessed 26 July 2016].

Pearce, N., 2008. Corporate influences on epidemiology. *International Journal of Epidemiology*, 37(1).

Peltzman, S., 1976. Toward a more general theory of regulation. *Journal of Law and Economics*, 2, pp. 17–34.

Perelman, M., 2011. *The Invisible Handcuffs of Capitalism: How Market Tyranny Stifles the Economy by Stunting Workers.* New York: Monthly Review Press.

Petracca, M., 1991. The rational choice approach to politics: a challenge to democratic theory. *The Review of Politics*, 53(2), pp. 289–319.

Piketty, T. & Saez, E., 2003. Income inequality in the United States, 1913–1998. *Quarterly Journal of Economics*, 118(1), pp. 1–39.

Pollin, R., 1998. The natural rate of unemployment: it's all about class conflict. *Dollars and Sense Magazine*, 219, September/October.

Pollin, R., 2003. *Contours of Descent: US Economic Fractures and the Landscape of Global Austerity.* London: Verso.

Pollin, R., 2004. Review of *The Roaring Nineties: A New History of the World's Most Prosperous Decade. Challenge*, 47(4), pp. 113–23.

Poole, W., 1988. Monetary policy lessons of recent inflation and disinflation. *Journal of Economic Perspectives*, 2(3), pp. 73–100.

Potter, W., 2010. *Deadly Spin.* New York: Bloomsbury Press.

Prescott, E., 1986. Theory ahead of business cycle measurement. *Federal Reserve Bank of Minneapolis Quarterly Review*, 10(4), pp. 9–22.

Prescott, E., 1999. Some observations on the Great Depression. *Federal Reserve Quarterly Review*, 23.

Prescott, E., 2004. Why do Americans work so much more than Europeans? *Federal Reserve Bank of Minneapolis Quarterly Review*, 28(1), pp. 2–13.

Prescott, E. & Ohanian, L., 2014. U.S. productivity growth has taken a dive. *Wall Street Journal*, 3 February.

Pressman, S., 2004. What is wrong with public choice? *Journal of Post Keynesian Economics*, 27(1), p. 3–18.

Quiggan, J., 2010a. Five zombie economic ideas that refuse to die. *Foreign Policy*, 15 October. Available at: http://www.foreignpolicy.com/articles/2010/10/15/five_zombie_economic_ideas_that_refuse_to_die.

Quiggin, J., 2010b. *Zombie Economics: How Dead Ideas Still Walk Among Us.* Princeton, NJ: Princeton University Press.

Rawe, J., 2004. Where the best ideas take wing. *Time Magazine*, 11 October, p. 68.

Rayack, E., 1987. *Not So Free To Choose.* New York: Praeger Publishers.

Reagan, R., 1981. *Inaugural Address.* [Online] Available at: http://www.reaganfoundation.org/reagan-quotes-detail.aspx?tx=2072 [Accessed 29 April 2016].

Reich, R., 2010. *Aftershock: The Next Economy and America's Future.* New York: Knopf.

Renwick Monroe, K., 1991. *The Economic Approach to Politics: A Reexamination of the Theory of Rational Action.* New York: HarperCollins.

Reuben, S., 2010. *Reducing Environmental Cancer Risk: President's Cancer Panel 2008–2009,* Washington, DC: US Department of Health and Human Services.

Rich, A., 1997. *Perceptions of Think Tanks in American Politics: A Survey of Congressional Staff and Journalists,* s.l.: Burson-Marstellar Worldwide Report.

Rich, A., 2004. *Think Tanks, Public Policy, and the Politics of Expertise*. New York: Cambridge University Press.

Robinson, J., 1971. *Economic Heresies*. New York: Basic Books.

Rogers, J. & Dresser, L., 2011. ALEC exposed: Business Domination Inc. *The Nation*, 1–8 August.

Rogoff, K., 2002. *An Open Letter to Joseph Stiglitz*. [Online] Available at: https://www.imf.org/en/News/Articles/2015/09/28/04/54/vc070202 [Accessed 11 August 2016].

Roubini, N. & Mihm, S., 2010. *Crisis Economics: A Crash Course in the Future of Finance*. New York: Penguin Press.

Rowley, C., 2012. The intellectual legacy of Gordon Tullock. *Public Choice*, 152, p. 29–46.

Sachs, J., 2008. *Remarks by Jeffrey Sachs at a Discussion on the World Economy*. Columbia University, s.n. [Online] Available at: http://www.earth. columbia.edu/worldeconomy/.

Sager, A. & Socolar, D., 2005. *Health Costs Absorb One-Quarter of Economic Growth, 2000–2005, Data Brief No. 8 – 9 February*, s.l.: s.n.

Sahay, R. et al., 2015. *Rethinking Financial Deepening: Stability and Growth in Emerging Markets*, s.l.: International Monetary Fund.

Samuelson, P., 2009. *Don't Expect Recovery Before 2012 – With 8% Inflation*. [Online] Available at: http://www.digitalnpq.org/articles/ economic/331/01-16-2009/paul_samuelson [Accessed 9 July 2012].

Sandmo, A., 1990. Buchanan on political economy: a review article. *Journal of Economic Literature*, 28(1), pp. 50–65.

Sargent, T., 1979. *Macroeconomic Theory*. New York: Academic Press.

Sargent, T., 1999. *The Conquest of American Inflation*. Princeton, NJ: Princeton University Press.

Sargent, T., 2010. *An interview with Thomas Sargent*. [Online] Available at: https://www.minneapolisfed.org/publications/the-region/interview-with-thomas-sargent [Accessed 12 May 1016].

Sargent, T. & Wallace, N., 1975. Rational expectations, the optimal monetary instrument and the optimal money supply rule. *Journal of Political Economy*, 83, pp. 241–54.

Sargent, T. & Wallace, N., 1976. Rational expectations and the theory of economic policy. *Journal of Monetary Economics*, 2, pp. 169–83.

Scaff, L. & Ingram, H., 1987. Politics, policy, and public choice: a critique and a proposal. *Polity*, 19(4), pp. 613–36.

Schaefer, A., 1998. Robert Merton, Myron Scholes and the development of derivative pricing. *Scandanavian Journal of Economics*, 100(2), pp. 425–45.

Schoen, C. et al., 2005. Taking the pulse of health care systems: Experiences of patients with health problems in six countries. *Health Affairs*. [Online] Available at: http://www.providersedge.com/ehdocs/ehr_articles/taking_the_pulse_of_health_care_systems.pdf.

Scholes, M., 2008. Economist debates: financial crisis. Opening statement. *The Economist*, 17 October.

Scholes, M., 2016. *Myron S. Scholes.* [Online] Available at: https://www.gsb. stanford.edu/faculty-research/faculty/myron-s-scholes [Accessed 7 June 2016].

Schwab, K., 2010. *The Global Competitiveness Report 2010–2011.* Geneva: World Economic Forum.

Sen, A., 1995. Rationality and social choice. *American Economic Review,* 85(1), pp. 1–24.

Shah, A., 1997. Black, Merton and Scholes: their work and its consequences. *Economic and Political Weekly,* 32(52), pp. 3337–42.

Shaikh, A., 1979. The poverty of algebra. In: I. Steedman et al., eds. *The Value Controversy.* London: Verso, pp. 266–300.

Shaikh, A., 2010. The first great depression of the 21st century. In: *Socialist Register 2011.* London: The Merlin Press, pp. 44–63.

Shen, Y., 2002. The effect of hospital ownership choice on patient outcomes after treatment for acute myocardial infarction. *Journal of Health Economics,* 21(5).

Shiller, R., 1981. Do stock prices move too much to be justified by subsequent changes in dividends? *American Economic Review,* 71(3), pp. 421–36.

Shiller, R., 2013. Sharing Nobel honors, and agreeing to disagree. *New York Times,* 27 October, p. BU6.

Shiller, R., 2015. *Irrational Exuberance,* 3rd edn. Princeton, NJ: Princeton University Press.

Shughart, W. & Tollison, R., 2015. *On the Extraordinary Scholarly Life and Times of Gordon Tullock.* Fairfax, VA, s.n.

Silverman, E., Skinner, J. & Fischer, E., 1999. The association between for-profit hospital ownership and increased Medicare spending. *New England Journal of Medicine,* 341(6): 420–26.

Sinclair, U., 1934. *I, Candidate for Governor: And How I Got Licked.* Berkeley: University of California Press.

Sjoblom, K., 1985. Voting for social security. *Public Choice,* 45, pp. 225–40.

Skidelsky, R., 2009. *Keynes: The Return of the Master.* New York: PublicAffairs.

Sklar, M., 1988. *The Corporate Reconstruction of American Capitalism 1890–1916.* New York: Cambridge University Press.

Smith, Y., 2010. *Econned: How Unenlightened Self Interest Undermined Democracy and Corrupted Capitalism.* New York: Palgrave Macmillan.

Snowdon, B. & Vane, H., 1998. Lucas, Robert E.: transforming macro-economics. *Journal of Economic Methodology,* 5(1), pp. 115–46.

Snowdon, B. & Vane, H., 2005. *Modern Macroeconomics: Its Origins Development and Current State.* Cheltenham, UK: Edward Elgar.

Solomon, D., 2009. Crash course. *New York Times,* 14 May.

Sommer, J., 2011a. The slogans stop here. *New York Times,* 29 October.

Sommer, J., 2011b. Good morning. You're Nobel Laureates. *New York Times,* 3 December, p. BU1.

Sommer, J., 2013. Eugene Fama, king of predictable markets. *New York Times,* 26 October, p. BU6.

Spotton Visano, B.,2006. *Financial Crises Socio-Economic Causes and Institutional Context*. New York: Routledge.

Stanford University, 2001. *Eight Hoover Fellows appointed to the U.S. Defense Policy Board Advisory Committee*. [Online] Available at: http://www.hoover.org/press-releases/eight-hoover-fellows-appointed-us-defense-policy-board-advisory-committee [Accessed 18 March 2016].

Stein, B., 2006. In class warfare, guess which class is winning. *New York Times*, 26 November.

Stewart, I., 2012a. *In Pursuit of the Unknown: 17 Equations that Changed the World*. New York: Basic Books.

Stewart, I., 2012b. The mathematical equation that caused the banks to crash. *Guardian*, 12 February.

Stigler, G., 1971. The theory of economic regulation. *Bell Journal of Economics and Management Science*, 2(1), pp. 2–21.

Stigler, G., 1974. Free riders and collective action: an appendix to Theories of Economic Regulation. *Bell Journal of Economics and Management Science*, 5(2), pp. 359–65.

Stigler, G., 1982. *George J. Stigler – Biographical*. [Online] Available at: http://www.nobelprize.org/nobel_prizes/economic-sciences/laureates/1982/stigler-bio.html [Accessed 16 November 2015].

Stigler, G., 1986. Why have the socialists been winning. In: K. Leube & T. Moore, eds. *The Essence of Stigler*. Stanford, CA: Hoover Institution Press, pp. 337–46.

Stiglitz, J., 1975. The theory of screening, education, and the distribution of income. *American Economic Review*, 65(3), pp. 283–300.

Stiglitz, J., 1979. Equilibrium in product markets with imperfect information. *American Economic Review*, 69(2), pp. 339–45.

Stiglitz, J., 2001. Information and the change in paradigm in economics. *Nobel Prize Lecture*, pp. 472–540.

Stiglitz, J., 2003. *The Roaring Nineties*. New York: W.W. Norton & Co.

Stiglitz, J., 2010a. The non-existent hand. *London Review of Books*, 22 April, pp. 17–18.

Stiglitz, J., 2010b. *Freefall*. New York: W.W. Norton & Co.

Stiglitz, J., 2010c. Lessons from the global financial crisis of 2008. *Seoul Journal of Economics*, 23(3), pp. 321–39.

Stiglitz, J., 2011. Of the 1%, by the 1%, for the 1%. *Vanity Fair*, 31 March.

Stiglitz, J., 2013. *The Price of Inequality*. New York: W.W. Norton & Co.

Stiglitz, J., 2014. *Reforming Taxation to Promote Growth and Equity*, s.l.: Roosevelt Institute.

Stiglitz, J., 2015. A Greek morality tale: why we need a global debt restructuring framework. *Guardian*, 4 February.

Stockhammer, E., 2004. Financialisation and the slowdown of accumulation. *Cambridge Journal of Economics*, 28(5), pp. 719–41.

Summers, L., 1998. *Treasury Deputy Secretary Lawrence H. Summers Testimony Before the Senate Committee on Agriculture, Nutrition, and Forestry on the*

CFTC Concept Release, Washington, DC: Senate Committee on Agriculture Nutrition and Forestry on the CFTC Concept Release.

Summers, L., 2000. *Remarks of Treasury Secretary Lawrence H. Summers to the Securities Industry Association,* s.l.: Press Room, US Department of the Treasury.

Summers, L. & Summers, V., 1989. When financial markets work too well: a cautious case for a securities transaction tax. *Journal of Financial Services Research,* 3, pp. 261–86.

Tasini, J., 2006. The DLC won't talk about corporate power. *Huffington Post,* 25 July.

The Economist, 2006a. Milton Friedman: a heavyweight champ, at five foot two. *The Economist,* 23 November.

The Economist, 2006b. Joe has another go. *The Economist,* 7 September.

The Royal Swedish Academy of Sciences, 1995. *Rational Expectations have Transformed Macroeconomic Analysis and Our Understanding of Economic Policy.* [Online] Available at: http://www.nobelprize.org/nobel_prizes/economic-sciences/laureates/1995/press.html [Accessed 10 May 2016].

The Royal Swedish Academy of Sciences, 1997. *The Sveriges Riksbank Prize in Economic Sciences in Memory of Alfred Nobel 1997: Robert C. Merton, Myron S. Scholes.* [Online] Available at: http://www.nobelprize.org/nobel_prizes/economic-sciences/laureates/1997/press.html [Accessed 7 June 2016].

Thompson, N., 2008. Hollowing out the state: public choice theory and the critique of Keynesian social democracy. *Journal of Contemporary British History,* 22(3), pp. 355–82.

Thurow, L., 1996. *The Future of Capitalism.* New York: Penguin Books USA Inc.

Tollison, R., 1982. Rent seeking: a survey. *Kyklos,* 35, pp. 575–602.

Tomaskovic-Devey, D., Lin, K. & Meyers, N., 2015. Did financialization reduce economic growth? *Socio-Economic Review,* pp. 1–24.

Tuccille, J., 2002. *Alan Shrugged: The Life and Times of Alan Greenspan, The World's Most Powerful Banker.* Hoboken, NJ: John Wiley & Sons.

Tullock, G., 1965. *The Politics of Bureaucracy.* Washington, DC: Public Affairs Press.

Tullock, G., 1967. The welfare costs of tariffs, monopolies, and theft. *Western Economic Journal,* 5, pp. 224–32.

Tullock, G., 1967. *Toward a Mathematics of Politics.* Ann Arbor: University of Michigan Press.

Tullock, G., 1971. The coal tit as a careful shopper. *The American Naturalist,* 105, p. 77–80.

Tullock, G., 1974. *The Social Dilemma: The Economics of War and Revolution.* Blacksburg, VA: Center for Study of Public Choice.

Tullock, G., 1980. Rent seeking as a negative-sum game. In: J. Buchanan, R. Tollison & G. Tullock, eds. *Toward a Theory of a Rent Seeking Society.* New York: The Free Press, pp. 16–35.

Tullock, G., 2003. *Gordon Tullock, Co-founder, School of Public Choice Economics.* [Online] Available at: http://archive.fcpp.org/posts/gordon-tullock-co-founder-school-of-public-choice-economics [Accessed 18 March 2016].

Udehn, L., 1996. *The Limits of Public Choice: A Sociological Critique of the Economic Theory of Politics.* New York: Routledge.

Union of Concerned Scientists, 2008. *Interference at the EPA: Science and Politics at the US Environmental Protection Agency,* Cambridge, MA: Union of Concerned Scientists.

United Nations, 2011. *UN International Human Development Indicators.* [Online] Available at: http://hdr.undp.org/en/data/ [Accessed 15 March 2011].

University of Chicago, 2007. Gary S. Becker receives Presidential Medal of Freedom. [Online] Available at: http://www-news.uchicago.edu/releases/07/071029.becker.shtml [Accessed 17 March 2016].

US Bureau of Economic Analysis, 2016. *Personal Saving Rate [PSAVERT], retrieved from FRED, Federal Reserve Bank of St. Louis.* [Online] Available at: https://fred.stlouisfed.org/series/PSAVERT [Accessed 5 August 2016].

US Department of Housing and Urban Development, 2010. *Report to Congress on the Root Causes of the Foreclosure Crisis.* Washington, DC: US Department of Housing and Urban Development.

Vaillancourt, R. & Linder, S., 2003. Two decades of research comparing for-profit and nonprofit health provider performance in the United States. *Social Science Quarterly,* 84(2).

Van Horn, R., 2011. Chicago's shifting attitude toward concentrations of business power (1934–1962). *Seattle University Law Review,* 34, pp. 1527–44.

Varoufakis, Y., 2011. *The Global Minotaur: America, the True Origins of the Financial Crisis and the Future of the World Economy.* London: Zed Books.

Varoufakis, Y., 2016. *Full Transcript of the Yanis Varoufakis, Noam Chomsky New York Public Library discussion e, Celeste Bartos Forum* [Interview] (26 April). [Online] Available at: https://yanisvaroufakis.eu/2016/06/28/full-transcript-of-the-yanis-varoufakis-noam-chomsky-nypl-discussion/.

Wade, R., 2001. Showdown at the World Bank. *New Left Review,* 7, pp. 124–37.

Waldie, P., 2008. Friedman under attack. *Globe and Mail,* 21 October.

Warren, E., 2006. The middle class on the precipice: rising financial risks for American families. *Havard Magazine,* 28, January-February.

Warsh, D., 1993. *Economic Principals: Masters and Mavericks of Modern Economics.* New York: The Free Press.

Warsh, D., 1993. Regulating government. In: *Economic Principals: Masters and Maverics of Modern Economics.* New York: The Free Press, pp. 97–100.

Weil, D., 1996. If OSHA is so bad, why is compliance so good? *The RAND Journal of Economics,* 27(3).

Weinsten, J., 1968. *The Corporate Ideal in the Liberal State 1900–1918.* Boston, MA: Beacon Press.

Weiss, G., 2012. *Ayn Rand Nation.* New York: St. Martin's Press.

WHO (World Health Organization), 2008. *Inequities are Killing People on Grand Scale, Press Release.* [Online] Available at: http://www.who.int/mediacentre/news/releases/2008/pr29/en/index.html [Accessed 3 August 2011].

Wigmore, B., 1985. *The Crash and Its Aftermath: A History of Securities Markets in the United States, 1929–1933.* Westport, CT: Greenwood Press.

Woodward, B., 2000. *Maestro: Greenspan's Fed and the American Boom.* New York: Simon and Schuster.

Woolhandler, S. & Himmelstein, D., 1997. Costs of care and administration at for-profit and other hospitals in the United States. *New England Journal of Medicine,* 336(11).

Wright, M., 1993. A critique of the public choice theory case for privatization: rhetoric and reality. *Ottawa Law Review,* 25(1), pp. 1–38.

Zingales, L., 2014. Preventing economists' capture. In: D. Carpenter & D. Moss, eds. *Preventing Regulatory Capture.* New York: Cambridge University Press, pp. 124–51.

Index